Interdependence on Trial

Interdependence on Trial

Studies in the Theory and Reality of Contemporary Interdependence

Edited by

R.J. Barry Jones
Peter Willetts

 Frances Pinter (Publishers), London

First published in Great Britain in 1984 by
Frances Pinter (Publishers) Limited
25 Floral Street, London WC2E 9DS

ISBN 0 86187 508 7

Typeset by Folio Photosetting, Bristol

Printed in Great Britain by SRP Ltd., Exeter

Contents

To all those who have made the International Relations Theory Group such an important and rewarding experience over the years, whether by participation, contribution, the provision of facilities or financial assistance.

Preface

This study of interdependence – its meaning and reality – is the work of the International Relations Theory Research Group. The group was encouraged to embark upon its study of interdependence by a number of influences. First, the intrinsic attraction of the subject: the widespread usage of the term 'interdependence'; the significance of its manifold referents; and, of no little significance, the vagueness of meaning that seems to attach to the word. Second, the stimulus that the group received from its earlier study of 'change' in international relations and the publication of the fruits of that work as *Change and the Study of International Relations* (Frances Pinter, 1981). Third, by the enthusiasm of the ESRC (formerly SSRC), which has consistently funded the work of the group, to see the work that it supports flower into publications of value and interest.

Appreciation must therefore be expressed to many for their varied contributions to the preparation of this volume. The breadth of this debt is suggested by the dedication and can only be reinforced by this preface.

R.J. Barry Jones
Reading
May, 1984

Notes on Contributors

R.J. Barry Jones lectures on International Relations and Politics at Reading University. His recent publications include articles on International Political Economy, and he has edited *Change and the Study of International Relations* (with B. Buzan) (Frances Pinter, 1981) and also *Perspectives on Political Economy* (Frances Pinter, 1983). He is currently preparing work on relations between Multinational Corporations and the British Government, and the role of governments in contemporary industrial and economic developments.

Richard Little lectures on International Relations at the University of Lancaster. He is the author of a seminal study of international intervention – *Intervention: External Involvement in Civil War* (Martin Robertson, 1975). He is also the author of a number of articles on philosophical issues in the study of International Relations and on international aid.

John McLean lectures on International Relations at the University of Sussex. He is the author of a number of articles on Marxist approaches to International Relations.

Michael Smith lectures on International Relations at Lanchester (Coventry) Polytechnic. He has co-edited a number of books including *The Nature of Foreign Policy* (with J. Barber) and *Perspectives on World Politics* (with R. Little and M. Shackleton) (Croom Helm, 1980). He is also the author of *Atlantic Community in Crisis: a Redefinition of the Atlantic Relationship* (New York, Pergamon, 1979).

Steve Smith lectures on International Relations at the University of East Anglia. Amongst his many publications is *Foreign Policy Adaption* (Saxon House, 1981).

John Vogler lectures on International Relations at Liverpool Polytechnic and was a contributor to *Change and the Study of International Relations*.

Peter Willetts lectures in International Relations at The City University, London. He is the editor of the Global Politics Series of books for Frances Pinter Ltd, and has written extensively on non-alignment, including two books, *The Non-Aligned Movement* and *The Non-Aligned in Havana*. Recently he edited a set of case-studies on transnational relations, *Pressure Groups in the Global System*.

1 Introduction

R.J. BARRY JONES and PETER WILLETTS

THE EMERGENCE OF THE NEW 'INTERDEPENDENCISM'

It is rare indeed for one term, or idea, to attract such widespread popular and academic appeal as that secured by 'interdependence' in recent years. Rare, too, is quite such a range of usage and diversity of definition as that attaching to this concept. It is, however, just these features of the notion of 'interdependence' that have stimulated the International Relations Theory Research Group and led to the present volume of essays.

The chapters in this volume range across many of the central issues that arise from the recent fashion for 'interdependence'. Contributors address themselves to the questions: why has such an interest emerged in recent years; how best, and most precisely, may the term be defined; how much empirical support is there for one or other of the possible conceptions; what are the practical implications of the development, if real, of empirical 'interdependence'; and, finally, what, if any, are the implications for the theory and study of international relations of the emergence of the concept of 'interdependence'?

Much of the initial impetus for the contemporary academic enthusiasm for 'interdependence' stemmed from North America. The early seed corn fell upon abundantly fertile ground: many of diverse backgrounds, positions and interests were soon to be heard uttering the contemporary shibboleths of 'interdependence'. The diversity inherent in current usage cannot, however, be overemphasized. Interdependence does not mean all things to all men but quite different things to those of differing stations and interests.

The contrasting perspectives, interests and purposes of those who have promoted one or another conception of inter-dependence constitute a fascinating subject for speculation and investigation. The interpretation given to the early North American enthusiasm for interdependence is itself a matter of theoretical (and, indeed, political) disposition. There are those who see the adoption of interdependence as an intellectual response to the practical setbacks experienced by the United States of America during the latter 1960s and early 1970s. Interdependence, in this vein, may thus be viewed as a rationalization of failure in Vietnam and the enforced abandonment of dollar convertibility into gold.

To those whose attention is drawn more towards scholarly processes, a marked weakening of the pace and quality of theoretical advance in the study of international relations, during the years immediately preceding the great American conversion to interdependence, may be discerned. The heady days of behaviouralism and of mammoth number-crunching projects were waning fast. Such approaches were now seen to produce rather trivial fruits, while Vietnam revealed reality to be of such complexity and messiness as to be beyond the mechanicists' apprehension. This view dovetails neatly with arguments that the novelty of the concept of interdependence has been grossly overstated in much of the recent literature.

Those scholars and critics who hold to notions of a global capitalist, and essentially exploitative, order would go much further than their less 'critical' colleagues. Such radical analysts would see in such references to interdependence an attempt to obscure the underlying reality of the global political-economic order. Faced with a practical and intellectual challenge from the South, Northern 'interdependencists' were, it would be argued, really doing no more than attempting to counter an adversarial conception of North–South relations with an approach that stressed the basic mutuality of interests amongst all groups of societies within the contemporary system. Such a stratagem would, moreover, be common to such apparently diverse positions as those of the 'liberal reformists' of the Brandt Commission *and* exponents of 'Reaganite' beliefs in the mutual benefits deriving from an unfettered, global *laissez-faire* system.

Advocates of interdependence within the Southern countries can also be seen to have varying motives and purposes. The range of such purported purposes is wide. Proclamations of global interdependence could well be seen as a tactic to persuade the North to concede on many of the demands for a New International Economic Order (NIEO) and to persuade faint hearts amongst Southern allies that the NIEO is not a hopeless cause. However, reference to international economic interdependence might also be viewed, more cynically, as a means by which self-interested Southern elites persuade their populations that the general pattern of established economic conditions, within and without the state, must continue with but marginal modification.

Whatever the motives of diverse 'interdependencists', and whatever the definition of the phenomenon that might ultimately be adopted, it will already be clear that the notion of interdependence is intimately bound up with judgements about the nature and effect of the contemporary international economic order. Indeed, the concept will be seen to have many implications for the analysis of the power relationships that exist, and might be developed, between the nations of the world and between nation states and other such salient global actors as multinational corporations (MNCs). The wary of mind would, however, be cautioned to search for the ideologies or special interests that lie behind so many current claims concerning interdependence.

DEFINITIONAL DIVERSITY

The mixed motives and purposes (albeit often hidden from casual observation) of its various proponents partly underlie the diversity of definition that may be distilled from the current range of usage of the term interdependence. When coupled with the definitional divisions that will always develop within any group of scholars, this diversity becomes formidable.

One of the most profound questions to be identified by various of the contributions to this volume is the contrast between actor-based and holistic conceptions of interdependence. The issue here is that between that of interdependence defined solely, or primarily, in terms of the manifest inter-relationships between two or more nation states and the contradictory view that any such attempt serves only to obscure the underlying (or overarching) structures of the global political economy that actually condition the appearances of 'interdependence' but that cannot be identified solely through such features. This issue is part of an epistemological and methodological debate of such moment that it cannot be avoided in any consideration of interdependence, in theory or reality.

Many will be intellectually disposed to continue working within an actor-based approach to, and definition of, interdependence. Here, however, a number of pressing definitional and conceptual issues remain to be resolved. The literature reveals a basic division between those who would define interdependence in terms of those connections between societies that reveal themselves in the covariance of economic conditions and indicators, and those who would, in clear contrast, identify interdependence as a condition of serious mutual dependence between two or more societies. The definition of interdependence as international and transnational *interconnectedness* suffers from a number of shortcomings that are discussed more fully in subsequent chapters. It is also limited to economic (and possibly cultural) relations between societies. Interdependence conceived as *mutual dependence*, in contrast, may be applied with equal effect to the condition of mutual nuclear deterrence as to instances of serious economic dependence. There are also many analysts who feel that the notion of mutual dependence better captures the meaning that most people would impute to the term 'interdependence'.

Whether interconnectedness or mutual dependence be the chosen definition of interdependence, there remain many conceptual pitfalls into which the unwary student may all too easily slip when using the term. Loose usage often appears to imply that such interdependence as exists has a blanket effect upon the societies concerned: that if two societies are dependent upon one another for one or two commodities or services, then this has profound consequences for the whole structure of their relations. Such an assumption may, of course, be quite unwarranted and, given that an actor-based approach is still being employed, would require empirical substantiation. Indeed, it is quite possible that instances of interdependence will remain highly specific in their effects upon participating societies. Whatever the case, it has to be established in fact.

In like manner, many uses of the term 'interdependence' imply that the relationships under consideration exhibit, if not complete symmetry, then a high measure of balance. In contemporary international relations perhaps the only example of perfectly symmetrical and balanced interdependence is that of mutual nuclear deterrence. Here, symmetry is a function of the dependence upon one another for the avoidance of nuclear bombardment. Balance is secured when both sides prove capable of deterring one another simultaneously. Throughout much of the economic domain, patterns of interdependence characteristically manifest neither symmetry nor balance. Indeed, that which is most interesting and significant in the contemporary international economic order is often to be found precisely in the asymmetries and imbalances that do abound.

Additional problems, of considerable complexity, are also encountered when instances of interdependence are to be analysed or classified. Robert Keohane and Joseph Nye's seminal *Power and Interdependence*[1] introduces a distinction between 'sensitivity' and 'vulnerability' in relations of inter-dependence. This highlights the malleability of much of economic reality: the possibility that dependencies may be modified over time in response to policy initiatives, technical innovations, the development of new sources, or changes in a host of relevant conditions. Time and opportunity are clearly critical in this respect and must always be considered in any statements about interdependence.

The term 'sensitivity', however, introduces a further issue and area of possible confusion. Keohane and Nye imbue the terms with an 'objective' meaning. 'Sensitivity' here is essentially a short-term phenomenon: exposure to externally induced costs before there has been time and opportunity to initiate remedial policies (vulnerability being the continued exposure to such externally induced costs even after remedial policies have been sought or implemented).[2] However, there is a strong sense in which the term 'sensitivity' carries subjective impli-cations. That is, many recent statements about international interdependence are really reports of the *perceptions* of policy-makers and their publics which do not always correspond precisely with underlying realities. The complex and often dynamic relationship between subjective sensitivity, on the one hand, and 'objective' sensitivity and vulnerability, on the other, constitutes one of the most interesting and important aspects of the study of contemporary interdependence and indeed of the global political economy.

The notion of sensitivity thus remains important and may be

employed with effect if its objective and subjective dimensions are held clearly distinct and if its possible empirical overlap with some instances of interconnectedness, on the one hand, and aspects of vulnerability, on the other, are recognized. Used in such a manner, sensitivity may thus be seen to have a number of interesting dimensions. Any actual condition of sensitivity, on any issue, will be a function of three features: the *immediacy* of the effect of the pertinent external development upon the dependent actor; the *salience* of the issue to the affected actor; and, finally, the short-term *adaptability* of the actor in the face of the problems created by the given development. Each of these three aspects of sensitivity, it should be noted, rest both upon objective features of the situation in which actors find themselves and upon their subjectively-based perceptions and policy orientations.

Conceptions of contemporary interdependence, and of the international political economy, do not, however, have to remain wedded to an actor-based approach. Indeed, as has already been suggested, a holistic approach may be both acceptable and essential. Which holistic vision of the global political economy will be adopted remains, however, a matter of considerable significance and not a little controversy.

Keohane and Nye's vision of contemporary reality is distilled in their concept of 'complex interdependence'. To these writers much of the modern world exhibits three central characteristics: (1) there are multiple channels of contact and communication connecting societies; (2) there is now an absence of a clear hierarchy of significance amongst the issues of international policy that concern governments; and (3) military force is not now used, or if used is of diminished effectiveness, in those areas of international relations in which 'complex interdependence' prevails.[3] Two problems, however, confront the claims of such a notion of 'complex interdependence' to offer an effective, holistic conception of the contemporary global system. First, that its view of current and future realities owes more to wishful thinking than to realistic appraisal. Second, that it is not a genuinely holistic conception and amounts, in fact, to little more than a list of purported conditions rather than a systematic and powerful theory of the development, dynamic and fundamental character of contemporary reality.

Many contemporary analysts would assert the superior claims of one or other of a number of holistic conceptions of the modern world system, based upon Marxist ideas. Latin American Dependencia Theory offers one such approach, the 'world system of capitalism' perspective, another. One of the many interesting features of such conceptions is their capacity to support two 'levels of analysis' simultaneously. At one level they are able to locate specific patterns of international interdependence within a conditioning, and determining, structure of global politico-economic relations which transcends and overarches visible nation-to-nation relationships. At a 'lower' level such perspectives also facilitate the exposure of those relationships between individuals and groups that cut across national boundaries and which serve to sustain a global capitalist system. From such perspectives, specific interdependencies are seen to be mere symptoms, or consequences, of far more profound patterns and processes within the global political economy.

While Marxist-based approaches do not necessarily monopolize the realm of holistic perspectives upon the global political economy, they do remain the most prominent and most fully elaborated. There are, however, some aspects of the recent concern with global interdependence that may give some of the appearance of holism but which do not rest upon the kinds of theoretical foundations that underpin such approaches. It is here that various facets of global 'common fate' are to be encountered. As will become clear from subsequent chapters, however, there are a number of differing forms of such 'common fate', with quite different implications and imperatives: from exposure to common external threat, through joint determination of consequences, to the transmission to others of effects that are already being experienced by oneself. Whatever the form of 'common fate', analytical caution should always be exercised for there are far too many unexpected vagaries in economic and technological development, and human policy-making is far too quixotic, for firm predictions to be made even from those conditions that seem to have the clearest and strongest practical implications.

It must be clear, then, that the term interdependence may be employed in a wide variety of ways, some of which may be mutually incompatible. It may, however, still be possible and desirable to offer some basic working definitions which will then serve to anchor both discussion and debate. Moreover, such a definition, if it purports to relate to no more than manifest conditions, will remain open to interpretation, explanation, or even criticism, from many perspectives.

Most of the contributors to this volume conceive of interdependence as a function of mutual dependencies, to whatever extent they exist. The initial definition must therefore be that:

> *dependence* exists for an actor when a satisfactory outcome on any issue requires suitable developments elsewhere;

> *interdependence* exists for two or more actors when each is dependent upon at least one other for satisfactory outcomes, on any issue(s) of concern.

It is important to note, however, that these definitions do not accord precisely with those offered elsewhere in this volume. This is particularly significant with respect to the contribution by Peter Willetts and this difference reflects the very special concerns which inform and direct his discussion.

It is not only actors that may be bound together. Suitable developments on one issue may be linked to appropriate developments on other issues, whether such developments be within the actor (*internal*) or outside the frontiers of the actor (*external*). A condition of *linked-issue* interdependence may also occur where satisfactory developments on a number of linked issues, within each of the participating actors, are dependent upon appropriate developments elsewhere within the set of interdependent actors.

THE REALITY OF INTERDEPENDENCE

Many popular statements about interdependence, by whatever definition, rest upon insecure empirical foundations. In some cases, ambitious declarations precede serious and systematic investigation. Other claims are either contradicted by such empirical evidence as is available or, perhaps more frequently, rest upon data which are open to differing, if not clearly contrary, interpretations.

The cases considered in the contribution to this volume illustrate the variety of specific conditions to be encountered in the modern world. Where the evidence does not actually contradict popular suppositions, it frequently paints a picture of far greater complexity than may have been imagined. Thus those who were intellectually weaned during the heyday of OPEC might be surprised to find that the world is not characterized by the 'commodity power' that was then predicted. Indeed, the contemporary scene is characterized by acute Southern dependence upon continued financial flows from the North and upon Northern supplies of technology, know-how information and advanced products. Only in the case of a very few strategic minerals is the North seriously materially dependent upon the South.

Interdependence amongst the Advanced Industrial Countries also presents an extremely complex picture. It is open to serious questions as to whether many of the economic transactions between such societies mark significant interdependence or, rather, patterns of competitive, and largely wasteful, trade.

East–West economic relations pose the analyst with an even more thorny problem. The development of these relations has been proceeding apace and clearly carries portents of a most significant kind. However, nowhere is the development of economic association more clearly a subject of political interest and control. This feature alone qualifies East–West trade for the most careful handling by the analyst and for the greatest caution regarding projections into the future.

Economic interdependence between and amongst Southern societies remains a matter of considerable interest and aspiration. Many Southern spokesmen advocate the complementary development of their societies as the most effective strategy for the overall development of the South. Such advocates argue that it is only through disengagement from economic relations with the 'exploitative' North, and concentration on collective economic self-help and self-development, that the South will be able to meet the pressing challenges with which it is faced. However, such a programme of South–South trade and development has achieved but limited progress thus far, with projects fostered by Southern-based multinational corporations marking some of the more prominent advances in this direction.

The discussion of the reality of interdependence thus far has been confined to those forms manifest in the immediately apparent. Holistic conceptions of the global political economy have, however, a more complex connection with reality. Empirical data will provide only indicators of underlying, or overarching, 'realities' and the manner in which such indication is furnished will, itself, be established by the perspective that proclaims such 'realities'. The reality of interdependence by a holistic conception will, therefore, remain an inherently complex matter.

All discussion of the 'realities' of interdependence, by whatever definition, will continue to require qualification by one abiding consideration. Conditions in the real world that we inhabit are characteristically and chronically liable to change. That which presents itself as a hard, and apparently immutable, reality today may well be transformed tomorrow.

THE IMPLICATIONS OF INTERDEPENDENCE

Contemporary interdependence has been held to have implications both for practical international relations and its study. On the practical side, the range of arguments reflects the spectrum of possibilities. In the realm of North–South relations the reader may choose at will between arguments that the prevailing pattern of interdependence furnishes the South with an ultimately irresistible weapon with which to compel the North to accept fundamental change in the international economic order and the opposing view that contemporary interdependence facilitates the continued Northern domination of the South.

Controversy of equal intensity is to be encountered in discussions of the effects and significance of most of the dimensions of contemporary interdependence. The development of East–West interdependence is one such issue of moment. Some argue that any further development of this relationship poses a fundamental threat to the military and political well-being of the West, while others contend that progress in this area can only contribute to prosperity, mutual confidence and, hence, improved security in the longer term.

An issue of particular interest has been posed by Keohane and Nye in their argument that the development of 'complex interdependence' is marked by a decline in the use and utility of force between the involved societies (an issue which has recently been the subject of particular attention by Barry Buzan, of Warwick University, and which he has discussed with the International Relations Theory Research Group). The argument which lies at the heart of Keohane and Nye's position is that the development of the conditions that underlie 'complex interdependence' are such as to reduce the use and utility of force. This argument, which closely parallels the traditional 'liberal' claim that the growth of free trade and a mutually advantageous international division of production will encourage global harmony and peace, is contentious on at least two grounds. First, it may be argued empirically that the use of force does not seem to have declined that dramatically when the whole of the modern international system is reviewed: merely that peace has been preserved within a few favoured enclaves. Second, it may be argued theoretically that, even in areas where force does appear to have been eliminated (at least for the time being), the view of Keohane and Nye rests upon an unwarranted presumption. In short, while Keohane and Nye argue that the growth of economic interdependence has led to the relative redundancy of force, the contrary argument may have equal, if not greater, weight. Such a counter argument would assert that it is special political conditions that initially establish a period of peace within a given area and that this peace, in turn, permits trade (and hence increased levels of economic interdependence) to flourish. It is in maintaining an erroneous pattern of causality that the weakness of the argument of Keohane and Nye, and their followers, may thus be identified.

Arguments about the relationship between peace and interdependence are, of course, of considerable practical importance (importance, that is, if it is to be assumed that a correct appreciation of the processes and dynamics of international affairs may lead to more effective policy-making). If the views of Keohane and Nye, or other 'liberals', are to be accepted, then anything that halts, or even threatens to reverse, the progress of free trade or the growth in interdependence is to be feared deeply. In contrast, those who are critical of the view that interdependence (or free trade) encourages, and even requires, peace may entertain two thoughts. First, that the real sources of peace within international regions (and, hence, of economic intercourse) must be sought in deeper or broader realms. Second, that far from contributing to peace, the growth of interdependence may actually stimulate such difficulties and frictions as to halt the further growth of trade and productive specialization and engender dangerous politico-economic frictions. Clearly, whatever the individual's final judgement, such arguments are of no inconsiderable significance.

The analysis of international relations may also be affected profoundly by contemporary interdependence in two possible ways. There is, firstly, the contention that the growth of empirical interdependence has exposed serious shortcomings in the intellectual armoury of traditional students of international relations. Contemporary interdependence, it would be argued, involves processes and subjects that lie outside the competence of such analysts. New features of the world have to be addressed and a new conception of the international realm deployed. Of equal import is the second argument that modern notions of interdependence occasion a basic change of view about all international relations, past as well as present. In part, but only part, this argument rests upon a recognition of the unsound, and over-sharp, separation between politics and economics that, it is held, was maintained for far too long within the musty preserves of the 'traditional' scholars of international relations.

Many and profound, then, are the implications of contemporary ideas about interdependence. The term clearly denotes something of considerable significance in international relations and the concept has many implications for the study of the subject. It is for these reasons that, whatever areas of scepticism and unease may remain, the term cannot merely be written off as too vague or diverse of meaning, or as no more than an ideologically conditioned impediment to a clear understanding of contemporary reality. A working definition of interdependence, and associated concepts, has been offered in this paper. These definitions, however, refer to only a narrow set of empirical conditions. It may, therefore, remain essential to maintain catholicity in the use of the term 'interdependence' if the richness of empirical and theoretical variety is to be apprehended. The analyst must still, therefore, be cautioned to handle the term in a careful and critical manner. If such an approach to the idea of interdependence can be sustained, then it may yet serve to unlock and highlight much that is central in the contemporary international political economy.

THE CONTRIBUTIONS

The contributions to this volume encompass a wide range of issues, both theoretical and empirical. Not all are agreed upon the most appropriate definition of interdependence, nor in their conclusions about its possible implications, empirical or theoretical. However, in combination these varied contributions should offer the reader a valuable and stimulating review of many of the central issues generated by modern notions of interdependence.

The earlier contributions identify and discuss in detail the major conceptual and theoretical issues raised by contemporary ideas about interdependence. These discussions are more than mere abstruse excursions, however, for they highlight the nature and complexity of many features of contemporary international conditions.

Barry Jones offers a wide-ranging review of the many possible definitions and implications of the term 'interdependence', as currently employed. The diversity of contemporary usage is strongly emphasized, as are the widely diverging practical implications of different conceptions, or forms, of interdependence. The relationships between various notions of interdependence and the empirical world are also somewhat more complex and problematical than is often supposed. In some instances, the accumulation of appropriate empirical evidence is a relatively straightforward matter. However, even here it is often the case that the implications of such evidence are either contrary to popular suppositions or, if not clearly contradictory, are complex and ambiguous. Elsewhere, the relationship between concept and 'reality' is intrinsically problematical, with the specification of appropriate evidence being determined by the governing theory and the evidence accumulated being no more than indicative of underlying 'realities'.

A number of firm conclusions can be distilled from Jones's lengthy contribution. First, that great definitional care needs to be exercised in any use of the term 'interdependence'. Second, that most significant instances of manifest interdependence are asymmetrical and seriously imbalanced. Third, that a holistic approach will be required if central features of the global political economy are to be apprehended and that such a holistic perspective will have to include an acknowledgement that the system is, for good or ill, basically a 'capitalist' system. Finally, that the relationship between theory and reality is, in the arena of contemporary interdependence, a far more complex matter than is often imagined.

The contributions of Steve Smith, Peter Willetts and Richard Little complement one another well. They offer clear and forceful statements of the two sides of the argument concerning the novelty of the concept of interdependence and its effects upon the study of international relations. Smith argues that the emergence of contemporary interdependence has a significant effect upon the formulation and conduct of foreign policy and, thence, has powerful implications for its study and analysis. 'Traditional' foreign policy analysis is, particularly, challenged by the manner in which modern interdependence erodes the distinction between domestic and foreign policy issues and influences; undermines the pre-dominance of politico-military issues over economic in foreign relations; displaces security issues as the main determinant of international orientations; and, hence, shifts the focus of analytical attention away from crisis decision-making. While Smith concedes that the debate is far from finished, he concludes that modern interdependence does confront traditional foreign policy analysis with severe problems.

Peter Willetts is concerned with the emergent 'global society' which is developing from a number of normatively based concerns and interests within contemporary international relations. His focus is not, therefore, upon economic or ecological forms of interdependence but upon 'cognitive interdependence': that dimension of international relationships wherein certain values may be satisfied only through mutually complementary forms of behaviour.

Richard Little's contribution contrasts with Steve Smith's. Little argues, forcefully, that many have been hasty in accepting the view that recent ideas about interdependence mark, or entail, a sharp break with established ways of studying and analysing international relations. This erroneous assumption rests, in part, upon the acceptance of a stereo-typical, and unwarranted, view of many of the traditional, and particularly Realist, approaches to analysis. Worse, by shunning the falsely condemned wisdom of the Realists, the acolytes of the new interdependence have denied themselves much of value. The paradoxical effect of this is, in Little's view, that the Realists themselves continue to have more to say about the relationship between power and interdependence in contem-porary international relations than the 'interdependencists'.

The debate over the intellectual implications of modern interdependence may, of course, be over-trumped by the contention that both sides of the argument share the same, insecure, epistemological and methodological premises and, therefore, the same basic flaws. This, in essence, is what John MacLean seeks to do in his chapter. His argument opens with a criticism of many of the popular approaches to interdepen-dence as resting upon actor-based, and hence reductionist, definitions of the phenomenon. Such actor-based conceptions are, he then argues, inimical to a proper appreciation of the complex structures that underlie, and condition, the inter-national relationships that are immediately visible to the observer. The global political economy can thus be properly comprehended only through the lenses of a structural and holistic perspective or theory; and a model based upon Marxist notions offers the best such perspective. MacLean's final act is to develop an analysis of the United Nations Educational Scientific and Cultural Organization (UNESCO) — its history and current difficulties — within the framework of a Marxist perspective: seeking to demonstrate that such a perspective is essential for effective analysis in this case.

The attention of the later contributors is directed primarily towards those areas of contemporary international relations which are, or might be expected to be, characterized by marked interdependence. The purpose of these discussions is to evaluate the extent and effect of such interdependence in each case, both for its own sake and as a means of establishing points of general importance about contemporary inter-national processes and conditions.

Mike Smith is concerned to identify a number of differing

views about the nature of relations within the North Atlantic area and the contrasting conceptions of the interdependence upon which they rest. In each of the three distinct notions of 'Atlanticism' there is seen to be a substantial gap between concept and reality: in the demonstration of which Smith is able to report much of interest about North Atlantic relations during the post-war era.

John Vogler explores the collective management of the electromagnetic spectrum, through which the transmission of telecommunications takes place. Behaviour and outcomes, within this arena, are seen to be governed by a combination of a recognition of the real, 'common fate' danger of damaging 'transmitted effects'; the technical and allied strengths of some of the major participants; and, finally, the influence of the institutions and organizations that have been established to administer such matters. However, the continued influence of organizational characteristics and opportunities would seem to be a result of the recognition, by the more 'powerful' participants, of the damaging 'transmitted effects' that might be precipitated by the collapse of the institutions that currently administer the electromagnetic spectrum.

NOTES

1. R.O. Keohane and J.S. Nye, *Power and Interdependence: World Politics in Transition* (Boston, Little, Brown, 1977), see especially pp.12-19.
2. Ibid., pp. 12-13.
3. Ibid., Ch. 2, and especially pp. 24-5.

2 The Definition and Identification of Interdependence
R.J. BARRY JONES

INTRODUCTION

The term 'interdependence' is now firmly entrenched in the thoughts and words of politicians, rhetoricians and international relations analysts. The reformist polemic of the Brandt Commission's *North–South: A Programme for Survival*[1] and such analytical excursions as Keohane and Nye's *Power and Interdependence*[2] rest, equally, upon the idea that the international system exhibits a condition that can properly be entitled interdependence; a condition, moreover, which is held to have been intensifying during recent decades. The meaning of the term, however, remains far from clear[3] and, for any given definition, empirical indicators are often ambiguous or elusive.

Acknowledgement of the diversity of meaning, if not downright confusion, attaching to the term 'interdependence' is, however, no warrant for its abandonment or for the neglect of its subject matter. It is rare that terms are conjured entirely from thin air. Concepts usually have some substantive referents in the empirical world and in the case of interdependence such referents are some of those features of contemporary international relations that underlie many basic changes and that may foreshadow serious conflicts. The study of interdependence, in one or other of its possible manifestations, may thus direct attention towards matters of considerable significance.

Progress in the study of interdependence, however, requires the identification and clear differentiation of the alternative meanings that can attach to the term. Such conceptual analysis should also reveal the extent to which alternative definitions rest upon differing normative orientations or contrasting theoretical presumptions.

Appropriate empirical indicators of interdependence will reflect the definition adopted. Naïve empiricism is too insecure a methodological position to allow confidence in any self-presenting empirical measures, or indicators, of any form of interdependence.[4] Empirical indicators remain, to an extent, arbitrary measures of phenomena that have been imbued with significance by some theory of reality. Such theoretical direction of empirical analysis is nowhere more clear than in the case of the 'contested concept' of interdependence, where diverse definitions emphasize different measures and indicators.

The empirical difficulty of identifying interdependence is compounded by the abstraction and holism inherent in some of its definitions. The structures of 'dependency' envisaged by the Dependencia theorists[5] will not be apparent at the level of everyday transactions but will be evidenced, in contrast, by indirect indicators. A system-wide condition of interdependence will, in like manner, not be demonstrated by simple measures of any given transactions or relationships but will, rather, require illumination through quantitative and qualitative aggregation of various evidence.

The second section of this chapter will survey a number of contrasting definitions of interdependence, many of which are explicit within the established literature; others of which have to be distilled from diverse sources and statements.

Such a survey requires the establishment of many critical distinctions. Interdependence has to be differentiated from integration; true interdependence from mere interconnectedness; symmetrical or balanced interdependence from asymmetrical or imbalanced instances; and discrete relations of mutual dependence from sets of relationships that constitute holistic phenomena.

A general excursion around the topic also has to pay careful attention to the varied implications that may be identified with interdependence, by one definition or another. Such supposed implications may be challenged on one, or both, of two grounds: firstly, that the suggested effects do not necessarily follow from the conditions of interdependence with which they have been linked; or, secondly, that even where such links do exist, the underlying conditions of interdependence are far from stable or irreversible. It is, furthermore, often assumed without proof that the hypothesized conditions of interdependence do, in fact, obtain. Should these conditions themselves be uncertain, then the entire edifice of the 'interdependencists' crumbles.

From the discussion in this chapter, a number of basic

themes and lines of argument will be seen to emerge. First, that most of the more interesting and significant forms of contemporary interdependence exhibit substantial asymmetry and imbalance. Second, that a number of central features of current global interdependence can be appreciated properly only if a holistic perspective is adopted: a holistic perspective, moreover, which exhibits some, if not all, of the features of Dependencia Theory. However, it should also be noted that this conclusion does not imply that more discrete forms and definitions of interdependence are to be neglected or rejected, merely that a holistic perspective will often prove a necessary part of effective analysis.

It will be seen, finally, that the discussion seeks to cast doubt upon many of the more sweeping conclusions that some have sought to draw from the existence, and possible further development, of international interdependence. Particular scepticism is directed towards two propositions. First, that the existing condition of North–South interdependence requires, and will therefore call forth, a new era of enlightened co-operation and mutually beneficial reform of the international economic order. Second, that the progress of a free trade system, and concomitant extension of the global division of labour, will guarantee harmony and well-being, regionally or internationally. Indeed, in sharp contrast, it may be more valid to conclude that the growth of interdependence (or inter-dependencies), up to a certain point, may create such frictions, sensitivities and worrying vulnerabilities as to generate disharmony and potential conflict.

DEFINITIONS AND CONCEPTS OF INTERDEPENDENCE

Normative considerations

The condition of interdependence carries contrasting norma-tive considerations for its various discussants. Many see the development of higher levels of interdependence as occasion-ing, or prompting, the coming together of peoples in more harmonious and co-operative approaches to common prob-lems and undertakings: from the management of the global 'commons' through to the banishment of war. In marked contrast, others identify less happy implications of interdependence; be they the exposure of the industrialized countries to threats of the withdolding of essential resources,[6] or the continued structural deprivation and subordination of the majority of the Less Developed Countries (LDCs).

Unfortunately, many of the contrasting perspectives upon interdependence rest, fundamentally, upon basic judgements about the benign or malign character of the relationships under consideration. It is, therefore, extremely difficult to develop an unclouded view of the empirical reality that is addressed from such perspectives, each perspective itself governing the basic description of that reality. Thus a perspective that views interdependence as a relationship of structural dominance (and diversity) will specify the condition as essentially malignant. Judgements upon the goodness, or otherwise, of interdependence will, equally, rest upon an appropriate definition and its associated theoretical perspective.

Definitional issues

Where a term is afflicted by diversity, and even confusion, in usage, some robust conceptual ground-clearing is usually warranted. Interdependence must initially be distinguished from integration. The political integration of societies entails a degree of common governance which goes far beyond that which is implied by interdependence. Economic integration may similarly be defined to signify commonalities of rule, regulation and practice not necessarily associated with interdependence.

Other important issues concerning the definition of inter-dependence cannot, however, be disposed of as neatly as that of integration. One of the more intractable issues within recent literature has been the controversy between those who define interdependence as 'mutual dependence' and those who view it more in terms of close 'interconnectedness', or 'interlinkage', between societies.[7] If mutual dependence is the concept to be adopted, then there is also the question of symmetry or asymmetry, balance or imbalance. Where asymmetry or imbalance is held to prevail it may then become a question of how much is permissible in a relationship before it should properly be deemed one of dominance or one-way depen-dence, rather than proper *inter*dependence.

Overarching the issues between interdependence and

interconnectedness, and between interdependence and dominance/dependence, is the question of whether inter-dependence is a relationship between discrete actors, which may or may not be aggregated into complex patterns, or whether it is a condition that is a property of a global system which can be properly conceived only within some form of holistic analytical perspective. At issue, too, is the question of whether interdependence can be conceived as incorporating those elements of global common fate which carry implications for all, but which are not strictly speaking a function of inter- or trans-national relations, but which are a contextual condition.

Mutual dependence or interconnectedness?

The literature on interdependence is permeated by a basic tension between two contrasting views of the concept. The first view identifies interdependence as existing only where there is some measure of mutual dependence, with dependence signifying an actor's reliance upon some other(s) for support, or the satisfaction, of a basic need. The disruption of, or adverse development within, such a relationship of dependence would be intrinsically costly to the dependent actor.

The contrasting position emphasizes situations in which effects in one society are occasioned by pertinent develop-ments in other societies: situations in which patterns of interconnectedness or interlinkage ensure the transnational transmission of developments.

Such a distinction between interdependence as mutual dependence and interdependence as interconnectedness is important, initially attractive, but persistently problematical. In practice, a pattern of interconnectedness between two or more societies may incorporate dependencies. The intercon-nectedness of the global oil market ensures the rapid transmission of changes in the price of crude oil across national frontiers, but also embraces the dependence of oil-importing countries upon continued flows from the supplying countries and the dependence of the oil-supplying countries upon continued purchases by the consuming countries.

Mutual dependence and interconnectedness are not, however, always associated. Many patterns of interconnected-ness cannot be equated with real dependence without serious departure from any normal interpretation of the latter term: the world market for used postage stamps may be highly interconnected across national frontiers without implying any serious dependence for any of the involved societies (merely stamp dealers). Again, on a point that will be taken up subsequently, movement from the economic domain to that of politico-military relations suggests areas of strategic interdependence in which, as with the case of mutual nuclear deterrence, the level of mutual dependence may be inversely related to the level of contacts and transactions (as conventionally conceived).

Politico-military interdependence is, however, a special phenomenon. The focus of this discussion is upon economic interdependence, wherein the analytical distinction between mutual dependence and interconnectedness is important. Central, here, is the differentiation of two significantly different conditions, both of which may be deemed forms of interdependence. In the first instance, two societies might be dependent upon one another in some critically important respects, even though these dependencies constitute but a small proportion, in volumetric terms, of their external relationships and transactions. Such a situation might, though would not necessarily, reflect considerable dissimilarity between the societies concerned. In the second instance, two societies, possibly quite similar in political and economic morphology, might sustain high levels of interaction and transaction without being significantly dependent, in a normal sense of the term, upon one another.

Sensitivity and vulnerability

Any consideration of the distinction between mutual dependence and interconnectedness leads inexorably into the issue of sensitivity. The concept of sensitivity has been accorded a central role in many discussions of interdependence[8] and certainly directs attention towards a number of important issues. Unfortunately, discussions of interdependence have often failed to give full consideration to the possible identity between sensitivity and some forms of interconnectedness, or to establish the critical distinction between the objective and the subjective connotation of sensitivity.

Keohane and Nye attempt, unsuccessfully, to clarify the

issue of sensitivity. They offer a definition which confines the term 'interconnectedness' to those relationships in which there are no '. . . significantly costly effects' (given an assumed opposition between significant and vanishingly trivial).[9] Most usages of interconnectedness assume the inclusion of effects with real costs and this allows the retention of the term as generic for a set of economic relationships (including, but not identical with, real interdependence).

Sensitivity is clearly an important notion in considerations of the immediate economic and political significance of any pattern of economic interrelationship. Keohane and Nye's introduction of the term 'sensitivity interdependence' is not, however, as useful in this respect as might initially appear, for it is not clear that it is distinct from mere interconnectedness. Keohane and Nye's suggestion that sensitivity interdependence is distinctive and may be contrasted clearly with vulnerability interdependence is, therefore, not as secure as might be supposed. A large part of this problem resides in the failure to distinguish clearly between the objective and the subjective facets of sensitivity.

Keohane and Nye define sensitivity in the following terms: 'Sensitivity involves degrees of responsiveness within a policy framework — how quickly do changes in one country bring costly changes in another and how great are the costly effects?'[10] Such a notion emphasizes the transnational transmission of costs while conditions (including the sensitive nation's policies) remain as they are currently. Now this is a view of interdependence which accords with many of the implications of interconnectedness perspectives upon interdependence,[11] for such sensitivity interdependence clearly requires some measure of interconnectedness between the societies concerned and suggests, implicitly, some level of contingency (one development occasioning another, elsewhere). Sensitivity interdependence is, in Keohane and Nye's usage, also definitionally exclusive of those more substantial forms of interdependence which incorporate real vulnerability, wherein: 'Vulnerability can be defined as an actor's liability to suffer costs imposed by external events even after policies have been altered.'[12]

Sensitivity interdependence would thus be basically those instances of international economic interconnectedness which have potentially costly implications (i.e. most) but which are not necessarily relations characterized by real vulnerability. Sensitivity interdependence for Keohane and Nye is, therefore, a form of interconnectedness in which the relevant international linkages cause a notable degree of mutual responsiveness and/or a form of short-term vulnerability to external developments and/or pressures.

More serious, however, is the ambiguity inherent in the common usage of the term sensitivity. While Keohane and Nye ignore this difficulty, it remains one which must be addressed in any serious discussion of contemporary interdependence.

The condition of some entity may be said to be sensitive, in an objective sense, when it is highly responsive to developments in its environment: a ball on a smooth surface being sensitive to lateral forces. In the political economy, such objective sensitivity would imply the responsiveness of an economy, unmediated by political authorities. Such objective sensitivity is a large part of the subject matter of those who study interconnectedness (in non-vulnerability forms). Subjective sensitivity, in contrast, has everything to do with the perceptions and reactions of political authorities and their publics. The difficulty is that subjective sensitivity might be the corollary of objective sensitivity, in the policy responses that governments are disposed to make to transnationally transmitted economic developments, or it might be a reflection of some more basic economic vulnerability. Thus the subjective sensitivity of importing nations towards oil in the post-1973 years reflected both a concern about short-term price movements and their effects, and a more deep-seated concern about long-term strategic-economic dependence and the associated dangers of suffering embargoes or resource exhaustion.

The introduction of the notion of subjective sensitivity, however, confronts the analyst with all the difficulties associated with the relationship between 'objective' and 'subjective' phenomena in human affairs. Whether or not the student wishes to embrace the doctrine that all social, economic and political events are conditioned exclusively by the subjectivities of the participants, it must be acknowledged that actors' perceptions and expectations may so influence behaviour as to modify developments, at times, in a significant manner. Thus, subjective sensitivities will clearly exert some

influence upon the reactions of populations and the calculations of governments, whatever their long-term impact upon
developments.

Sensitivity is thus a central, if rather confused and somewhat
uncertain, issue in discussions of interdependence. Sensitivity
interdependence may be no more than patterns of potentially
costly (but non-vulnerability) interconnectedness. However, it
may be important to analyse the varying patterns and causal
conditions of subjective sensitivity, for they constitute a
significant part of the politics of interdependence. It may thus
be of particular value to investigate the conditions under
which potential costs are ignored, tolerated, misperceived or
exaggerated by populations or their political leaders.

Costs: the ambiguous cornerstone of interdependence

The discussion thus far has suggested that costs play a critical
role both in the conceptual analysis and in the practical
politics of interdependence. Indeed, careful consideration of
the costs involved in maintaining or disrupting a given
international relationship may provide the most useful basis
for classifying such relationships.

Reference to costs can, in principle, be employed in the
identification of true interdependence and its differentiation
from other forms of interconnectedness, the extent and
irreducibility of costs being the criteria. Costs might also
provide the basis of a number of other discriminations
between, and within, various interdependence relationships.
Unfortunately, costs fail to provide watertight discriminatory
criteria or indicators, for they are neither sufficiently unam-
biguous nor as certain in the development over time to permit
confidence in any simple classificatory scheme based upon
them.

The first problem is that of the ambiguity of costs. It is
inherently difficult to establish clear thresholds between those
costs that can be considered trivial and those that ought to be
deemed significant in different patterns of interconnectedness.
Clearly, many patterns of international interconnectedness
carry considerable potential or actual costs for their participants.
Contemporary international financial interconnectedness
exposes national economies to the danger of rapid, and
adverse, movements of capital and associated pressures upon

currency values in money markets. Such possibilities, further-more, subject national governments to substantial and serious constraints upon their freedom of manoeuvre in economic policy (as the experiences of the French Socialist government of President Mitterrand clearly demonstrated).

Interconnectedness may thus be associated with very substantial costs. It is, however, interesting that many of these costs (though not all) are those attendant upon the maintenance, rather than the disruption, of the pertinent relationships.

A further, equal difficulty is posed by the need to differentiate between costly interconnectedness on the one hand, and real, persisting vulnerabilities on the other. The first problem encountered in this task is that costly interconnectedness and long-term vulnerability (and dependence) may be associated empirically. Thus, the global responsiveness exhibited within many commodity markets may be associated with the serious, long-term dependence of some of the participating societies upon continued exports or imports of the relevant commodity. However, this is not the sole difficulty encountered in seeking to employ costs as *the* arbiter of true dependence (or interdependence). A serious, additional problem is the un-certain development of costs over time, for they may be far from constant.

The attempt by analysts to avoid the problem of the variation of costs over time undermines the apparent defini-tional clarity of 'vulnerability'. This weakness in the concept of vulnerability is compounded by conflating two distinct notions — of availability and cost — within the definition of the term. Keohane and Nye offer the argument that: 'The vulnerability dimension of interdependence rests on the relative availability and costliness of the alternatives that various actors face.'[13] Availability carries a binary, or absolute, implication — availability or unavailability — regardless of any attempt to convert it into a variable by qualifying it with the adjective 'relative'. The notion of costs, in contrast, is clearly one that can accommodate infinite variation.

The problem with conflating availability and cost is that while an available policy will clearly have an identifiable cost, an unavailable policy will not. The question for Keohane and Nye, therefore, is whether they wish to make the lack of such a policy that would remove future costs the criterion of vulnerability or whether the criterion is to be the costliness of those policy options that are both available and suitable for eliminating (or significantly reducing) an adverse condition, development or relationship. The former condition is absolute, therefore analytically attractive, but unlikely in practice; the latter condition is relative, therefore less precise, but more realistic.

The basic problem here is that, given sufficient time, ingenuity can be allowed to flourish and long-term policies brought to fruition. It is improbable, then, that it will prove impossible to find some avenue of escape from what once appeared to be daunting vulnerability. Only in the most extreme of conditions will dependencies prove irreducible or inescapable.

It is just such possibilities of escape, and their attendant analytical complications, that prompt Keohane and Nye to hedge their bets and maintain a degree of ambiguity on 'vulnerability'. At one point they support the availability criterion, arguing, in a previously given quotation, that: 'Vulnerability can be defined as an actor's liability to suffer costs imposed by external events even after policies have been altered,'[14] while subsequently veering back towards the *level of* costliness criterion in their statement that: 'Vulnerability dependence can be measured only by the costliness of making effective adjustments to a changed environment over a period of time.'[15]

A worthwhile definition of real (or vulnerability) dependence must, therefore, add time to availability and cost as the criteria of real dependence. However, time contributes considerable complexity to the new equation, for it adds the costs attendant upon the delay before a new policy can be fully implemented (and its effects felt) to the intrinsic costs of pursuing that policy. Thus a series of nuclear power stations will be intrinsically costly to build and operate, but there may also be other costs incurred while awaiting the completion of such facilities, especially if shortages of other energy sources threaten to arise.

Reference to cost is thus rendered a less than certain criterion for classifying interdependence relationships by the combined effects of time and the profound changes that might follow upon innovations or policy initiatives. Other forms of interconnectedness are equally affected by such possibilities. The alteration of attendant costs over time, and with changed conditions, also undermines some of the more extravagant claims made by those who have perceived the remorseless advance of global interdependence or proclaimed its irresistible and multifarious implications.

Reference to costs may thus fail to provide the 'philosopher's stone' for interdependence analysts. However, costs do remain a useful point of reference in the differentiation and indentification of disparities amongst and within various forms of interdependence.

The comparison of the intrinsic costs allows an important distinction to be drawn between symmetrical and asymmetrical, balanced or imbalanced, forms of interdependence. Naïve discussions of interdependence often imply a perfectly, or at least highly, symmetrical or balanced condition (balanced, at least, in terms of the weights of the costs and benefits to the involved parties). In contrast, the more perceptive of analysts are at pains to emphasize the asymmetry and imbalance which characterize most instances of interdependence in the real world.[16] Indeed, most actual interdependencies occupy a middle position along the continua from perfect symmetry to asymmetry, and balance to imbalance.

In determining the location of any interdependence relationship on the symmetry–asymmetry, balance–imbalance continua, judgement will rest upon the identification and comparison of the potential costs to the participants. Costs might be comparable in terms of type or weight: participants may face similar costs in any relationship; in another, dissimilar but equally serious or weighty costs might be involved. Balance in any relationship will be a function of the comparative weight, or seriousness, of the potential costs to each of the participants regardless of the qualitative type of those costs (for an exporting nation the extent of loss of overall export markets would be of greater consequence than the loss of any one overseas market, *per se*).

The significance of relative levels of costs reinforces the view that interdependence must be conceived as a feature of specific relationships: a feature which can be identified only through the detailed examination of such relationships rather than by grand generalization. Bland assertions of the existence of a general condition of interdependence in the contemporary international system might thus be dismantled.

Once specific relationships are examined, highly unequal relationships may be identified. The costs for various participants may be found to differ in intensity and type: costs attendant upon both maintaining the relationship or disrupting it. Such an approach might be more discriminating with regard to contemporary realities and more indicative of their future development. The range of feasible, or desirable, policy options for governments might also be better indicated.

An important feature of contemporary international economic interdependence may be identified through an examination of relevant costs. The costs involved in the disruption of various patterns of international trade may be quite different in type and intensity when one form of society is compared with another. For many Advanced Industrial Countries (AICs), the costs arising from any disruption of imports of raw materials, basic foodstuffs or energy resources might be far greater than those resulting from any curtailment of imports of manufactured goods or advanced services (which might well be produced, or producible, domestically). Such AICs might also suffer far lower overall costs than would many Less Developed Countries (LDCs) for any comparable level of lost export opportunities up to a threshold (at a fairly high level) at which the relativities of costs might be dramatically reversed.

For the LDCs, overall, their weak financial reserves and lack of general shock-absorbing capacity makes them more sensitive to, and hence experience more acute costs from, quite small changes within established international economic relationships (as the great burden imposed upon many LDCs by the post-1973 oil price increases demonstrated so sharply, or as the impact of food price increases continues to illustrate).

A consideration of costs may thus contribute much to the analysis of interdependence. However, the relevant costs remain less than perfect indicators. Time may permit such changes of policy, or alterations of conditions, as to transform the pattern of costs inherent within any relationship (thus the dependence of Nigeria upon foreign sources of luxury automobiles will continue only for as long as there is a local Nigerian elite desirous of, and able to import, such vehicles).

Alternatives to the state-to-state vision of interdependence

Thus far the discussion has rested implicitly upon the assumption that interdependence is, or should properly be seen to be, a state-to-state phenomenon: bilateral or multi-lateral. There are, however, two prominent alternative views of the interdependence that does exist within the contemporary global system: two perspectives which achieve a synthesis of sorts within the Dependencia Theory.[17]

One alternative to the state-to-state approach to inter-dependence is based upon disaggregating the nation-state into its component interest groups, organizations and classes. Such an approach avoids the reification of the state and the unwarranted assumption that all, or indeed any, such nation-states are unitary, cohesive and internally homogenous entities. One serious form of over-simplification may thus be avoided and a more discriminating analysis facilitated; an analysis that permits the identification of diverse interests within societies and the serious consideration of alternative socio-economic conditions.

The second major alternative to the state-to-state view of interdependence rests upon some holistic conception of the global system. Here, the essence of the interdependence with which any state is faced is not to be discerned in any one or more of its bilateral relationships with other states, but in its overall relationship to, and location within, a complex of global conditions and relationships, the sum of which is greater than the addition of its component parts.[18]

Keohane and Nye's imagined condition of complex inter-dependence, with its multiple channels of contact, mixed hierarchies of issues and reduced role for force,[19] constitutes a dilute form of holistic perspective, for the characteristics thus identified are clearly those of a system rather than a part of any one, bilateral relationship within the system. More powerful holistic perspectives exist, however. One such locates any individual society within a global system that is inherently biased structurally and that sustains substantially unequal distributions of critical resources and capabilities. Such a biased structure might itself be seen to rest upon, and thence perpetuate, principles of action (e.g. capitalist or socialist) that further condition the circumstances with which any individual state will be confronted. Linkages across issues will also be characteristic of, and easier to identify within, such a holistic perspective; as with the danger of loss of financial aid by any Less Developed Country that might threaten to expropriate those assets of Northern multinational corporations that exist within its frontiers.

In the hands of the Dependencia Theorists, both alternatives to the state-to-state approach meld into one critical perspective. A capitalist world system is seen to have produced, over time, a fundamentally imbalanced structure in which the advanced capitalist states benefit systematically from their economic relations with a wide range of societies that have been positively underdeveloped through their historical association with their 'exploiters'. The world capitalist system is now seen to constitute a holistic phenomenon which conditions the experiences and opportunities of member societies. A global structure of asymmetrical and imbalanced interdependence has thus been created in which capitalists, within advanced capitalist states, are dependent for their continued accumulation of capital and wealth upon the underdeveloped world. The short-term well-being of the populations of the advanced capitalist societies is also dependent upon the maintenance of the established pattern of North–South exploitation.

To Dependencia Theorists, the existing order places the underdeveloped countries in a 'Catch-22' of dependence for short-term survival (through the continued export of primary commodities and cheap manufactures, as sources of revenues with which to purchase necessary basic imports) upon a pattern of economic relationships that systematically disadvantages and 'exploits' them.

Part of the cement of the structure of North–South 'dependency' and 'exploitation' consists in the group-to-group relations of interdependence that have developed transnationally between certain elite groups in both the advanced capitalist societies and the Less Developed Countries.[20] Here, while the greater part of the population of the underdeveloped countries is systematically disadvantaged by global capitalist exploitation, local elites may remain substantial beneficiaries from the relationships, institutionalized or otherwise, that have been established with elite groups in the advanced capitalist societies. An intimate and mutually beneficial symbiosis has thus been created between elite groups, those in the South guaranteeing the economic interests of those in the North, while those in the North provide various forms of largesse and politico-military support for their Southern affiliates.

The primary and positive interdependence of elite groups in North and South contrasts with the antagonistic positions into which non-elite groups are forced towards one another. Non-elites within the North are largely co-opted by the Northern elites through the high standard of living with which, under prevailing conditions, they are provided. The high standard of living within the North is, in turn, partly sustained by the continued exploitation of the South or, more properly, of the resources and non-elite groups of the South. Non-elite groups in the South continue to be controlled by their domestic elites and confronted by the dismal paradox of relying upon being exploited (through their exports to the North) to secure the funds with which to purchase the basics of life.

Beyond this vision of a global structure of exploitation and imperialism, which is by no means uncontroversial or incontrovertibly established, there is another, more diffuse, sense in which the international system places member states in a condition of interdependence. Wherever states are subject to a measure of common fate they may be dependent upon one another for desirable outcomes or the collaborative efforts necessary to secure beneficial developments.[21]

A degree of common fate exists when conditions can be influenced by a set of actors; the decisions of one actor, or a set, influencing conditions not only for itself but also transmitting similar effects (even if unintended) to others (the generation of pollution, with widespread effects, by states in the Mediter-ranean Basin being an outstanding example).

A second type of common fate can be identified in those developments which are determined by simultaneous, or mutually regarding, decisions by pertinent actors (an arms race in the politico-military sphere, the promotion of global recession by states all determined to maintain deflationary economic policies in pursuit of competitively low rates of domestic inflation and/or the avoidance of balance of payments deficits).

Common fate may not, however, be a matter of human volition, for it may reflect joint exposure to a development which is not the result of any decisions or actions by humanity but which is truly 'given' by nature (the approach of a destructive meteor).

Where common fate does reflect human decision-making and action, however, it continues to exert a significant influence upon the deliberations of governments and upon the developments that impose themselves upon the peoples of the contemporary global system.

Interdependence: myth or reality?

While no one phenomenon, or conception, presents itself automatically and unambiguously as interdependence, it is clear that the concept, in one guise or another, captures some important features of contemporary international reality. Diversity of meaning and variety of empirical referent are, however, both chronic and persistent. Such difficulties should not, however, encourage the spurious, tautological repudiation of interdependence offered by certain 'ultra-Realist' analysts of international relations but, rather, prompt careful investigation of the empirical conditions suggested by alternative definitions.

IDENTIFICATION

The identification of any form of interdependence or interconnectedness will remain a function of the definition and approach adopted. While all measurement is, to an extent, theory governed, it is generally the case that many of the more simple and straightforward measures may reveal little more than the trivial. In the case of interdependence, some of the more interesting formulations are either not essentially empirical conceptions (as with Dependencia Theory and its analytical-Marxist basis), require complex aggregations of data, or can only rest upon indirect, rather than direct, indicators.

Interconnectedness

General interconnectedness is relatively easy to indicate, as has been demonstrated by Richard Rosecrance and his colleagues. However, it should be noted that the Rosecrance approach depends not upon the demonstration of the mechanisms through which interconnectedness may be established, but upon the identification of common movements in such factors as prices in a number of countries. Even here, then, indirect indicators rather than direct measures, or identifiers, are being employed.

Rosecrance's group chose to establish the interconnectedness of the global economy by investigating the degree to which variations in wholesale prices, consumer prices, interest rates and wage rates showed similarities in the major industrialized economies during the period 1890–1975. Similarities in variation were established primarily by correlations (Pearson's 'r') of indices of the four factors and of changes in those indices (deltas) supplemented, in the case of interest rates, by a measure of the degree of convergence.[22] An additional indication of interconnectedness was also provided by establishing the percentages of each country's trade with each other.

The findings of the Rosecrance group challenge the arguments both of those who maintain that interconnectedness has advanced steadily during the post-World War II era and of those who hold the contrasting view that interconnectedness has, if anything, diminished during the twentieth century. The picture revealed by Rosecrance *et al.* is that of a mixed record, with evidence of sharp discontinuities between phases of growing and diminishing interconnectedness, coupled with variations in the qualitative nature of the characteristic patterns of interconnectedness.[23] After an ephemeral intensification of interconnectedness during the period 1950–8, the '. . . gradual and progressive detachment of individual national policies'[24] has been discerned.

Mutual dependence

Statistics that are suggestive of dependencies and mutual dependencies abound. Suggestion is not, however, always firm indication. Simple measures of such phenomena as trade flows and nations' import ratios for given commodities usually require qualification or elaboration before they may be presented as firm indicators of real needs that must be met or genuine benefits that might be lost.

The qualifications and elaborations required in the trans-formation of statistics on international economic transactions into indices of real dependencies involves both theory and extensive knowledge of the economic structure, resource distribution and prevailing technologies of production. The security of analysis is also weakened by the possibility of discontinuous developments in politico-military affairs, as well as in technological possibilities and requirements. The problems associated with these possibilities are, furthermore, exacerbated by the extension of time span. An awareness of the actual possibilities of technical innovation does no more than moderate these difficulties.

Mutual dependence can, moreover, be discussed sensibly only when specific dependencies and their interrelationships are identified. Only when the types and weights of the costs facing all parties have been measured is it possible to establish the symmetry and balance or, more probably, the extent of asymmetry and imbalance and, hence, indicate the political potentialities inherent in the given pattern of interdependence.

While the most pertinent asymmetries and imbalances can be indicated only within a specified relationship, or set of relationships, some of the general flavour of asymmetrical interdependence in the contemporary global system can be provided by relatively simple measures of the composition of trade.

Asymmetries in the trade relations between the North and the South may be indicated by the proportions of exports being directed to one another, as depicted in Table 2.1. Thus while the LDCs (rows 1 and 2) remain dependent upon the AICs for some 50–65 per cent of their export markets and, hence, their earnings of foreign exchange, the AICs are dependent upon the LDCs for only 28 per cent of their export markets. Subsequent evidence will reveal the complex situation relating to the import dependencies of the AICs and the LDCs upon one another. However, one prominent asymmetry is indicated in Table 2.2, which demonstrates that while the proportions of primary goods and manufactured merchandise amongst *imports* are roughly similar for both AICs and lower income LDCs, the proportions within *exports* vary significantly for the two types of country. The table does indicate that this latter condition is less true for the 'upper middle income' countries.

Table 2.1 *Destination of merchandise exports, 1960 and 1981 (% of totals)*

To From	1. AICs		2. LDCs		3. CPEs		4. High income oil exporters	
	1960	*1981*	*1960*	*1981*	*1960*	*1981*	*1960*	*1981*
1. Low Income Countries	51%	50%	27%	41%	21%	5%	1%	4%
2. Middle Income Countries	68%	65%	25%	29%	7%	4%	—	2%
3. Advanced Industrial Countries	67%	65%	30%	28%	3%	3%	—	4%

AICs: Avanced Industrial Countries;
LDCs: Less Developed Countries;
CPEs: Centrally Planned Economies.
Source: World Bank, *World Development Report*, 1983 (Oxford, Oxford University Press, 1983), Table 12, pp. 170–1.

Table 2.2 *Composition of imports and exports for selected groups of countries, 1980*

	AICs	Low Income Countries	Middle Income Countries	CPEs (1979)
Imports				
Primary commodities	48%	45%	37%	37%
Manufactured goods, etc.	52%	55%	63%	64%
Exports				
Primary commodities	28%	55%	63%(55%)*	37%
Manufactured goods, etc.	72%	45%	37%(45%)*	63%

* Upper Middle Income Countries
Note: World Bank classification of 'Middle Income Countries' ranges from Kenya (with a GNP per capita of $420 in 1981) to Trinidad and Tobago (with a GNP per capita of $5670). This group includes such countries as Israel, Greece and South Africa.
Source: *World Development Report, 1983*, ibid., Tables 10 and 11, pp. 166–9.

Amongst the AICs, potentially significant asymmetries may also arise, like that within Japanese–European trade as it had developed by 1970. In that year Japanese exports to Europe were worth some $US 2920 million, while European exports to Japan were worth a mere $US 1710 million:[25] evidence of a growing disparity between levels of export dependence of one upon the other.

Reference to statistics on general global trade patterns may suggest something of the overall character and condition of the international political economy. It is, however, necessary to embark upon rather more detailed studies, at a lower level of generality, before a discriminating picture of the more pertinent interdependencies may be constructed.

The statistics on the Centrally Planned Economies (socialist bloc primarily), given in Table 2.2, illustrate this need for more detailed, and discriminating investigation. The simple figures suggest a broad similarity between the economies and economic relations of the AICs and the CPEs. It is, however, common knowledge that the CPEs exhibit quite different approaches to internal economic management, and to patterns and processes of international economic transaction, from those characteristic of the AICs.

Historically, the Stalinist regime in the USSR directed economic developments in Eastern Europe towards intra-bloc interconnectedness, and even interdependence, and away from interdependence with societies outside COMECON. Most recently, however, dramatic evidence has been provided of the extent to which the opening-up of East–West trade and financial links may encourage singular patterns of interdependence, or dependence (Poland in early 1981 proving herself to be dramatically dependent upon receipts of foodstuffs and medicines from the West, while many Western financial institutions were simultaneously shown to be acutely dependent upon Poland continuing to honour her considerable international debts).

The location of any statistics within their appropriate politico-economic context is thus necessary for their accurate interpretation. It may also be important to disaggregate general patterns of trade and 'interdependence', as far as proves possible, to establish the precise nature and significance of any specific dependence. Many of these requirements may be illustrated by considering North–South 'economic interdependence' in terms of a 2 x 2 matrix, differentiating export dependencies from import dependencies for both parties to the relationship.

The import dependence of the AICs

The dimension of interdependence that has most attracted the attention of analysts in the North (and that stimulated much of the contemporary concern with the phenomenon) is that of the Advanced Industrial Countries' dependence upon imports of various commodities, particularly raw materials and energy resources, from the Less Developed Countries. Embargoes by oil-exporting countries during 1973 and 1974 demonstrated the vulnerability of import-dependent industrial societies to the dislocation of their complex economic and, thence, socio-economic systems.

The initial hysteria over resource shortages, price rises and even embargoes was followed by reassuring claims (or subtle propaganda) to the effect that the suppliers of such basic commodities were as dependent upon those to whom they sent the resources as were those who received them upon their senders. With time and further reflection, however, it has become apparent that the vulnerability of AICs is a more complex matter than initially envisaged. Real vulnerability depends upon the existence of a real import dependence, the pattern of supply of the resource in question and the related prospect of supplies actually being disrupted. Even where it is clear that one or more AICs do suffer from an import dependence, reserves of the resource in question must be inadequate if there are to be shortfalls in supply, or the producing nations must be willing and able to control supplies in such a way as to exert pressure for economic or political purposes. The initial condition of import dependence will, moreover, be qualified by the availability or the cost of substitutes, coupled with the existence of any alternative sources of supply of the original commodity.

The ratio of imports to consumption is the conventional index of import dependence. While common in the literature, simple import/consumption ratios tend to inflate the degree of dependence in one obvious way, by neglecting both direct exports and re-exports of the relevant commodity,[26] and, less obviously, by neglecting the indirect re-export of the commodity as part of manufactured goods. These distortions will occur, however, only where imports are less than 100 per cent of domestic consumption of the given primary commodity or energy source (when the effect of re-exports will be on absolute dependence levels rather than import/consumption ratios).

The level of import dependence of the major Advanced Industrial Countries is clearly high for a number of important raw materials, even when indicated by simple import/ consumption ratios, as outlined in Table 2.3.

Table 2.3 *AICs' imports as a percentage of consumption, 1975*

	USA	EEC	Japan
Aluminium	84	75	100
Chromium	91	98	98
Cobalt	98	98	98
Copper*	net exporter	98	90
Iron*	29	55	99
Lead*	11	85	73
Manganese*	98	99	88
Nickel*	72	100	100
Petroleum	37	93	100
Tin*	84	93	97
Tungsten	55	100	100
Zinc*	61	70	53

* One of the ten most important materials in engineering: see Table 5, p. 50, of R.W. Arad, U.B. Arad, R. McCullich, J. Pinera and A.C. Hollick, *Sharing Global Resources* (New York, McGraw-Hill, 1979).
Source: *Sharing Global Resources*, ibid., Table 3, p. 43, derived from 1977 International Economic Report of the President.

The AICs import dependence for these important raw materials and energy resources has been rising during recent years. However, the sources of most of these vital materials are diverse in political, economic and geographical respects. Table 2.4 illustrates these two features of AIC import dependence, in the case of the United States (differences in some figures reflect differing sources).

The very diversity of suppliers for many of the more critical resources complicates and generally reduces the possibility of producer cartels that might prove strong enough to force

Table 2.4 *Net US imports of selected minerals as a percentage of consumption, 1950–75, and major foreign suppliers*

Mineral	1959	1960	1970	1975	Major foreign sources 1972–5
Aluminium	58	68	83	84	Jamaica, Australia, Surinam, Canada
Chromium	95	85	89	90	USSR, S. Africa, Philippines, Turkey
Cobalt	90	66	98	98	Zaïre, Belg.-Luxemburg, Finland, Norway
Iron	4	15	21	29	Canada, Venezuela, Japan, EEC
Lead	40	33	22	11	Canada, Peru, Australia, Mexico
Manganese	77	89	95	98	Brazil, Gabon, Australia, S. Africa
Nickel	90	72	71	72	Canada, Norway, New Caledonia
Tin	82	82	81	84	Malaysia, Thailand, Bolivia
Tungsten	80	32	50	55	Canada, Bolivia, Peru, Thailand
Zinc	41	46	54	61	Canada, Mexico, Australia, Peru, Honduras

Source: D. Pirages, *The New Context for International Relations: Global Ecopolitics* (North Scituate, Mass., Duxbury Press, 1978), Table 5.3, p. 169, based upon US Dept. of Interior, *Mining and Mineral Policy, 1977*, p. 24.

substantial price increases or to impose severe restraints upon supplies. Controversy thus continues to surround the possibility of effective producer cartels. Some observers believe that there are few potential cartels that have a high probability of materialization, as Table 2.5 indicates. It is, therefore, far from clear that the Advanced Industrial World has been on the verge of a determined and effective onslaught, based upon control of supplies of a significant number of primary resources, particularly at a time of global recession which has depressed the prices of most such commodities. Thus it is that estimates of the 'risk factor' attaching to various minerals that are strategically critical to the Advanced Industrial Countries range from the moderate to the merely slight, as Table 2.6 indicates.

Resource exhaustion could confront the Advanced Industrial World with a serious problem, which was the import of *The Limits to Growth* and allied studies.[27] Such prognoses remain controversial, however,[28] and recent indications are of a mixed, but far from desperate, situation, as Table 2.7 indicates.

The import dependence of the Advanced Industrial Countries

Table 2.5 *Some assessment of the feasibility of producer cartels*

Feasibility	Economist Intelligence Unit	OECD Sect General	Helge Hveem
High	Bauxite	Tin Diamond Phosphate rock Antimony Manganese	Bauxite Phosphate rock
Medium (to high)	Bananas Iron ore Natural rubber Pepper Sugar Tin	Silver Chromite Bauxite	Rubber Tungsten Bananas Iron ore Copper Tea Spices (pepper) Cocoa
Medium (to low)	Cocoa Tea	Cobalt Mercury Uranium Zinc Copper	Jute Hard fibres Coffee Sugar Manganese Tin Lead Zinc
Low	Coffee Copper Wool	Lead Tungsten Iron ore	Cotton Wool Oilseeds Groundnuts Timber Nickel Fruits
Other	Phosphate rock Cloves		Uranium

Source: A. Gunder Frank, *Crisis in the Third World* (London, Heinemann, 1981), Table 3.2, p. 124, sources — various.

may, therefore, be a far less straightforward and serious matter than was often thought in the mid-1970s. Subjective sensitivity does not, however, always reflect objective vulnerability and a comparative study of financial flows from the USA, West Germany and Japan reveals a gross disparity between flows to five selected resource-rich LDCs and five resource-poor LDCs and, in addition, a notable jump in flows to the resource-rich

Table 2.6 *'Northern' mineral supplies risk factors (risk factors on a scale 1–100)*

Mineral	Risk factor	Mineral	Risk factor
Chromium*	41.5	Tungsten	13.9
Manganese	36.7	Tantalum	13.6
Cobalt*	35.3	Silver	11.6
Copper	28.8	Indium	10.5
Platinum group	28.8	Rhenium	9.9
Gold	26.4	Iron	9.5
Aluminium	23.0	Lead	9.0
Columbium	22.3	Mercury	8.8
Tin	21.8	Gallium	7.7
Diamond	19.0	Rare earth minerals	6.6
Nickel	18.8	Magnesium	5.9
Titanium*	17.7	Zirconium	5.9
Beryllium	17.6	Selenium	4.6
Vanadium	17.6	Cadmium*	4.5
Molybdenum*	16.1	Silicon	4.3
Germanium*	15.5	Tellurium	3.8
Zinc	14.9	Bismuth	3.7
Uranium	14.2	Lithium	3.6
		Antimony*	3.2

* Minerals of major strategic importance to the North.
Note: 'Risks' are risks of serious disruption of supplies.
Source: *South*, No. 36 (1983) 73.

Table 2.7 *Known reserves in 1970 and growth rates 1950–70 for critical raw materials*

	Known reserves at present usage rate (years)	Growth of known reserves since 1950 (% per annum)
Aluminium	100	6.6
Chromium	420	11.0
Copper	36	6.7
Iron	240	14.0
Lead	26	6.4
Manganese	97	2.0
Tin	17	2.9
Zinc	23	5.1

Source: C. Freeman and M. Jahoda, *World Futures: The Great Debate* (London, Martin Robertson, 1978), Table 6.12, p. 199, sources — various.

Table 2.8 *Financial flows from USA, West Germany and Japan to 5 resource-rich and 5 resource-poor LDCs — % of total financial flows to all developing countries, 1972–5*

Source country	Recipient countries	
	Resource-rich	Resource-poor
USA		
1972	5.5	0.5
1973	4.7	0.4
1974	4.6	0.2
1975	13.9	0.2
W. Germany		
1972	6.4	0.6
1973	5.8	0.2
1974	10.5	1.0
1975	18.2	0.5
Japan		
1972	13.2	0.6
1973	16.4	0.1
1974	35.8	0.5
1975	35.0	0.6

Source: H. Munoz, 'Strategic dependency: relations between core powers and mineral exporting countries', pp. 191–213 in C.W. Kegley and P. McGowan (eds), *The Political Economy of Foreign Policy Behavior* (Beverly Hills, Sage, 1981), Tables 8.4, 8.5 and 8.7, pp. 203–7.

recipients after the oil shocks of 1973-4, as Table 2.8 demonstrates.

The dependence of the Advanced Industrial Countries is thus real in the cases of a number of critical resources. Subjective sensitivity to possible shortages or strategic embargoes has also been demonstrated in recent years. The situation is, however, far too complex and varied to sustain any simple vision of Northern dependence upon the South, or of the emergence of Southern cartels possessed of sufficient power to force a transformation of the global economic order.

The export dependence of the AICs

The dependence of Advanced Industrial Countries upon given markets for their exports has often been a matter of considerable expressed concern when discussing such possibilities as the adoption of protectionist policies, withdrawal from such associations as the EEC, or the adoption of sanctions against such international malefactors as South Africa. In each case it is the threat to established export markets that is at the heart of arguments for care, caution, and restraint.

A number of measures may serve as indicators of various aspects of the export dependence of the AICs. A general picture may be provided by the ratios of exports to Gross National Product for individual AICs and selected examples are provided in Table 2.9.

Table 2.9 *Export / GNP ratios (%) for selected AICs, 1971*

	Exports (fob) ($US millions)	GNP	Exports/GNP (%)
All AICs	*643 100*	*4 404 332*	*14.6*
USA	113 323	1 702 020	6.66
Canada	38 128	194 600	19.59
EEC	*324 810*	*1 386 750*	*23.42*
Belg-Luxemburg	32 847	68 150	48.20
France	55 817	346 760	16.10
W. Germany	102 032	445 910	22.88
Italy	36 969	170 770	21.65
Netherlands	40 167	89 520	44.87
Denmark	9 113	38 530	23.65
Eire	3 313	7 930	41.78
Great Britain	46 271	219 180	21.11
Other:			
Japan	67 225	555 060	12.11
Australia	12 868	94 120	13.68
New Zealand	2 795	12 960	21.73
Sweden	18 440	74 220	24.85
Switzerland	14 845	56 290	26.37

Source: *UNCTAD Handbook of International Trade and Development Statistics, 1979* (New York, United Nations, 1979), Tables 1.1 and 6.1a, pp. 2–11 and 473–9 resp.

Table 2.10 goes on to amplify the aggregate statistics, provided in Table 2.9, by indicating the proportions of those AICs' exports that are directed to various categories of importing states.

Such general statistics, however, require further elaboration before a clear picture may be provided of the patterns of export

Table 2.10 *Proportional destination of the exports of AICs, 1960 and 1980*

	AICs 1960	AICs 1980	CPEs 1960	CPEs 1980	High inc. oil exporters 1960	High inc. oil exporters 1980	LDCs 1960	LDCs 1980
Ireland	96	88	—	1	—	2	4	9
Spain	80	62	2	2	—	5	18	31
Italy	65	67	4	3	2	7	29	23
New Zealand	95	67	1	5	—	1	4	27
UK	57	71	3	2	2	5	38	22
Finland	69	68	19	20	—	1	12	11
Australia	75	61	3	6	1	3	21	30
Japan	45	48	2	3	22	7	51	42
Canada	90	85	1	3	—	1	9	11
Austria	69	71	13	11	—	2	18	16
USA	61	58	1	2	1	4	37	36
Netherlands	78	85	1	2	1	2	20	11
France	53	68	3	4	—	3	44	25
Belgium	79	85	2	2	1	1	18	12
Norway	80	88	4	1	—	1	16	10
Denmark	83	83	4	2	—	2	13	13
Sweden	79	79	4	4	—	2	17	15
W. Germany	70	75	4	4	1	3	25	18
Switzerland	72	72	3	3	1	3	24	22

Source: World Development Report 1982, op. cit., Table 11, pp. 130–1.

trade of the major AICs. While the proportion of total exports sent to other AICs has been increasing in general during recent years, and the proportion of exports sent to LDCs commensurately declining, movements have also taken place in the proportion of AICs' exports going to given AICs, or groups of AICs, as Table 2.11 indicates with regard to the USA, Europe and Japan. Notable amongst these developments is the relative self-enclosure of trade within Europe. Table 2.12 also illustrates the marked redirection, during the period 1975–70, of the trade of Australia and New Zealand away from Europe, and Britain in particular, towards America, Japan and, to a lesser extent, developing Asia.

Equally interesting is the growing imbalance between Japan's substantial export dependence upon Europe and North America on the one hand, and, on the other, the relatively trivial level of export dependence of both Europe

Table 2.11   *Percentage of exports from selected AICs to selected AICs and regions (with LDCs for comparison), 1974–7.*

From＼To	USA	EEC	EFTA	Japan	LDCs
USA					
1974	—	22.2	3.4	10.9	32.6
1977	—	21.9	3.3	8.8	35.3
EEC					
1974	6.9	50.5	11.9	1.2	15.1
1977	6.2	50.6	11.5	0.9	18.8
EFTA					
1974	5.7	45.7	19.2	1.6	11.9
1977	5.4	46.5	17.5	1.2	14.3
Japan					
1974	23.2	10.8	2.9	—	45.2
1977	24.7	10.8	3.1	—	46.3
LDCs					
(non socialist)					
1974	17.4	32.0	2.4	14.2	21.3
1977	21.2	28.0	2.6	12.9	23.0

Source: UNCTAD Handbook 1979, op. cit., Table 3.1, pp. 86–92.

Table 2.12   *Percentages of exports from Australia and New Zealand to selected AICs and regions, 1955–70*

From＼To	USA	Whole Europe	Japan	Australia N. Zealand	Latin America	African LDCs	Developing Asia
Australia &							
N. Zealand							
1955	6.94	66.12	6.94	4.49	0.57	0.94	7.14
1960	8.78	52.33	12.19	5.91	0.75	0.82	8.24
1965	11.25	43.22	13.94	5.63	0.92	0.95	9.08
1970	13.50	28.72	23.42	5.64	0.75	1.16	14.56

Source: UNCTAD, Handbook on International Trade and Development Statistics, 1972 (New York, United Nations, 1972), Table 3.1, pp. 46–61

and North America upon Japan (albeit given the relatively low overall proportion of exports to GNP in the case of North America).

Discussion of the export dependencies of the AICs thus has to accommodate a number of questions including the level of exports relative to GNP, the degree of concentration in goods and commodities being exported and the extent to which exports are concentrated in one export market or a small number.

While most AICs, with the notable exception of the USA, have medium to high export/GNP ratios, they are in general far less reliant either upon one consumer of their exports, or upon a narrow range of exports, than are most of the LDCs.[29] Furthermore, the resources of the AICs are such as to allow many of them to undertake a quite remarkable redirection of their exports, given sufficient time and determination, as the cases of Australia and New Zealand so dramatically demonstrate. Most AICs, with the possible exception of those very small AICs that have a very high export/GNP ratio, are also possessed of sufficient capabilities to allow them to manage with substantially reduced levels of international trade and, hence, exports. In such instances it is possible, as war-time experience has so often demonstrated, to redirect productive facilities from exports towards domestic consumption.

With so many qualifications, it is clear that the export dependence of the AICs is a complex but, for all save a few committed international traders, a far from immutable condition.

The import dependence of the LDCs

The continuing import dependence of the LDCs is both considerable and serious and it remains a matter of acute concern to the governments, and often the peoples, of the LDCs. The 67.1 per cent of manufactured goods in the LDCs' overall level of imports are supplied, overwhelmingly, by the Advanced Industrial Countries. Many of these manufactured imports remain necessary for the maintenance of the economic infrastructure or as development capital.

Of even greater immediate seriousness, however, is the relatively high level of dependence of many LDCs on imports of staple foodstuffs. As Table 2.13 indicates, Less Developed Countries in Africa and Asia remain heavily dependent upon imports of grains (while North America continues to be a massive exporter). The pincer effect of reliance upon outside sources of food, manufactured goods and (for most) energy sources leaves many LDCs in a condition of critical import

Table 2.13 *World net grain production/consumption (in millions of metric tons)*

	1974–5
AICs	+54.5
North America	+75.8
West Europe	−18.7
Australia and N. Zealand	+12.1
Other Developed	−14.7
CPEs	−12.8
LDCs	−37.5
Africa and Middle East	−19.0
Latin America	−1.5
Asia	−17.1

Note: + indicates surplus producer/exporter;
         − indicates deficit producer/importer.
Source: Hansen, *The U.S. and World Development: Agenda for Action 1976*, (New York, Praeger, 1976), Table B2, p. 153.

dependence: a dependence which is of particular politico-economic significance given that the source of most of these vital resources continues to be the Advanced Industrial Countries.

The export dependence of the LDCs

Something of a paradox characterizes the continuing specialization of many LDCs upon the production and export of a narrow range of primary commodities. It is the AICs' dependence upon imports of just these commodities that is often supposed to provide the LDCs with their primary economic weapon in their attempt to extract concessions on a New International Economic Order from the AICs. However, it is also over-reliance upon exports of those same commodities that is widely held to be one of the characteristic, and most serious, sources of weakness for the majority of the LDCs.

The reality of contemporary global economic relations is that, while much of the South does remain highly dependent upon the export of a narrow range of primary commodities, it is only in a very few cases that the North is dependent primarily upon the South for vital supplies.[30] The supposed interdependence between North and South is thus marked in reality by a substantial and serious imbalance.

Table 2.14 *Selected LDCs, indices of commodity concentration for 1968 and 1976*

Country	Indices of commodity concentration	
	1968	*1976*
Mauritius	0.958	0.847
Netherlands Antilles	0.926	0.915
Colombia	0.609	0.530
Egypt	0.456	0.307
Ghana	0.686	0.751
[Iceland]	0.715	0.609
Burma	0.486	0.471
Trinidad and Tobago	0.680	0.633
Thailand	0.323	0.220
Panama	0.581	0.492
Honduras	0.460	0.358
Brazil	0.400	0.237
Costa Rica	0.379	0.377
Malaya	0.362	0.283
Nigeria	0.382	0.926
Kenya	0.275	0.296
Tanzania	0.262	0.266
Indonesia	0.407	0.645
Turkey	0.351	0.264
Mexico	0.147	0.174
Libya	0.999	0.948
Argentina	0.207	0.164
AICs (for comparison)		
Japan	0.122	0.181
West Germany	0.129	0.133
Great Britain	0.105	0.095
USA	0.107	0.110

Formula: 'Hirschman Index', 0 = minimum; 1 = maximum
Index: H_j (for country j)

$$H_j = \frac{\sqrt{\sum_{i=1}^{182}\left(\frac{x_j}{X}\right)^2} - \sqrt{\frac{1}{182}}}{1 - \sqrt{\frac{1}{182}}}$$

where x_j = the value of exports of commodity i

$$X = \sum_{i=1}^{182} X_j$$

182 = number of SITC commodities.

Source: *UNCTAD Handbook, 1979*, op. cit., Table 4.5, pp. 293–6.

Table 2.15 *LDCs exports accounting for more than 20% of a nation's export earnings, 1975*

Country	Export	% of export earnings	Country	Export	% of export earnings
Algeria	Petroleum	91	Jordan	Phosphates	41
Bangladesh	Jute	53	Kuwait	Petroleum	93
Barbados	Sugar	42	Liberia	Iron ore	75
Bolivia	Tin	41	Libya	Petroleum	100
	Petroleum	26	Malawi	Tobacco	42
Burma	Rice	44	Malaysia	Rubber	37
	Teak	22	Mauritania	Iron ore	82
Burundi	Coffee	87	Mauritius	Sugar	85
Cameroon	Cacao	25	Morocco	Phosphates	47
	Coffee	24	Nicaragua	Cotton	25
Cent. African)	Cotton	23	Nigeria	Petroleum	93
Republic)	Coffee	23	Panama	Bananas	21
Chad	Cotton	65	Philippines	Sugar	26
Chile	Copper	67		Coconut	20
Colombia	Coffee	42	Rwanda	Coffee	63
Congo	Petroleum	54	Saudi Arabia	Petroleum	100
Costa Rica	Bananas	27	Senegal	Phosphates	26
Dominican				Peanuts	21
Rep.	Sugar	65	Sierra Leone	Diamonds	54
Ecuador	Petroleum	57	Somalia	Bananas	20
Egypt	Cotton	37	Sri Lanka	Tea	49
El Salvador	Coffee	33	Sudan	Cotton	46
Ethiopia	Coffee	31		Peanuts	22
Gabon	Petroleum	86	Syria	Petroleum	69
Gambia	Peanuts	92	Togo	Phosphates	76
Ghana	Cacao	54	Tunisia	Petroleum	51
Guatemala	Coffee	25		Phosphates	20
Guyana	Sugar	50	Uganda	Coffee	76
	Bauxite	32	Uruguay	Wool	23
Haiti	Coffee	33	Venezuela	Petroleum	95
Honduras	Bananas	21	W. Samoa	Copra	57
Indonesia	Petroleum	74		Cacao	26
Iran	Petroleum	74	Zaïre	Copper	66
Ivory Coast	Coffee	24	Zambia	Copper	90
Jamaica	Bauxite etc.,	68			
	Sugar	21			

Source: Arad *et al.*, op. cit., Table 2, pp. 120–2, from IMF, *International Financial Statistics*, December 1976.

The dependence of many LDCs upon commodity exports is quite remarkable. Michael Michaely's 1954 seminal study of commodity concentration revealed some marked coefficients of concentration[31] (the higher the coefficient the smaller the number of important commodity exports, by value). Table 2.14 updates this picture. Figures for 1975 indicate a broadly similar situation for most of the LDCs, as Table 2.15 indicates and

Table 2.16 *Selected LDCs coefficients of geographic concentration of export markets, 1954*

Country	C_{jx}*	Largest customer
Panama	95.5	USA
Colombia	79.8	USA
Honduras	78.0	USA
Mauritius	77.6	Great Britain
Nigeria	74.0	Great Britain
Mexico	73.7	USA
Costa Rica	62.4	USA
Rhodesia and Nyasaland	58.4	Great Britain
Trinidad and Tobago	50.0	Great Britain
Ghana	47.9	Great Britain
Libya	47.9	Great Britain
Burma	47.6	India
Thailand	43.5	Malaya
Brazil	41.5	USA
Tanganyika	39.5	Great Britain
Kenya and Uganda	38.8	Great Britain
Indonesia	38.3	Holland
Netherlands Antilles	33.6	USA
Argentina	32.1	?
Turkey	29.3	?
Malaya and Singapore	26.0	Great Britain
Egypt	26.0	?

$$*C_{jx} = 100 \sqrt{\sum_s \left(\frac{X_{sj}}{X_j}\right)^2} = \text{Coefficient of geographic concentration}$$

Where X_{sj} = exports of country j to country s

$\qquad X_j$ = total exports of country j.

Source: Michaely, op. cit., Table 3, pp. 19–20.

details. Such concentration in commodity exports is serious, for LDCs will be dependent upon them for their earnings of foreign currencies and, hence, their ability to pay for imports. Concentration, however, renders the LDCs vulnerable to changes of taste in consuming countries, to the introduction of substitutes or to fluctuations in the prices of the relevant commodities (for whatever reasons).

Not only are many LDCs concentrated in the commodities that they export but they are also noticeably concentrated in the countries or regions to which they export (beyond, that is,

Table 2.17   LDCs with more than 30% of their exports to the USA, 1974

Year	Country	% Exports to USA	Year	Country	% Exports to USA
1973	Mexico	69	1973	Jamaica	41
1972	Haiti	67	1972	Venezuela	40
1971	Dominican Rep.	64	1972	Ecuador	38
1973	Panama	45	1974	S. Korea	34
1971	Surinam	45	1972	Peru	33
1972	Trinidad	45	1973	Nicaragua	33
1974	Philippines	42	1973	Costa Rica	33

Source: Pirages, op. cit., Table 6.4, p. 199, from *UN Yearbook of Trade Statistics, 1974*, and *UN World Trade Annuals.*

their general dependence upon Northern markets). Michaely identified some high coefficients of geographical concentrations of exports from the data regarding trade in 1954, as shown in Table 2.16.

Concentrated export markets have remained a problem for the LDCs over subsequent years, as Tables 2.17 and 2.18 indicate. Such concentration in export markets renders LDCs vulnerable in two respects. The first area of potential vulnerability is that of sensitivity to economic changes in the importing country, including any alterations in its general level of economic activity or shifting consumption patterns. The second danger is that of major consuming nations using threats to reduce, or curtail, imports from the exporting LDC as a means of exerting economic or political pressure.

The extent of both dangers is conditioned by the precise level of reliance upon the export markets in a given AIC, or group of AICs, the general importance of exports to the LDC in question and, most critically the possibilities of switching exports to alternative markets. The second danger is further conditioned by the extent to which the AIC, or group of AICs, is dependent upon the imports from the given LDC (and the degree to which the AIC depends upon sending exports to the pertinent LDC). Despite their low likelihood, such possibilities require consideration in any discussion of dependencies and a formula for incorporating them is provided by Neil Richardson.[32] It is, moreover, always open to a LDC to accept a reduction of its exports if it is willing and able to forego

Table 2.18   *Exports of LDCs to the EEC, 1965–76*

Country	Exports to EEC as % of total exports 1965	1976	Country	Exports to EEC as % of total exports 1965	1976
Africa			Liberia	61	60
Benin	84	67	Mauritania	94	75
Burundi	40	36	Nigeria	74	40
Chad	59	40	Senegal	87	64
Ethiopia	19	25	Sudan	46	42
Malawi	12	60	Togo	81	90
Rwanda	35	12	Zambia	67	60
Somalia	51	15			
Upper Volta	78	62	*Caribbean*		
Zaïre	83	59	Bahamas	5	10
Cent. Afr. Rep.	60	72	Barbados	42	19
Gambia	70	80	Guyana	30	31
Kenya	53	46	Jamaica	29	19
Niger	60	69	Surinam	9	40
Sierra Leone	89	71	Trinidad & Tobago	30	8
Tanzania	48	41	Madagascar	54	37
Uganda	32	42	Mauritius	77	69
Cameroon	79	66			
Congo	80	64	*Pacific ACP*		
Gabon	65	60	Fiji	27	40
Ghana	43	38	Papua New Guinea	44	32
Ivory Coast	66	61	W. Samoa	33	42

Source: Tables 1, 2, 3 and 4, pp. 147, 148, 149, C.G. Twitchett, 'Patterns of ACP/EEC Trade', pp. 145–81, in F. Long, *The Political Economy of EEC Relations with African, Caribbean and Pacific States; Contributions to the Understanding of the Lomé Convention on North–South Relations* (Oxford, Pergamon, 1980).

the imports hitherto purchased with the revenues received.

Geographical and commodity concentration in exports is a source of strategic economic weakness and general vulnerability for many LDCs. Commodity concentration, in particular, brings vulnerability to price fluctuations or even secular decline in commodity price levels which, in turn, will undermine earnings of foreign revenues. Such developments as these plunge LDCs into acute, and chronic, balance-of-payments' difficulties. Faced with critical import requirements and deteriorating balances of payments, the LDCs become increasingly dependent upon overseas, and largely Northern, sources of financial assistance.

Table 2.19 *Financial conditions and financial flows for selected LDCs, 1981, ($US millions)*

	Balance of payments	GNP	Gross Inflow	Repayment	Net inflow	Net private Direct inflows
Bangladesh	-1 016	12 698	513	52	461	—
Ethiopia	-254	4 480	149	24	125	—
Nepal	-19	2 250	64	2	61	—
Burma	-317	6 479	431	83	348	—
Mali	-140	1 311	116	36	110	4
Zaïre	—	6 258	260	90	170	—
Burundi	—	966	30	3	27	—
India	-4 040	179 452	1 987	647	1 340	—
Somalia	-30	1 232	175	13	163	—
Sierra Leone	-143	1 152	64	41	24	8
Pakistan	-936	29 575	673	331	340	107
Sudan	-648	7 296	540	52	489	
Kenya	-736	7 308	476	177	299	61
Indonesia	-736	79 235	2 356	1 001	1 355	133
Zambia	-649	3 480	248	187	61	—
Egypt	-2 135	28 145	3 487	1 570	1 918	746
Thailand	-2 560	36 960	1 461	226	1 235	291
Morocco	-1 839	17 974	1 704	602	1 103	59
Zimbabwe	-635	6 264	330	41	289	4
Jamaica	-337	2 596	408	243	165	-12
Ivory Coast	-1 693	10 200	1 168	489	679	48
Colombia	-1 943	36 432	1 361	257	1 104	209
Costa Rica	-372	3 289	603	80	523	46
Turkey	2 175	70 070	1 816	510	1 306	150
Rep. of Korea	-4 419	66 130	6 087	1 820	4 266	59
Malaysia	-2 911	26 128	1 874	138	1 736	1 317
Algeria	249	41 944	2 781	2 399	382	315
Brazil	-11 762	267 510	8 997	3 619	5 378	2 317
Mexico	-12 933	160 200	13 416	3 782	9 634	2 254
Argentina	-3 973	72 192	1 845	1 092	753	902
Venezuela	3 998	64 988	2 059	1 352	706	160
Singapore	-1 750	12 576	169	107	62	1 797
Trinidad	357	6 804	88	26	62	166

Note: — denotes lack of data
Source: *World Development Report, 1983*, op. cit., Tables 1, 14 and 15, pp. 148–9, 174–5 and 176–7.

The financial dependence of the LDCs

The desperate economic straits of many LDCs is indicated, albeit imperfectly, by their balance-of-payments' deficits and their ratio to a country's GNP. For many non-oil-exporting

LDCs, the balance-of-payments' deficit remains huge.

Faced with considerable, continuing balance-of-payments deficits, LDCs are faced with painful short-term restrictions upon imports or reliance upon financial support from outside, primarily from Northern states or Northern-dominated financial institutions. Table 2.19 indicates some of the dimensions of the LDCs' current financial plight.

Balance-of-payments deficits add a critical weight to dependence. Such deficits reflect the past economic weaknesses of Less Developed Countries and the costs of their current efforts to survive and to develop. Much of the financial assistance necessary to cover the LDCs' import bills has been in the form of loans (both public and private) rather than outright grants. A considerable, growing burden of external debts and repayments has resulted and has created a vicious cycle of new borrowing, undertaken to cover current repayments.

Table 2.20 highlights the extent of current LDC indebtedness and repayment burdens by showing, amongst other features, the relationship between selected LDCs' export earnings and their debt service payments. Financial assistance from outside, and particularly from the North, makes 'good behaviour' a cardinal condition, as the recent experiences of Manley's Jamaica so amply demonstrate. Such 'good behaviour' may range from honouring foreign debts, through tolerating 'free enterprise zones', to not impeding the flow of primary resources to the AICs.

The considerable financial dependence of much of the South upon the North, and Northern dominated institutions, is a significant part of North–South 'interdependence': a major asymmetry that has barely been moderated by recent efforts by OPEC in the fields of aid and financial activity globally.

Group-to-group interdependence

Interthreaded with the asymmetrical and imbalanced interdependence that exists between North and South is the close pattern of contact and reciprocal interest that has developed between various groups within the two sets of countries. These patterns may remain difficult to identify in detail but become open to examination, in principle at least, once the 'state' is disaggregated into its component groups and their trans-

Table 2.20 *Debts and debt servicing of the LDCs, 1981*

	Debt service as % of exports	Debt service as % of GNP	External debt as % of GNP
Bangladesh	6.9	0.8	31.2
Ethiopia	7.6	1.0	18.7
Nepal	1.6	0.2	9.5
Burma	22.1	2.4	28.7
Mali	3.8	0.8	64.9
Malawi	24.5	5.4	42.0
Zaïre	—	4.1	77.0
Burundi	—	0.5	16.1
India	—	0.6	10.8
Somalia	6.1	1.3	70.9
Tanzania	7.2	2.1	28.3
Sierra Leone	24.4	4.5	31.0
Pakistan	9.6	1.8	29.2
Sudan	5.0	1.0	59.3
Kenya	17.1	4.5	34.4
Indonesia	8.2	2.4	19.0
Zambia	24.0	9.4	73.1
Egypt	22.6	6.5	43.7
Thailand	6.7	1.7	14.4
Morocco	30.1	8.2	52.4
Zimbabwe	4.4	1.1	13.8
Jamaica	22.5	13.2	53.6
Ivory Coast	22.2	10.9	54.4
Colombia	13.9	6.1	38.0
Costa Rica	15.3	7.8	92.6
Rep. of Korea	13.1	5.8	32.1
Malaysia	3.1	1.7	19.2
Algeria	24.9	9.5	35.2
Brazil	31.9	3.1	16.0
Mexico	28.2	3.7	18.5
Argentina	18.2	1.3	8.7
Venezuela	12.4	4.4	16.9
Singapore	0.8	1.8	10.2
Trinidad	6.5	1.4	9.7

Source: *World Development Report, 1983*, op. cit., Table 16, pp. 178–9.

national relationships with groupings elsewhere brought to the fore.

The most prominent form of group-to-group interdependence in North–South relations is that between the managers and major owners of Northern multinational corporations (MNCs) and certain elite groups within the South that have linked their interests (and fates) with the multinationals that operate within the frontiers of their countries.

The picture that characterizes such special patterns of interdependence is that identified by Galtung.[33] The elites of Northern MNCs are highly interdependent with elites in the Southern nations. Other groupings within Northern countries are partially assimilated to the interests of the MNC elites through their reliance upon continued cheap imports of basic resources from the South. Non-elite groups within the North thus share a short-term identity of interests with the MNC owning and operating elites.

Non-elite groups within the South are placed in an essentially antagonistic relationship with all other involved groups: those in the North and elites in the South. Southern non-elites are 'forced' to produce primary commodities by a combination of political repression and economic compulsion: the necessity of maintaining production of such commodities as a means of securing vital imports.

MNCs may also create, or extend, a measure of interdependence amongst the Advanced Industrial Countries, as they promote an increased division of labour between the plants that they control but which are located in different countries. Here, the MNCs are fostering a measure of dependence of AICs upon one another (sometimes also involving LDCs) that may be quite unnecessary by any other criteria. The effect, however, is to create a condition of increasing interdependence within each MNC, in which it becomes increasingly dependent upon continued flows of components between plants located in different countries: a complex dependence which is diminished only by multiple sourcing of any particular component or input for subsequent stages of manufacturing or processing.

The induced interdependence wrought by MNCs also affects the workers employed by such global juggernauts, for they, too, require continued transnational flows of components and inputs for the maintenance of their jobs. The consumers of the MNCs' end-products are similarly made dependent upon the contributory transnational flows. Such a state of interdependence, however, says nothing about the alternative arrangements that might have proved equally satisfactory for workers and consumers alike, without exposing them to increased vulnerability to overseas sources of disrupted flows of components and other essential resources, or to the manipulations of MNCs.

Statistics relating to the level of MNC earnings from overseas operations are indicative of the extent of the special interdependence that has been fostered by them and their overseas clients. Table 2.21 indicates the growing reliance of US corporations upon earnings from their overseas operations.

Table 2.21   *Foreign earnings as a share of total earnings of US corporations, 1957 and 1966–74 ($US billions*)*

Years	Total	Foreign	Foreign shares %
1957	45.4	3.9	8.6
1966	78.6	5.2	6.7
1967	75.6	5.5	7.3
1968	82.1	6.5	7.9
1969	77.9	7.5	9.6
1970	66.4	8.0	12.1
1971	76.9	9.0	11.7
1972	89.6	10.8	12.1
1973	98.6	16.9	17.2
1974	93.6	25.1	26.9

Source: *American Multinationals and US Interests*, op. cit., Table 1.3, p. 10.
* Thousand millions

Further indicative of the pattern of special 'interdependence' fostered by Northern MNCs is the evidence of six of Britain's top firms which make more than 25 per cent of their profits from their overseas operations,[34] while eight of the top ten American corporations earn more than 25 per cent of their profits similarly, with six making more than 50 per cent in this manner.[35]

With such levels of profits from overseas interests, it is clear that owners and managers of MNCs are, in a real sense, dependent upon their overseas subsidiaries (whether they be in the North or the South) and the people who man, sustain and protect them. This dependence, coupled with the general significance of such MNCs for their home countries, gives this special form of 'interdependence' its broader, and frequently critical, economic and political significance.

Interdependence and 'common fate'

Many of the forms of interdependence considered thus far turn, in some degree, upon actual transactions — material or financial — between societies. Even loose economic inter-connectedness and interlinkage rest upon the cement of financial flows and trade in merchandise. Common fate, however, may constitute a most important form of interdependence which can exist in the absence of any immediate, tangible transactions between societies or does not, at least, depend upon them.[36]

Many issues of long-term politico-military security reflect forms of common fate that may be identified only through the implications of their disappearance or modification. The problems of cumulative pollution illustrate common fate in the ecological domain.

Irrespective of the level of conventional economic trans-actions amongst the states bordering the Mediterranean Sea, the effects of the pollution generated by some is transmitted to others.[37] All Mediterranean states are thus subject to a form of common fate which can be qualified by measures of various level of pollutants and their detrimental consequences.

The common fate that is also inherent in resource depletion and/or the production of adequate levels of renewable resources may be suggested by comparisons of projected needs with either proven reserves, established stockpiles or provisions for future production. Such common fate (even if its impact varies across societies) in food production is illustrated by Table 2.22, which indicates levels of food security, specified in terms of grain reserves between 1961 and 1976. (It is worth noting here that much of the interconnectedness considered by Rosecrance and his colleagues constitutes common fate in the sense now being discussed.)

The form of common fate indicated by such statistics and projections has, however, some interesting peculiarities. The sources of such inadequacies in resources may not be universal and their effects may well be unequally distributed. Food shortages might be attributable, according to inter-pretation, to excessive population growth in some countries

Table 2.22   *Indicators of world food security, 1962-76 (millions of metric tons and days)*

	Reserve stocks of grain, etc.	Grain equivalent of US idled cropland	Total reserves	Reserves as days of grain consumption
1962	176	81	257	105
1964	153	70	223	87
1966	151	78	229	84
1968	144	61	205	71
1970	188	71	259	89
1972	130	78	208	69
1974	108	0	108	33
1976	100	0	100	31

Source: Hansen, op. cit., Table B.1, p. 152.

(primarily certain of the LDCs), or to the misdirection of agricultural production from basics into luxury commodities (from staples to, say, bananas and tobacco) by others (mainly MNCs). Consumable food in the poor countries is thus replaced by luxuries for consumption by those who are already over-fed. Whatever the source of any food shortages, the effects will be felt most severely by those who are both heavily dependent upon the importation of staples and who lack the wealth to make effective bids for basic foodstuffs in increasingly competitive international markets.

Many such indicators of common fate, in one form or another, could be offered. Many such were the basis of the alarmist studies of impending disaster in publications like *The Limits to Growth*.[38] All, however, illustrate an inescapable, and very real, condition of contemporary interdependence: albeit a condition that will remain uncertain and that will continue to attract controversy.

Beyond the many areas of common fate that involve the decisions and actions of human agents are those that impose themselves upon humanity. Great natural disasters and threats from outer space fall into this broad, but often rather exotic, category. The examples of such common fate quoted do, however, illustrate that while such phenomena are of potentially great significance for mankind, they remain far from the everyday concerns of most governments and peoples.

CONCLUSION

The measures chosen for interdependence depend, centrally, upon the theory or approach adopted at the outset. Few phenomena illustrate this principle more clearly. Many measures and indicators attest to the existence of one or other international relationship that can lay some claim to the term 'interdependence'. Some such measures can, however, be no more than indirect indicators of underlying and complex patterns of interrelationship between and amongst states or, indeed, amongst groups located within various of the involved societies.

The empirical material surveyed in this chapter reveals much that is suggestive of notable international interconnectedness and interdependence: of patterns of import and export dependence affecting AICs and LDCs alike; of the serious financial dependence of the South upon the North; and, lastly, of the peculiar form of interdependence that characterizes a structure of Dependencia. In most areas, moreover, asymmetry and imbalance is the rule in the relationships manifest in the real world.

The extent to which any condition corresponds to that of long-term, irreducible interdependence must, however, remain an open question. Few conditions are immutable given sufficient will, imagination and time. Furthermore, the differing involvement in any pattern of international interdependence of various groups within any society may, when coupled with continuing international strains, furnish a major source of the political impulse to bring about fundamental changes: groups with differing stakes in contemporary 'interdependence' may well respond differently to developments within, or affecting, such relationships.

A discerning study of interdependence should, therefore, demonstrate that it may not be all things to all men, either analytically or practically.

NOTES AND REFERENCES

1. Independent Commission on International Development Issues, *North–South: A Programme for Survival* (London, Pan Books, 1980).
2. R.O. Keohane and J.S. Nye, *Power and Interdependence: World Politics in Transition* (Boston, Little, Brown, 1977).

62   *R.J. Barry Jones*

3. For discussions of the various meanings of interdependence see: E.L. Morse, 'Interdependence in World Politics', in J.N. Rosenau, K.W. Thompson and G. Boyd (eds), *World Politics: An Introduction* (New York, Free Press, 1976); D.A. Baldwin, 'Interdependence and power: a conceptual analysis', *International Organization, 34* (1980), 471-506; P.A. Reynolds and R.D. McKinley, 'The Concept of Interdependence: Its Uses and Misuses', pp. 141-66 in K. Goldmann and G. Sjostedt (eds), *Power, Capabilities, Interdependence: Problems in the Study of International Influence* (Beverly Hills, Sage, 1979).
4. On the weaknesses of naive empiricism see the chapters by R.J. Barry Jones, R. Little and J. MacLean in B. Buzan and R.J. Barry Jones (eds), *Change and the Study of International Relations: the Evaded Dimension* (London, Frances Pinter, 1981).
5. On which see Tony Smith, 'The underdevelopment of development literature: the case of Dependencia Theory', *World Politics, 31* (1979), 247-88.
6. For instance, see C. Fred Bergsten, 'Oil is not the exception', in C. Fred Bergsten, *Toward a New International Economic Order: Selected Papers of C. Fred Bergsten, 1972–1974* (Lexington, Lexington Books/D.C. Heath, 1975).
7. An issue which is well discussed in Baldwin, op. cit., especially pp. 475-6.
8. In particular, Keohane and Nye, op. cit., especially Ch. 1.
9. Ibid., p. 9.
10. Ibid., p. 12.
11. See especially R. Rosecrance, *et al.*, 'Whither interdependence', *International Organization, 31* (1977), 425-71 and especially pp. 426-7.
12. Keohane and Nye, op. cit., p. 13.
13. Ibid.
14. Ibid.
15. Ibid.
16. Ibid., pp. 10-11.
17. See in particular: Andre Gunder Frank, *On Capitalist Underdevelopment* (Bombay, Oxford University Press, 1975); Andre Gunder Frank, *Dependent Accumulation and Underdevelopment* (London, Macmillan, 1978); and Samir Amin, *Accumulation on a World Scale: A Critique of the Theory of Underdevelopment, Vols. 1 and 2* (New York, Monthly Review Press, 1974).
18. See, in particular, the critique offered by Mary Ann Tetreault, 'Measuring interdependence', *International Organization, 34* (1980), 429-43; and the subsequent controversy: R. Rosecrance and W. Gutowitz, 'Measuring interdependence: a rejoinder', pp. 553-60, and Mary Ann Tetreault, 'Measuring interdependence: a response', pp. 557-60 both in *International Organization, 35* (1981).
19. Keohane and Nye, op. cit., especially Chs 1 and 2.
20. A point made with force, albeit from a differing perspective, by J. Galtung in 'A structural theory of imperialism', *Journal of Peace Research, 8* (1966), 81-117.
21. See the discussion by E.L. Morse, 'Crisis diplomacy, interdependence

and the politics of international economic relations', pp. 121-50, in R. Tanter and R. Ullman (eds), *Theory and Policy in International Relations* (Princeton, Princeton University Press, 1972).

22. The lower the convergence the higher the equalization amongst rates, the convergence being the product of dividing the absolute value of the sum of the differences in rates between each two countries by the number of dyads (pairs of countries).

23. Rosecrance *et al.*, 'Whither interdependence', op. cit. (note 11), especially pp. 441-3.

24. Ibid., p. 442.

25. D.P. Calleo and B.M.Rowland, *America and the World Political Economy* (Bloomington, Indiana University Press, 1973), Table 8.2, p. 211.

26. Nazli Choucri's index of dependence — see: Choucri, 'Population, Resources and Technology: Political Implications of the Environmental Crisis', pp. 9-46, especially p. 42, in D.A. Kay and E.B. Skolnikoff (eds), *World Eco-Crisis: International Organizations in Response* (Madison, University of Wisconsin Press, 1972).

27. D.H. Meadows *et al.*, *The Limits to Growth* (London, Pan Books, 1972); M. Mesarovic and E. Pestel, *Mankind at the Turning Point* (London, Hutchinson, 1975).

28. See especially H.S.D. Cole *et al.*, *Thinking About the Future: A Critique of 'The Limits to Growth'* (London, Chatto and Windus/Sussex University Press, 1974); and C. Freeman and M. Jahoda, *World Futures: The Great Debate* (London, Martin Robertson, 1978).

29. Galtung, op. cit., Appendix, pp. 110-11.

30. Commodities like bananas cannot really be considered to be of vital importance to their importing countries, primarily in the North.

31. M. Michaely, *Concentration in International Trade* (Amsterdam, North-Holland Publishing 1962), p. 1.

32. N.R. Richardson, 'Economic dependence and foreign policy compliance: bringing measurement closer to conception', pp. 87-110 in C.W. Kegley and P. McGowan, *The Political Economy of Foreign Policy Behavior* (Beverly Hills, Sage, 1981).

33. Galtung, op. cit.

34. R. Murray, *Multinational Corporations and Nation States* (London, Spokesman Books, 1975), Table II, p. 46.

35. C. Fred Bergsten, T. Horst and T.H. Moran, *American Multinationals and American Interests* (Washington, Brookings Institute, 1978), Table 1-4, pp. 11-13.

36. Morse, 'Interdependence in world politics', op. cit., and 'Crisis diplomacy . . .', op. cit.

37. See, for instance, Map 53, 'Fouling the nest', in M. Kidron and R. Segal, *The State of the World Atlas* (London, Pan Books, 1981).

38. Meadows *et al.*, *Limits to Growth*, op. cit.

3   Foreign Policy Analysis and Interdependence

STEVE SMITH

INTRODUCTION

In many ways the rise of the phenomenon of interdependence, along with the associated development of transnationalism, has represented a most fundamental challenge to the study of international relations. Certainly, in terms of the development of the discipline since 1918, there have been major debates and disputes over the correct focus of attention or the most appropriate methodology, but the problems caused by inter-dependence and transnationalism seem to relate to areas that were largely immune from earlier controversy. This chapter aims at assessing the extent to which interdependence poses a serious problem for one area of international relations, that is, foreign policy analysis.

INTERDEPENDENCE AND THE RISE OF ECONOMIC ISSUES

Before concentrating on foreign policy analysis and the effects of interdependence on our ability to explain the foreign policies of states, it is necessary to make two introductory comments. The first is to point out that interdependence and the phenomenon of transnationalism are essentially related in terms of their historical development. Whilst it is true that it is theoretically possible for interdependence to occur without any development of transnationalism, it is clear that the two expanded concurrently in the late 1960s and early 1970s. In other words, the forces in the international system that have led to a realization of the impact of actors other than the state are essentially the same as those that have resulted in the development of interdependence: the most obvious common causal link is the increased role of economic factors in international relations. Of course, many would argue that economic forces have always been of significant importance in international relations; the point here is not to argue this contention, rather it is to assert that in the literature of the subject-area the role of economic forces has, over the last fifteen years, been seen as of rising importance. This indicates a linkage that will be examined below, namely, the relationship between empirical developments and theoretical developments. To make the central assumption of this chapter explicit, the literature of international relations shifted during the early 1970s from a concentration on military–security issues, specifically the East–West conflict, to a concentration on economic–resource issues, thereby highlighting North–South relations. A secondary assumption is that this transformation in the literature had two interrelated theoretical strands, that of transnationalism and that of interdependence.

Now, the implication of this transformation in the literature — most clearly seen in Seyom Brown's book, *New Forces in World Politics* and reflected in Maghroori and Ramberg's excellent reader on this literature, *Globalism vs Realism: International Relations' Third Debate*[1] — was to cast doubt on the utility of the state-centric view of the subject area. Transnationalism and interdependence in essence eat away at the central assumptions and parameters of the state-centric perspective. This point is often misrepresented in the literature in that the attack on state-centrism is portrayed as just another area of debate in the literature. It is far more serious a challenge than this implies. Although one can point to the succession of major debates in international relations, the often-missed point is that in none of these cases was the attack on such a fundamental assumption of the discipline as is represented by the challenge of interdependence and transnationalism. The so-called major debates between Idealism and Realism and Realism and behaviouralism, or even that between scientific-classical approaches, did not involve a debate over who was the major actor in international relations. An excellent example of this is seen in discussions of the level of analysis problem. For Singer[2] the major methodological issue revolved around the question of how best to explain the behaviour of states; in his notion of a system, the constituent actors were states and only states. The same assumption is to be found in the pioneering works of Kaplan and Rosecrance in systems theory,[3] Deutsch and Haas in integration theory,[4] and Snyder, Modelski and Rosenau in foreign policy analysis.[5] In all of these works, each of which was offered as an innovative way of explaining aspects of international relations, and all fitting under the banner of behaviouralism, there was no attempt to question the centrality of the state as the focus of attention for any explanatory theory of international relations.

Similarly, if you look at the debates between Idealists and Realists, you find that the clear assumption on each side is that the state is the actor in international relations. Even the 'great debate' between the classical and the scientific schools, as represented by the Bull–Kaplan exchange in *World Politics*,[6] and the induction–deduction debate between Young and Russett,[7] accept as a *given* that the state is *the* actor. The paradox is that despite the heat (if not light) generated by the debates in the discipline, the centrality of the state-as-actor, and all the epistemological and methodological baggage that this entails, was never really subjected to serious examination. This paradox is neatly summed up in the title of the unpublished 1973 paper by Handelman, Vasquez, O'Leary and Coplin, 'Color it Morgenthau'.[8] Their argument is that, despite the seeming differences between the myriad of approaches to studying international relations, each accepts the central assumptions of the Realist paradigm relating to the subject of study and the issue-areas involved in that study. It is, of course, exactly these assumptions that are questioned by the interdependence–transnationalist literature. In other words, the current debate in the literature focuses on a set of assumptions that have, either implicitly or explicitly, been accepted by the successive paradigms in international relations; in this sense, the rise of interdependence and transnationalism poses a fundamental challenge to the basic assumptions of the discipline. This has been reflected both in the resistance to the interdependence/transnationalist literature, which is based exactly on the grounds of the relative salience of actors and issues, and in the clearly felt need in the transnationalist/interdependence literature to create an alternative paradigm of international relations; again, this is one based firmly on a conception of who acts and in what issue-areas. These factors will be returned to later.

The second qualification relates to the distinction between empirical evidence and theory. Much of the confusion concerning the concept of interdependence arises from the fact that it is used to refer to two rather different phenomena. The first is to relate to a set of empirical, primarily economic, events which affect the nature of international political processes. In this sense we can talk of interdependence as an empirical phenomenon. As such it is argued that it alters the nature of international relations in that it gives rise to new issues, new constellations of actors, and new problems for governments. This empirical change is usually seen as occurring incrementally through the 1950s and 1960s, giving rise to a qualitative change in international relations in the 1970s. Now, this issue can be, and has been, debated in terms of whether or not interdependence has increased and whether this fundamentally alters international relations. The point, though, is that it is seen as an empirical event or set of events. In this connotation it makes sense to talk of the nature of international politics in an interdependent world as being, in many ways, different to previous patterns of behaviour. It will be accepted that this interdependence varies in impact from type of state to type of state, from issue to issue, and from time to time; nevertheless, in this context the use of the term relates to empirical evidence.

The second use of the term, and this has been both the more dominant and the more problematic in the literature, relates to a new way of explaining international relations. In this way, interdependence provides a basis for explaining international phenomena in terms of certain linkages between what were previously treated, for the purpose of analysis, as hermetically sealed states and societies. As such, it claims to offer increased explanatory power, much in the same way as bureaucratic politics was offered as a 'new' perspective from which to explain foreign policy phenomena. The value of interdependence as a theoretical concept does not, therefore, depend solely upon evidence about empirical changes in the international system. It may be that the system has not fundamentally changed, but interdependence is useful to understand the past as well as the present.

THE IMPACT OF INTERDEPENDENCE ON FOREIGN POLICY ANALYSIS

In each of these uses, the concept of interdependence has had a massive effect on foreign policy analysis. On the one hand, the empirical phenomenon has had a significant impact on actual foreign policy behaviour. It is obviously now even less possible than ever for states to behave in international relations as if the state were both a self-contained and a sealed unit. The impact of interdependence has been very clearly illustrated in the Falkland crisis, where British and Argentinian policies have been fundamentally affected by a mass of interdependencies. Indeed, much of the contemporary foreign policy behaviour of Western states is based on sets of constraints and demands imposed by interdependence. The European reaction to the Soviet intervention in Afghanistan, the very differing reactions of Western states to the 1981–2 Polish crisis, and the continuing linkage between the Middle East policies of European states and their dependence on oil, are but some of the clearest examples of this phenomenon. On an empirical level, then, interdependence fundamentally affects the foreign policy behaviour of states.

On the other hand, interdependence, both as a phenomenon and as a concept, has a significant effect on the way we study and comprehend the foreign policy behaviour of states. Clearly, insomuch as the actual foreign policy behaviour of states is altered because of the rise of interdependence, foreign policy analysis will have to take account of this. However, potentially more destabilizing for the subject-area is the effect that the theoretical work emanating from the interdependence/transnationalist school has on the very assumptions of foreign policy analysis. Now it will be argued below that the impact of this theoretical reorientation will differ according to the methodology utilized in the analysis of foreign policy behaviour, but, to treat the subject-area in general for the time being, the attack on the state-centric viewpoint has serious implications for foreign policy analysis.

The first is that interdependence challenges the view, inherent in nearly all foreign policy analysis, of the distinction between domestic and international politics. I say nearly all because it is clear that a number of writers, specifically Rosenau and Hanrieder,[9] were pointing to this linkage for a number of years before interdependence became 'fashionable'. Nevertheless, the bulk of the literature of foreign policy analysis rests on a distinction between foreign and domestic policy, with the analysis of foreign policy being a distinct analytical enterprise with very little overlap with the study of domestic politics. The centrality of this assumption can be seen by the concentration in the literature on the specific inputs to foreign policy; it is commonly argued that the domestic environment for foreign policy-making is very different from that for domestic politics. Similarly, it is commonly argued that the extent of agreement on foreign policy issues is far greater than on domestic ones (hence the popularity of the concept of national interest). However, the phenomenon of interdependence calls this assumption into question by highlighting the linkage between domestic and international issues as a direct consequence of the linkages between domestic societies. As William Wallace succinctly entitled a recent paper, 'How foreign is foreign policy?'[10]

A second area of challenge emerges from the dominance of economic factors in interdependence. This challenges much of foreign policy analysis in that the dominant assumption is that one can distinguish between high politics, such as military and security issues, and low politics, that is economic and cultural issues. Of course, most analysts would want to qualify this assumption but, nevertheless, the literature of foreign policy analysis does tend to concentrate on the issue-area of military security. Indeed, for the whole Realist paradigm, it is exactly the predominance of this issue-area that both defined international relations and comprised its central problematic. Yet, it is this distinction that is at the centre of the interdependence challenge; the whole thrust of the interdependence literature is to the effect that it is no longer possible to distinguish rigidly between the central, i.e. military, area of foreign policy and the periphery, i.e. economics. Indeed, some of the best work on interdependence stresses exactly the reverse of this argument; that is to say, that economic problems arising from interdependence constitute the central feature of the foreign policies of advanced industrial societies.[11] This, of course, feeds back into the discussion of the distinction between foreign and domestic policies.

The third area of challenge, which builds directly on the previous two, relates to the dominant area for explanation in international relations. Foreign policy analysis has historically focused on explaining the orientation of states towards essentially security cleavages in the international system;

hence, much of the literature concerns the explanation of the political orientations of states. This is very clearly illustrated in the whole range of the foreign policy analysis literature, from the applications of the decision-making frameworks of Snyder *et al.*,[12] and Brecher *et al.*,[13] through the works on psychological aspects, such as Boulding, Holsti and Jervis,[14] to decision-making models, such as those of Allison and Janis.[15] In each of these examples the focus of study is on the political/military, specifically East–West, cleavage. To this extent, decisions concerning war and alliances were at the heart of the foreign policy analysis literature. As is so amply illustrated in Seyom Brown's book, *New Forces in World Politics*,[16] the rise of interdependence, however one links it causally to the era of *détente*, causes these issues to move off the centre-stage. The major focus of concern in international relations is said to be the politics not of security but of economics, as seen in not the East–West but the North–South cleavage. In this situation the focus for explanation of international relations shifts from the area that foreign policy analysis so far has centred on to an area in which the methodology, epistemology and even ontology of the subject seems less relevant.

A fourth effect of the development of interdependence is that it casts doubt on the situational focus of much foreign policy analysis, namely crisis decision-making. Most of the analytical techniques developed in foreign policy analysis were intended to provide better explanations of crises since, of course, these seemed to be the dominant area for explanation in the age of the cold war. Now, exactly because interdependence blurs so many conceptual boundaries, it also reorientates the notion of situational impact. While economic issues also generate crises, they more obviously emphasize incremental linkages within and between societies, and play down the centrality of crises as a focus for explanation; the thrust of much of the writing on interdependence is to argue that foreign policy will shift not as a result of crises, but more incrementally. The notion of crisis, as traditionally defined, plays a decreasing role in inter-state relations, partly because military issues become less important, but mainly because the kinds of issues dominating international relations are not amenable to crisis-type solutions.

The combination of these factors results in a situation in which many of the core assumptions of traditional foreign policy analysis are called into question. Specifically, what Vasquez[17] has termed the three fundamental assumptions of Realism, which, in turn, underpin both behavioural analysis generally, and foreign policy analysis specifically, are undermined. These are: (a) that nation-states or their decision-makers are the most important actors for understanding international relations; (b) that there is a sharp distinction between domestic and international politics; and (c) that international relations is concerned with power and war. The linkage between interdependence and transnationalism is clearly indicated in the similar undermining effect that each has on these assumptions. The central texts of the transnationalist literature, specifically Keohane and Nye[18] and Mansbach, Ferguson and Lampert,[19] argue that it is exactly these assumptions that are called into question by transnationalism. Thus, whereas Keohane and Nye's *Transnational Relations and World Politics* attacks the notion of the centrality of power and war as the dominant feature of international relations, Mansbach *et al.*'s *The Web of World Politics* offers quantitative evidence on the very limited role of the state in international interactions. The most powerful attempt to combine the related academic arguments of transnationalism and interdependence into a coherent alternative theory of international relations is found in Mansbach and Vasquez's *In Search of Theory*.[20]

The effect of these developments is seriously to call into doubt the assumptions of foreign policy analysis. This is so because, on the one hand, the actual role played by states in international relations is seen as being on the decline, given the rise of non-state actors. On the other hand, the traditional concern of states — military security — appears to be of declining relevance in the contemporary international system. Since foreign policy analysis concentrates axiomatically on states (and it is very difficult to stretch the subject to cover either international or transnational organizations), and as it focuses on security issues, then exactly because transnationalism and interdependence attack, in turn, each of these focal points, the subject has a very serious identity crisis.

This identity crisis is less marked in what may be called traditional foreign policy analysis (such as that which dominates work in the United States). However, one must not allow the patient's own diagnosis to determine whether or not there is a problem. Paradoxically, although there is less overt concern in the British literature about the destabilizing effects of interdependence than there is in the United States, it will be argued below that the problem is really more serious here.

To turn to foreign policy analysis as practised in the United States, it is abundantly clear that the subject underwent a fundamental crisis in the mid-1970s. Looking back at the development of foreign policy analysis in the United States, one can see a very noticeable trend towards a more 'scientific' approach from Snyder through Modelski to Rosenau and the Inter University Comparative Foreign Policy Report (ICFP). By the early 1970s, there was a very extensive and identifiable research community in foreign policy analysis utilizing one set of concepts, with a relatively clear view of direction (and certainly a high degree of hope), and able to get significant quantities of research grants. One does not have to rely on the statements of the founder of this school, J.N. Rosenau, about the extent to which there existed a paradigm (albeit in a very loose form); there is an excellent survey of this approach in Charles Kegley's recent monograph, *The Comparative Study of Foreign Policy: Paradigm Lost?*[21] There is a very interesting point to note here, which is that this paradigm or orientation was at the same time explicitly behavioural and state-centric. The linkage between these two points is crucial: it was state centric *because* it was behavioural. This is for the simple reason that at the time of the development of the subject, states were perceived to be the dominant actors and military and political issues were predominant for the USA and its government.

Yet, if one looks at the development of foreign policy analysis since, say, 1973, it is clear that a major problem occurs around that time. The quite astonishing rate of activity within the behaviouralist approach seems to stop suddenly in the period from 1975 to about 1979. There are several explanations for this, such as a drying-up of research money, methodological difficulties, and the exhaustion of the potential of various theories and models. These factors must not be underestimated in terms of their effect in undermining behavioural foreign policy analysis. To be sure, there were serious methodological problems in the approach — most notably over how to develop theory — and the role of these problems in leading to the disintegration of the approach in the mid-1970s is an important one. However, it is not at all clear that those engaged in the discipline were aware of these problems. What is evident is that the rise of the interdependence/ transnationalist literature called the assumptions of the approach into doubt. Certainly, if one looks at Rosenau's own work it is clear that this was the major cause; he wrote a series of papers in the mid-1970s on the problems of studying international relations in a transnational world. The virtual cessation of output from the behaviouralist school in the mid-1970s, along with the change of direction in the work of a number of its leading figures, amply illustrates the problems that interdependence and transnationalism caused for its coherence and identity. Thus, Modelski moves from foreign policy analysis to study MNCs; Rosenau concentrates on interdependence and transnationalism; McGowan moves to political economy; Kegley works on American foreign policy; Brecher becomes increasingly concerned with Israel's foreign policy; Hanrieder moves to work on arms control and West German foreign policy; Hermann and Wilkenfeld move into quantitative analysis.

The pattern is a very clear one: comparative foreign policy analysis loses a sense of direction and purpose at the time of the rise of the literature on interdependence and trans-nationalism. Since the extent to which the state is the dominant actor is being called into question, since the distinction between domestic and foreign policy no longer seems to hold, and since economics seems to be replacing security as the dominant issue of international relations, it is increasingly difficult for foreign policy analysis to claim that it is a central area of the subject. This is reflected in the increasing self-reflection of many of the pioneers of the discipline over the coherence of the area in a world which *seems* to be undergoing structural transformation. This point is worth stressing; a very important assumption of much of the interdependence/transnationalism literature was that the international political system was undergoing a once-and-for-all transformation. There was a clearly linear conception of the process of change. In this light, the assumptions of foreign policy analysis seemed to be outmoded, so as to reduce very seriously the utilty of a concentration on states and on security

issues for an explanation of international relations. This is seen
most clearly in a 1979 article by Jim Rosenau in which he states,

I am convinced that neither epistemological nor methodological
problems are the source of our difficulties in the field today. The need
to develop a new paradigm springs . . . from the dynamics of change
that are rendering the world ever more complex . . . . [One] still has to
contend with the declining capacity of governments, the rise of new
issues, the advent of new actors and the many interactive effects that
derive from mounting interdependence in an increasingly fragmented
world. These substantive dynamics are at work no matter how we
proceed.[22]

For Rosenau, then, the major problems of foreign policy
analysis find their source in the rise of interdependence.

This self-conscious reflection that characterized the more
behavioural approaches to foreign policy analysis has yielded
very positive benefits in that, after a lull of some five years,
there does seem to be a re-emergence of the subject-area, as
witnessed by the publication of a number of books dealing
with reformulated approaches to studying foreign policy
behaviour.[23] Much of the current work in comparative foreign
policy analysis is directed towards integrating the structural
features of interdependence with an examination of state
behaviour, an excellent example being the sixth volume of the
Sage Yearbook.[24]

However, such reflection was not mirrored in the more
traditional approaches to analysing foreign policy behaviour.
Although, of course, foreign policy analysis has many different
approaches, the most traditional is that which characterizes
most of the study of the subject in Britain. It is hardly
surprising, therefore, that the reaction of many writers whose
work is more historical than behavioural is to attack the whole
notion of interdependence. An alternative account of the effect of
interdependence can be found by looking at the objections to the
view that interdependence seriously reduces the explanatory
power of foreign policy analysis.

THE COUNTER-ATTACK ON THE IMPACT OF INTERDEPENDENCE

There are four main arguments to counter the charge that
interdependence calls into doubt the basic assumptions of

foreign policy analysis. The first is that despite the fact that economic issues are now far more a part of foreign policy than before, states, and only states, are responsible for making the major military decisions. It is pointed out that the rise of economic factors does not replace the central military problematic for states; indeed it can be argued that the salience of economic issues is itself a reflection of specific military and security configurations. A further aspect of this argument is well illustrated in Mansbach *et al.*'s *The Web of World Politics*,[25] in which they quantify the behaviour of actors in world politics; what they do is to count each target or actor in terms of the number of activities they perform. This allows them to conclude that state-to-state interactions account for 'only' some 44 per cent of international behaviour; the implication is that since 56 per cent of behaviour includes non-state actors, then a concentration on states can only provide a very limited picture of international relations. However, two qualifications need to be made to this argument. The first is that one of their findings is that non-state-to-non-state interactions account for only 11 per cent of behaviour; therefore, states are involved in 89 per cent of interactions. The second, and more general, is that their methodology does not allow one to distinguish according to the importance of the behaviour; thus an act of war is counted as one interaction, as is a visit by a religious leader to another country. The obvious point to make is that a mere quantitative account cannot account for the fact that the behaviour of states, although it may not be the majority of international behaviour, may still be the most important in terms of consequences.

A second point, following on directly from the first, is that interdependence may only have been seen as so important because of specific historical circumstances. The recent events in Afghanistan, Poland, the Falklands, and especially US–Soviet relations, call into question the idea of a once-and-for-all transformation from a military/security-based system to an economic-based one. In this sense, the interest in interdependence may be seen as a temporary phenomenon arising out of a particular configuration of security issues. Once this specific configuration vanishes, then the traditional military concerns again become the dominant area for explanation in international relations.

A third area of attack is found in the works of Bull and Northedge and concerns the role of the state in contemporary international relations. In a rather vitriolic article,[26] the flavour of which may be gained from its title, 'Transnationalism: the American illusion', Northedge disputes the view that the state is under attack. He argues that 'this curious delusion'

... is strengthened by the conviction of so many American political scientists that commonsense, the plain evidence of the senses, visible and stubborn facts, do not matter and must not be permitted to destroy the illusion, so long as they cannot be quantified. It is better — more scientific — to count letters and weigh parcels, year by year, between Thailand and Ecuador.[27]

The view that interdependence and transnationalism reduce the centrality of the state is, therefore, an American illusion. As Northedge puts it: 'If an American professor ... were to lecture on the demise of the nation-state in most of the countries in Africa or Asia today, he would in all likelihood be promptly locked up, if not sent before a firing squad.'[28] For Northedge, the state is not declining in importance, it is growing.

Hedley Bull has argued that '... it is wrong to speak as if the decline of the state, or the loss of its primacy to "other actors", could now be predicted.'[29] He cites three reasons for this: the first is that the state has often come under attack from other organizations, but has survived to continue to dominate the international system. The state 'has demonstrated a formidable capacity to withstand the challenges [of other actors].'[30] Thus, on the one hand, it is too early to say that an irrevocable transformation has occurred, as many such transformations have been (inaccurately) predicted through history. Interdependence and transnationalism may be just one more fashion. On the other hand, the state continues to possess a number of characteristics that suggest that its dominant role will continue; the most obvious of these are its monopoly of *legal* force, and the allegiance of its population.

A second factor is that the role of the state is in fact expanding rather than declining. This is so both geographically and functionally. At the geographical level, the state has now become the common political form for the whole international political system. At a functional level, the state is expanding into a vast number of areas; to quote Bull: 'The states system has extended its tentacles to deprive business corporations and bankers, labour organizations and sporting teams, churches and political parties of the *standing as autonomous actors that they one enjoyed*[31] (emphasis added). In other words, the functional extension of the state has actually increased its power (and thereby, of course, the ability of foreign policy theories to explain more salient behaviour); this is directly opposed to much of the interdependence literature.

A third reason is that any other actors still have to work within a framework of rules made by states. Again, to quote Bull, 'Ethnic groups, transnational political parties and international organizations may edge their way closer to the centre of the stage; but there are no agreed rules which define their place in a universal political order. Thus these putative challengers of the system of states find themselves coming to terms with it.'[32]

To these defences of the centrality of the state may be added the obvious one concerning whether or not interdependence is actually increasing. Although the assumption in the interdependence literature is that it is increasing over time, this has been strongly challenged by Kenneth Waltz, who argues that the international political system is now less interdependent than it was before the First World War.[33] To reiterate a point made previously, it is clear that interdependence is not a unitary phenomenon either in terms of the issue-areas to which it applies or to the actors in the system. Two actors may be interdependent in one issue-area and not in others, whilst the same two actors may be interdependent in one period but not in another. This problem seriously reduces the utility of aggregate data, especially if they are concentrating on economic factors.

CONCLUSION

In trying to bring these various themes together in order to assess the impact of interdependence on foreign policy analysis it is necessary to discuss two basic questions: the first is, 'Do states continue to dominate the international political system?'; the second is, 'Is military policy still the central focus for the study of international relations?' In answering the first, it must be accepted that there has been a significant transformation in the international political system. It is now clearly impossible to explain international events solely by referring to states. To this extent, interdependence and transnationalism have brought other actors into prominence. Whilst non-state actors are clearly important in explaining international relations, on many issues some states remain central, although it must be stressed that this will not apply over the whole range of issues. Indeed, it is evident that the role of the state is expanding both domestically and internationally; states are now seen as responsible for far more of their population's wants and needs than ever before. This does not mean that they can deliver the goods, but they are judged increasingly in terms of their ability to do so.

The answer to the second question is far less clear-cut. Two extreme views are clearly inaccurate: one argues that the 1970s witnessed a once-and-for-all transformation from a military-security system to an economic one. This, as recent events amply testify, is simply not the case. The other view argues that the system went through a period of specific military configurations which allowed interdependence to be seen as central; now that military and security issues have re-emerged this concentration on interdependence will fade. Again, this is to fail to understand just what interdependence means for the performance of foreign policy, as is witnessed by the obvious, and even painful, linkages between military and economic policy for Britain over the Falklands. The current situation is far more complex than either of these extremes suggests. The contemporary international system is one in which military *and* economic issues are central; to be sure, they differ in impact from issue to issue, from state to state, and from time to time, but it is simply not possible to arrange the issues facing governments in an overall and all-embracing hierarchy.

The current international system is, therefore, one in which a complex of issues and actors may be distinguished. The effect of interdependence, although by no means either universal or unitary, has been significantly to affect the actors and issues that students of international relations have to deal with in providing explanations of international events. Interdependence has created a situation in which the rigid distinctions between domestic and foreign policy, and between high and low politics, can no longer be seen as satisfactory ones. At the same time, it has not altered the salience of security issues, yet it has very seriously affected attempts by states to deal with them. This is most clearly illustrated in intra-Western relations, in which security issues and economic issues both vie for the attention of decision-makers and, at the same time, pull in very different directions. To cite just one example: it is clear that British military policy over the Falklands has been significantly influenced by British economic relations, specifically by the European Community countries tying the extension of sanctions against Argentina to British policy over the CAP.

This new complexity of issues and actors does represent a fundamental change from the cold war international system. So, whilst it is inaccurate to claim that this results in a new hierarchy of issues, it is equally misleading to pretend that it is only a temporary phenomenon caused by *détente*. To this extent, interdependence is a given for the medium-term future international system, albeit one that is of varying impact on actors and issues. It is therefore most profitable, in explanatory terms, to see it as a variable rather than as a parameter.

This distinction between interdependence as a variable and as a parameter leads us back to a discussion of foreign policy analysis. Now, exactly because behaviouralism has, by its methodological orientation, to focus on salient behaviour (however defined), it is much more likely to be able to cope with the impact of interdependence on foreign policy behaviour than is a traditional view of foreign policy analysis, which stresses the unique, and is based on the assumptions of a state-centric world. For traditional views of foreign policy analysis, the problem is a very serious one, since the central assumptions of state-centrism force analysts to downgrade the salience of interdependence, relying instead on notions of the ultimately determining impact of military issues. For behavioural foreign policy analysis the problem is one of evaluating how much of an explanation a concentration on states can provide. That is to say, that accepting a world of mixed actors and issues, the question becomes one of how central are states to specific issue-areas. To the extent that they are not, then foreign policy analysis cannot provide a comprehensive explanation: but, clearly, there are many issues in which states still dominate.

Interdependence, therefore, poses less of a problem for behavioural foreign policy analysis than it does for traditional accounts. Since the focus is behaviour, then the explanatory power of a reliance on states is determined by the role of states in determining that behaviour. After all, interdependence *per se* does not remove the explanatory power of theories; it only does so if those theories are still seen as dealing with all that is to be explained. What interdependence does is to force behavioural foreign policy analysts to re-examine the extent to which states account for international behaviour; there is no reason why it should reduce explanatory power in the areas in which states continue to dominate. Indeed, it is quite possible to develop alternative models and theories of foreign policy to include the major effect of interdependence on the domestic-international and high–low distinctions. The real problem faces those foreign policy analysts who continue to see the world as only composed of states or, at least, who see international relations as explicable by a reliance on state behaviour. Because interdependence does alter the nature of the international system, such approaches will be increasingly removed from reality and will simply not be able to account for the substance of international relations in a complex inter-dependent world.

For the behaviouralists, of course, the task of integrating foreign policy analysis within a revised conception of the role of the state in international relations remains, but it is the conclusion of this chapter that this is potentially a far easier task to achieve than is that which faces the state-centric approach. As such, interdependence may reduce the ability of foreign policy analysis to explain the central aspects of international relations, but it does not remove it. For those who cling to a state-centric view of the world the current complexities will remain unfathomable; for those who see the task of foreign policy analysis as explaining behaviour on the international stage, interdependence reduces explanatory power by reducing the role of the actor that the subject has, axiomatically, to be concerned with. A realization of this vast distinction between these two schools of thought in foreign policy analysis is but one illustration of the ways that the empirical phenomenon of interdependence and its theoretical reflection have a varying impact on, international relations theory and practice.

NOTES AND REFERENCES

1. Seyom Brown, *New Forces in World Politics* (Washington, Brookings Institution, 1974); R. Maghroori and B. Ramberg, *Globalism vs Realism: International Relations' Third Debate* (Boulder, Westview, 1982).
2. J. D. Singer, 'The level-of-analysis problem in international relations', pp. 77-92 in K. Knorr and S. Verba (eds), *The International System: Theoretical Essays* (Princeton, Princeton University Press, 1961).
3. See, for example, Morton Kaplan, *System and Process in International Politics* (New York, John Wiley, 1957); Richard Rosecrance, *Action and Reaction in World Politics* (Boston, Little, Brown, 1963).
4. See Karl Deutsch *et al.*, *Political Community and the North Atlantic Area* (Princeton, Princeton University Press, 1957); Ernst Haas, *Beyond the Nation State* (Stanford, Stanford University Press, 1954).
5. See Richard Snyder *et al.*, *Foreign Policy Decision Making* (New York, Free Press, 1962); George Modelski, *A Theory of Foreign Policy* (New York, Praeger, 1962); James Rosenau, 'Pre-theories and theories of foreign policy', in R. Barry Farrell (ed.), *Approaches to Comparative and International Politics* (Evanston, Northwestern University Press, 1966).
6. The original essays, along with others on the same topic, are reprinted in K. Knorr and J. Rosenau, *Contending Approaches to International Politics* (Princeton, Princeton University Press, 1969).
7. See Oran Young, 'Professor Russett: industrious tailor to a naked emperor', *World Politics,* 21 (1969), 486-511; and Bruce Russett, 'The young science of international politics', *World Politics,* 22 (1969), 87-94.
8. John Handelman, Michael O'Leary, John Vasquez and William Coplin, 'Color it Morgenthau: a date-based assessment of quantitative international relations research', unpublished paper presented to the International Studies Association Conference, 1973. For a published version, see John Vasquez, 'Colouring it Morgenthau: new evidence for an old thesis on quantitative international politics', *British Journal of International Studies,* 5 (1979), 210-28.
9. See James Rosenau, *Domestic Sources of Foreign Policy* (New York, Free Press, 1967) and *Linkage Politics* (New York, Free Press, 1969); Wolfram Hanrieder, *Comparative Foreign Policy* (New York, McKay, 1971), Ch. 7.
10. William Wallace, 'How foreign is foreign policy?', unpublished paper presented to the Political Studies Association Conference, 1977.
11. See, for example, Edward Morse, *Modernization and the Transformation of International Relations* (New York, Free Press, 1976).
12. See, for example, G. Paige, *The Korean Decision* (New York, Free Press, 1968).
13. See, for example, M. Brecher, *The Foreign Policy System of Israel* (Oxford, Oxford University Press, 1972), *Decisions in Israel's Foreign Policy* (Oxford, Oxford University Press, 1974), and *Decisions in Crisis* (Berkeley, University of California Press, 1980).
14. See K. Boulding, 'National images and international system', *Journal of Conflict Resolution,* 3 (1959), 120-31; O. Holsti, 'The belief system and national images', *Journal of Conflict Resolution,* 6 (1962), 244-52; R.

Jervis, Perception and Misperception in International Politics (Princeton, Princeton University Press, 1976).
15. See G. Allison, *Essence of Decision* (Boston, Little, Brown, 1971); I. Janis, *Victims of Groupthink* (Boston, Houghton Mifflin, 1972).
16. Brown, op. cit.
17. Vasquez, op. cit., p. 211.
18. See R. Keohane and J. Nye (eds), *Transnational Relations and World Politics* (Cambridge, Harvard University Press, 1972) and *Power and Interdependence* (Boston, Little, Brown, 1977).
19. R. Mansbach, Y. Ferguson, and D. Lampert, *The Web of World Politics* (Englewood Cliffs, Prentice-Hall, 1976).
20. R. Mansbach and J. Vasquez, *In Search of Theory* (New York, Columbia University Press, 1981).
21. Charles Kegley, The Comparative Study of Foreign Policy: Paradigm Lost? (Columbia, University of South Carolina, 1980).
22. James Rosenau, 'Muddling, meddling and modelling: alternative approaches to the study of world politics in an era of rapid change', *Millennium, 8* (1979), 132.
23. See, for example, M. East *et al.*, *Why Nations Act* (Beverly Hills, Sage, 1978); J. Wilkenfeld *et al.*, *Foreign Policy Behavior* (Beverly Hills, Sage, 1980).
24. C. Kegley and P. McGowan, *The Political Economy of Foreign Policy Behavior* (Beverly Hills, Sage, 1981).
25. See Mansbach *et al.*, op. cit.
26. F. Northedge, 'Transnationalism: the American illusion', *Millennium, 5* (1976), 21-8.
27. Ibid., 25.
28. Ibid., 26.
29. Hedley Bull, 'The structures that prevent collapse into anarchy', *Times Higher Education Supplement*, 30 September 1977, p. 13.
30. Ibid.
31. Ibid.
32. Ibid.
33. Kenneth Waltz, 'The myth of national interdependence', in C. Kindleberger (ed.), *The International Corporation* (Cambridge, MIT Press, 1970); also, see his *Theory of International Politics* (Cambridge, Addison-Wesley, 1979), Ch. 7.

4 The Politics of Global Issues: Cognitive Actor Dependence and Issue Linkage

PETER WILLETTS

The increasing usage of the term 'interdependence' with respect to global politics is predominantly associated with the technological and economic complexity of the modern world. Keohane and Nye mainly refer to 'problems of economic or ecological interdependence'; Kissinger made it the central concept of his speech at the UN Special Session, convened in early 1974 in response to the oil crisis; and Dadzie and Ramphal focus on interdependence in order to promote co-operation in North–South economic relations.[1] Yet, once a clear, analytical definition is given, we see that dependence and interdependence need not contain direct reference to economic matters as an essential part of the definition. Despite the reluctance that most authors have displayed towards producing a formal definition, it does seem worthwhile to do so. The following is offered as being compatible with the work of both Keohane and Nye and of Rosenau.[2]

Dependence exists for an actor with respect to a policy question when achievement of the optimal outcome, desired by that actor, requires appropriate behaviour by one or more other actors.

Actor interdependence exists for a set of actors, to each of which the same policy question is salient, when each of the actors is dependent for that question upon one or more of the other members of the set.

The fundamental feature of dependence is the constraint imposed upon freedom of action: actors cannot take unilateral, independent decisions without having to evaluate the degree of co-operation, willing or unwilling, which will be given by other actors. We are used to thinking of constraints being imposed by the lack of necessary material resources, but politics is also about non-material, non-economic constraints.

Discussions of interdependence rapidly move on to the concept of vulnerability, which is seen as the liability to suffer opportunity costs when independent action is attempted. The word 'costs', when used without qualification, is generally assumed to mean economic costs. Yet, although there is no clear unit of measurement like money, costs can equally well cover psychological resources, which can both be accumulated and be subject to deprivation by others. The aim of this chapter is to show that we may separate out an analytically distinct, non-economic realm for the use of the concept of interdependence: the cognitive realm.

THE LEGAL APPROACH TO INTERNATIONAL LEGITIMACY

Two very different traditions in the study of international relations have given attention to the cognitive outputs of international actors, that is the political decisions of actors and the arguments used to justify those decisions. The legal tradition has tended to emphasize how limited in scope is international law and how devoid of supranational authority are international institutions. The conservative approach within the legal tradition considerably underplays the scope of international law by declining to regard as law routinized interactions, which have not been codified at all or have been codified by something less than a full treaty.[3] In addition, the extent to which elements of institutional supranationality do exist and are utilized is also underplayed.[4] Whatever may be the balance of these arguments, inasmuch as international law has an impact, it represents a cognitive constraint upon independent action. In practice it is a clear norm of diplomacy that governmental actions have to be justifiable in terms of international law. For example, the United States' invasion of Grenada in October 1983 depended upon the assertions that it was acting in defence of its citizens and under the provisions of the Treaty establishing the Organization of Eastern Caribbean States. The fact that these assertions are of dubious legal foundation[5] is not so striking as the fact that it was deemed essential to put them forward. Indeed, without the legal justification it is unlikely that the invasion would have taken place.[6] But, important as arguments about international law may be, they do not have the impact of domestic law within each society. The tribunals before which the United States had to justify its position on Grenada were the UN Security

Council and General Assembly rather than the International Court of Justice. Thus the actual impact of international law is less through the direct impact of legal authority than as a contribution to debate by international actors about normative legitimacy.

THE BEHAVIOURAL APPROACH TO INTERNATIONAL LEGITIMACY

On the other hand, the behavioural tradition has tended to ignore international law, emphasizing what people do and how they arrive at decisions rather than the way decisions are justified. There is a literature on bureaucracies covering both operating procedures within bureaucracies and conflicts between them,[7] and there is a literature on how policy is perceived. The latter might be an appropriate starting-point to consider cognitive interdependence. There are two formal methodologies which have been developed. Leites in 1951 studied *The Operational Code of the Politburo* in the Soviet Union and George reviewed and systematized the approach a decade and a half later.[8] Despite the rather specific, practical concerns suggested by the term, an operational code is defined by answers to five questions concerning 'philosophical issues' and five questions on 'instrumental' or policy issues, all of which are highly abstract and general in nature.[9] This makes the approach inapplicable to the study of interdependence, a concept which is solidly grounded in debates about specific, empirical problems. Also operational codes are assumed to be highly stable,[10] while interdependence is primarily of interest to those who wish to explain change and the dynamics of the international system.

The second methodology is the construction of 'cognitive maps' of individuals by induction from documents or responses in interviews. The result is a diagram, or a matrix, of concepts in the individual's belief system and connections between the concepts, asserting whether or not a casual relationship is present between the pairs of concepts.[11] Cognitive maps suffer the opposite disadvantage to operational codes. The maps are ultra-specific: they apply to one individual 'with respect to some limited domain, such as a given policy problem'.[12] The analysis can only be made *post facto*. Although it is claimed that predictions can be made from cognitive maps,[13] this can only be with respect to events closely related to the specific topic of the map. It is not a methodology appropriate to the study of many issues in complex systems. Lastly, without a formal methodology, detailed conceptual work has been done on how information is processed and perceived by individuals and groups.[14] This is, perhaps, the most important work on cognition in global politics. However, it is again difficult to visualize its application at the global systematic level rather than in the study of particular actors.

COGNITIVE CONSISTENCY THEORY

One approach, which has run as a thread throughout all the behavioural literature on cognition in politics, is Festinger's cognitive consistency theory.[15] Yet it has not been extensively applied as a central concept in the study of global politics. The idea that we all have a psychological drive to make our perceptions of the world harmonious and will tend to change the normative evaluations and/or beliefs about the empirical nature of the world, in order to remove incongruities, is both highly parsimonious and of high analytical utility because it is so widely applicable. Cognitive consistency can be formulated in a general abstract manner, while readily becoming applicable to specific, empirical case-studies.

The idea that political actors all have a drive towards consistency also helps to transcend the level of analysis problem in global politics,[16] as pressures to achieve consistency are present in some form at each level of analysis. For the individual the drive is an internal psychological one, motivated by the desire for the security and the satisfaction of thinking that he/she has a coherent understanding of the world around us. For the group, there is the need to hold the allegiance of its constituent members, to establish a coherent identity and to project a credible view of the world as the basis for appealing for wider support to achieve the group's goals. All these requirements for political action can best be met by developing an acceptable policy platform for the group. The better the various planks of the platform are integrated each with the others, the more successful will the group be (*ceteris paribus*). At the systematic level, communication through consistent loops will produce positive feedback, strengthening the original perceptions, while communication through loops which appear as dissonant will produce negative feedback, tending to dampen the original action, i.e. to challenge the original perceptions. (We will consider some illustrations of this below.)

It must be emphasized that, in seeking to extend cognitive consistency theory to the analysis of global politics, we are not suggesting that psychological processes operate at all three levels of analysis. They can only operate within individual people and groups cannot be assumed to have the properties of individuals. What is being argued is that individuals, groups and larger systems all structure political debate in a similar manner: they are homologous. Any particular articulation of ideas, whether by the US President, by the Pope or by the Secretary-General of Amnesty International, will be coming in part from the individual, in part from a participant in a social group and in part in response to pressures from the global system. At all three levels the effect is the same as the promotion of cognitive consistency.

THE DIMENSIONS OF EVALUATION

A second body of work in social psychology is of interest and strengthens the idea that cognitive consistency theory might be applicable. Osgood developed the semantic differential technique to investigate inductively whether or not there are standard attitude dimensions by which we assess objects and ideas.[17] The respondents are given rating scales, which are bipolar with the ends represented by pairs of adjectives, such as weak/strong, fast/slow, new/old, etc., by which the items are assessed. The ratings of items can be subjected to factor analysis to discover any underlying dimensions. Osgood has shown that three factors consistently appear: they are affect (positive/negative evaluation), potency and activity. The finding is consistent across very varied studies, from market research to sociology and political science, and across varied social groups. The three dimensions would appear to suggest that most people will use Realist criteria for assessing other countries: 'Are they powerful?' (potency) and 'Are they a threat?' (activity). But closer reflection leads one to note that the first factor, with greater explanatory effect, is always the positive/negative evaluation, rather than potency, and that the evaluation is independent of potency. Thus the psychological drive behind coalition formulation would appear to be an attempt by each actor to achieve cognitive consistency in the patterns of positive/negative evaluations the various actors make of each other. In other words, there is no need to assume that alliances are formed solely on the basis of security concerns or economic interests. This undermines the Realist assumption that 'states' attempt to pursue an objective 'national interest'. Ideology is not necessarily rhetoric to justify policy arrived at by other criteria. It may well be that the evaluations contained in our ideologies are the basis for most political actors to take policy decisions.

AN ILLUSTRATION OF COGNITIVE DYNAMICS

If we are all prone to evaluate other groups of people or countries by a simple good/bad criterion, then simple, signed digraphs showing balance or unbalance might not be too unrealistic a representation of cognitive patterns. Let us consider an example for heuristic purposes, of a system containing four governments as the actors. As a simplification, it will be assumed that there is sufficient information flowing round the system and sufficiently similar dimensions of evaluation that the four actors all have the same perceptions of who is friendly and who is hostile to whom. (The diagrams solely portray cognitive factors and are not in any way meant to portray, as Realists do, the structure of 'power' relations.)

If events external to these cognitive systems lead B and D to come into conflict, there is then dissonance for all four governments. Dissonance exists in all paths which return to their starting-points via an odd number of minus signs, i.e. BDC and BDA involve dissonance. On the assumption that the disturbance is significant enough to affect the BD relationship for some time, the pressure is upon A and C to remove the cognitive stress. A can, on the one hand, become antagonistic towards both B and D or, on the other hand, attempt to remove the BD conflict, in order to restore balance. Both options are to some extent pursued by an attempt to

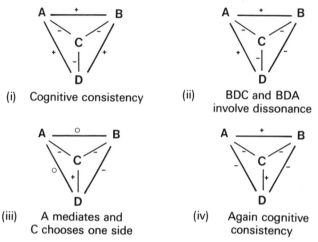

(i)   Cognitive consistency   (ii)   BDC and BDA involve dissonance

(iii)   A mediates and C chooses one side   (iv)   Again cognitive consistency

Figure 4.1   Cognitive consistency dynamics

mediate. For C, only taking sides with B or with D can restore balance and this will be done on the basis of the salient attributes of B and D and of their conflict.[18] If mediation fails and is abandoned, the situation in diagram (iii) means that A has now lost its freedom to choose and must take the opposite side to C, if it wishes to restore cognitive consistency. The abstract deduction of the dynamics fits well to several contemporary conflicts, when the various actor governments were as shown in Table 4.1.

Table 4.1   *Cognitive dynamics in contemporary conflicts*

	Falklands War 1982	Iran–Iraq War 1980	Ogaden War 1978	Kampuchea–Vietnam 1979
A	USA	PLO	USSR	USSR
B	Britain	Iraq	Ethiopia	Vietnam
C	Cuba	Israel	USA	USA
D	Argentina	Iran	Somalia	Dem. Kampuchea

(In the second case in the table, there have been persistent reports that Israel has supplied arms to Iran but they are not clearly substantiated. Relations of the two with the USA complicate those within the quartet.)

If we were to move even beyond a simple, four-actor model, the complexities and permutations would soon become too difficult to handle with two-dimensional diagrams. But our mental limitations are no reason for rejecting the proposition that each actor's striving for cognitive consistency in evaluation of other actors is part of the dynamics of international politics. What has been identified is a process which can be described as cognitive actor-interdependence. For each actor the evaluation of other actors is not an independent property of their own value systems, but is subject to the pattern of evaluations within the system as a whole.

THE RECOGNITION OF EVALUATIONS OF AFFECT IN THE REAL WORLD

We can observe in the global system many phenomena whereby governments publicly signal positive or negative evaluations of each other. The establishment of diplomatic missions is a weak positive evaluation, which appears to be restricted in its use only by a definite negative assertion of an 'enemy' evaluation or more frequently by a lack of resources to fund further missions. More subtle evaluative rankings can be shown by the status of the ambassador and the number of diplomats employed. Formal visits are only a positive sign but the communiqués they generate may include negative evaluations of third parties.[19] Both military alliances, such as NATO or the Warsaw Pact, and non-military coalitions, such as the Non-Aligned Movement or the Commonwealth, provide regular meetings to express mutual support and solidarity. (It is noteworthy that these alliances and coalitions try to avoid the cognitive dissonance of conflict within their organizations by avoiding recourse to voting procedures wherever possible.) Lastly, we find that frequently when military force is used it occurs on a multinational basis, even when some, or all but one, of the participating governments are providing such token forces that they have little military significance. This is true for the Soviet invasion of Czechoslovakia, the US intervention in Vietnam, the multinational forces in Sinai and the Lebanon, and most recently the US invasion of Grenada. The supposedly 'Great Powers' are dependent upon valued 'minor powers' to add legitimacy to their actions by positive identification with them.

Voting in the UN and its related agencies regularly forces an uncomplicated but coherent and comprehensive set of evaluations.[20] If the policy objective for each actor is to obtain a 'favourable' decision from an international organization, then logically they must all be dependent upon other members to obtain the required majority of votes. This is an example in the realm of cognitive interdependence of what is called 'common fate' interdependence. If the aim is to obtain a consensus decision then there is total mutual dependence of each upon the others. If the aim is only to obtain a sufficient majority, then only those within the majority share the common fate, while those in the minority are just dependent for support upon other members of the minority. The simplifying assumption that all actors are able to take part in the voting does not apply in the executive committees of international organizations. For example, Security Council debates often have non-members as participants, but then it is only the fifteen members of the Council which are in this type of interdependent system. Other speakers are dependent, without being interdependent. Situations where actors individually possess a veto do provide a limited possibility for that actor to avoid dependence. This arises where the actor merely has the objective of preventing any positive decision being taken. Then the common fate interdependence does not include the member(s) with the veto.

The empirical discussion so far has been remarkably government-orientated for an author who is committed to a pluralist, non-state-centric paradigm.[21] Partly this is because non-governmental organizations operating at the global level receive so little attention in the mass media that governmental, rather than NGO, coalitions spring more readily to mind. Partly, also, one would suspect that coalition formation among NGOs occurs with a much lower relative frequency than among governments. Certainly there are few parallels in the NGO world with the world of intergovernmental diplomacy,[22] in which general channels of communication are established to deal with any issues which may arise in global politics. That said, NGOs in various countries do form institutional coalitions by setting up INGOs and some INGOs themselves are constituted by a membership of more specialist INGOs. The broadest coalition of all arises at the UN in New York with

CONGO, the Conference of NGOs in Consultative Status with ECOSOC, and its various sub-committees.

Some of the coalitions of NGOs do, like intergovernmental coalitions, develop negative evaluations, including political conflict, with other NGO coalitions. For example, the IPPF (International Planned Parenthood Federation) is in conflict with the Catholic Church over birth control and IBFAN (International Baby Foods Action Network) is in conflict with ICIFI (International Council of Infant Food Industries). Such conflicts do not split the NGO world in the way that the cold war, Israeli-Palestinian relations or North–South relations split governments. Amnesty International and other NGOs may happily work with both IPPF and Catholics, with IBFAN groups and dried milk manufacturers, while avoiding cognitive dissonance, because Amnesty defines its own identity in a limited, specialized manner which excludes direct concern with other issues. (One may assume that Amnesty would not remain unaffected and uninvolved were a conflict to arise between two human rights organizations.) Governments might wish to concentrate on one or two priority issues, but they are prevented from doing solely that by their generalized, territorially-based mandate, by pressures from other governments and from NGOs to take positions, and by membership of the UN and its agencies where they are expected to vote on virtually all major contemporary issues.

If one is not a Realist and has a concept of actor interdependence, which is applied equally to cognitive constraints among governments and among NGOs, then logically it should also apply to relationships between governments and NGOs. There are both governments and NGOs concerned with disarmament, with development, with opposition to apartheid or with human rights. Should we not expect to find that coalitions across the governmental/NGO divide are operating on these issues? Much co-operation does occur, but it is often kept secret by both sides, it is usually on an *ad hoc* rather than a regular basis and it is rarely institutionalized. Indeed, the author is aware of only one such institution, the International Union for the Conservation of Nature and Natural Resources.[23] It would appear that governments and NGOs are perceived to be such fundamentally different units that coalition formation does not seriously cross the participants' minds. The Realist paradigm is in this respect a self-fulfilling prophesy. Cognitive dissonance of a different kind, between theory and the empirical world, would arise if NGOs were regularly and publicly given an equal status to governments. Sometimes the extent to which the distinction is internalized *on both sides* leads one to suspect that there are two great hyper-coalitions in world politics — all governments versus all NGOs. This problem requires further theoretical attention.

THE CONTRASTING PREDICTIONS FROM THE TWO THEORIES

Inasmuch as cognitive actor interdependence is operating to shape conditions, we would expect the resulting coalitions to be very different in composition from those based on security or economic interests. The problem is that, in practice, theories of rational power-maximization can, when applied to particular historical case-studies, provide an *ex post facto* explanation of virtually any pattern of events. However, when presented in a formal abstract manner, as in Riker's theory of minimum winning coalitions, there is a clear prediction that beyond a certain point, at which victory is assured, there is no utility in recruiting further members to a coalition.[24] Cognitive consistency theory, on the other hand, would lead one to predict that firstly a coalition will recruit all those actors for whom the members of the group have a positive evaluation and reject all those for whom there is a negative evaluation. After that has been achieved it may be possible to continue recruiting, by accepting members previously considered unacceptable, on the grounds that the enemy will lose more in status than the coalition will lose in coherence. In other words there is no theoretical maximum size for a coalition and it may well continue to grow until it is all-encompassing. The history of UN voting, particularly on decolonization, shows that this does occur.[25] Indeed, on a large number of issues the United States is now in a tiny minority of three or four governments — a situation which is impossible according to power theory.[26]

ISSUE LINKAGE AND ISSUE INTERLINKAGE

We may now turn from actor interdependence to issue

interdependence and ask what processes will produce, for any one actor, linkages from one issue to another. One of the first and best-known uses of the concept was by Rosenau in his book, *Linkage Politics*. He defined linkage as 'any recurrent sequence of behaviour that originates in one system and is reacted to in another'.[27] This is much too loose a concept. Firstly, it is ambiguous enough to cover both dependence by one actor upon another and linkage for a single actor between different issues. Secondly, it refers to connections, but omits reference to constraints which are necessarily present, if interdependence is to be a concept of theoretical significance. In a manner that is directly comparable to our definitions of dependence and of actor interdependence, we may offer definitions of linkage and of issue interdependence. One problem with the concept of interdependence is that it is not always clear whether it is being applied to actors or to issues. To make it plain that we are talking about an analytically distinct usage, we will reluctantly coin a new piece of jargon and refer to issue interdependence as issue interlinkage.

Linkage exists on a single policy question for an actor when the achievement of the optimal outcome on that question requires appropriate behaviour by the actor on one or more other policy questions.

Issue interlinkage exists for an actor on a set of policy questions when on each of the questions there is linkage for that actor to one or more of the other questions in the set.

It should be emphasized that we are now considering constraints which are not part of international relations but are internal to the politics of the individual actor.

THE OCCURRENCE OF ISSUE LINKAGES

A non-academic usage of the word linkage arose in the mid-1970s when Kissinger asserted linkage between Soviet actions in Europe and Cuban intervention in Angola and Ethiopia, supposedly under Soviet instructions. This falls under our definition as one category: unilaterally-imposed linkage. It 'exists on a policy question (*détente* in Europe) for an actor (the Soviet government) when achievement of the optimal outcome, desired by that actor (further agreements with the USA) requires appropriate behaviour (withdrawal of Cuban troops) on one or more other policy questions (the Angolan and

Ethiopian wars).' In this case the linkage was compounded by Soviet dependence upon Cuban agreement to withdraw.[28] Around the same time the OPEC governments unilaterally imposed a linkage upon the United States, so that if it wished to discuss energy supplies and prices it had to do so in a wider development context.[29]

While it is possible at times to identify cases of unilaterally imposed linkages, the category merges rather fuzzily into the more typical bargaining linkages, whereby as a result of negotiations among a group of actors a set of issues become linked for all the members of the group. In multilateral negotiations a single actor may well try unilaterally to impose a linkage, as when Malta at the Madrid Conference on Security and Co-operation in Europe tried to insist upon its desire for a conference on the Mediterranean.[30] Usually a negotiating agenda is such a mixture of items of general interest and items of interest to one or two actors, without conflict necessarily arising about its composition, that one could not distinguish several unilaterally-imposed items from mutual agreement to consider each others' concerns.

Bargain linkages are, of course, as old as politics itself, but they are more complex and more constraining in modern times because of the growth of permanent membership in international organizations. This is particularly true where the organizations cover a wide range of issues in their mandate and on their regular agendas. When time and other resources do permit, it may be possible to negotiate each item separately, producing acceptable compromises. However, at the sessions of the institutions a finite number of personnel, operating on a limited time-scale, are often under the pressure that a second-best agreement now is much preferred to no agreement at all or a marginally better agreement at the next session. The result is typically that one actor gains an outcome which is more favourable on an issue that is particularly salient, in return for a less favourable outcome on an issue that is more salient to another actor. Agreement on one issue is linked to and requires agreement on the other issue(s): a bargain is struck. Such is the nature of virtually every session of the European Community Council of Ministers, as when the British government accepts an increase in agricultural prices in return for the French government's acceptance of a budget rebate arrangement for Britain.

Such explanations are again incompatible with a Realist approach, firstly, because the capabilities applicable to each issue will not determine the outcomes on those issues and, secondly, because the differential saliences of issues, which are an essential part of the explanation, cannot be analysed in power terms. Salience for each actor is derived from the normative evaluation of issues and will determine whether or not bargain linkage can occur. If the relative salience rankings of various issues are the same or very close for all the actors, then bargain linkage becomes highly improbable. Each actor will give priority to the same issue and not be willing to be diverted by concessions on secondary issues. Fortunately, such situations are relatively rare and differential salience rankings are normal.

THE APPROACH OF MANSBACH AND VASQUEZ TO ISSUES

A stronger form of linkage, stronger because it is psychologically internalized, is cognitive linkage. Before we can discuss such linkages it is necessary to define what an issue is. Mansbach and Vasquez have sought to construct an 'issue paradigm'. They assert that politics involves contention over proposals for the disposition of stakes.

It is the perceptions of contenders concerning the way in which these various proposals about stakes are related that shape issues. Proposals that are seen as related (either because actors consciously claim that they are or behave as though they were) are perceived to constitute an issue . . . stated more formally: *An issue consists of contention among actors over proposals for the disposition of stakes among them.*[31]

Issues that have the highest salience in the political system can be referred to as *critical issues*. These are issues that are initially at the apex of the individual agendas of all or most of the high-status actors and that, in time, tend to draw in or redefine other issues.[32]

It would appear that we have here a two-stage process of aggregation. Stakes are aggregated into issues and issues are aggregated into critical issues. The discussion of issues is clear and rigorous, but the concept of critical issues is far from satisfactory.

One component of the concept of critical issues is that they 'dominate the attention of major actors.' This is curious for sophisticated and detailed work that is seeking consciously to replace the Realist, power paradigm. Within one paragraph they appear to use 'important actors', 'high-status actors' and 'powerful actors' as synonyms to 'major actors'.[33] Yet complete replacement of a power paradigm by an issue paradigm requires abandonment of the idea that power is a constant attribute of an actor across several issues.[34] (IBFAN has had more impact than the US government upon the baby foods issue and the IPPF has had more impact upon the global politics of birth control than the Soviet government.)

Thus an issue can only be critical, with reference to salience, by dominating the attention of the actors which are most active on the issue. This is not the same as dominating the global agenda and demolishes the assertion that 'critical issues tend to dominate an agenda for definite periods of time'. Still less can one accept that 'in global society, this cycle seems ... to be ... around twenty-three years'.[35] For the governments, companies and banks involved, the Siberian gas pipeline was a critical issue, but it was only of less than one year's duration from 14 December 1981 to 13 November 1982.

The second component of the concept of a critical issue was the drawing-in and redefining of other issues. Beyond a certain point stakes can only be aggregated by reference to abstract values. It seems preferable to label the result of such an aggregation as a 'hyper-issue'. Following Mansbach and Vasquez, we may say that issues which are seen to be related (either because actors consciously claim that they are or behave as though they were) are perceived to constitute a hyper-issue. The definition is that 'a hyper-issue consists of contention among actors over proposals for the identification of issues with the fulfilment of abstract values'. Thus, the imprisonment of Nelson Mandela, sporting contacts with South Africans, South African government and NGO member-ships of international organizations, etc., are all specific stakes related to the global politics of the apartheid issue. Similarly, abortion, equal pay, political participation, etc., are all specific stakes related to the global politics of women's rights. At a higher level, which can only be related to abstract values such as justice and equality, the issues of apartheid and women's rights are part of the hyper-issue of human rights. Other hyper-issues are communism (the cold war), development, peace and conservation.

THE AGGREGATION OF ISSUES

Once political contention moves beyond the attempt to coerce one's opponent, all actors seek to legitimize their position by reference to abstract values, in at least a vague form and sometimes in a highly sophisticated manner. Thus debate about the cognitive linkage of stakes into issues and of issues into hyper-issues is central to politics. Once such linkages are established they will become internalized in the minds of the actors. Just as cognitive dependence between actors is sustained by the attempt to maintain cognitive consistency, so, too, is cognitive linkage between stakes and between issues.

The Non-Aligned Movement has long been committed to the hyper-issue of the non-use of force in international relations. This provided linkage between Yugoslav and Indian promotion of *détente*, African fears of South African military might, and Arab hostility to Israeli expansionism. The Movement has also related many issues to the hyper-issue of self-determination. Thus the British were surprised to find how strong was their support in the UN, including among the members of the Non-Aligned, when they went to war over the Falklands with Argentina, one of the Movement's members. After the war was over, in the subsequent 37th Session of the UN General Assembly, Argentina did not even attempt to propose condemnation of Britain for re-establishing control of the Falklands islands. In the Latin American resolution proposing negotiations over sovereignty, they had to refer to non-use of force in order to obtain majority support (implicitly condemning the Argentinian invasion in April 1982) and to self-determination (implicitly accepting Britain's position that territorial control was not the only issue).[36] The United States government, too, had a shock in November 1983 when linkage of the Grenada issue to the hyper-issue of the non-use of force was so strong and linkage to the hyper-issue of communism was so weak, that not one of the NATO allies voted with the USA against the resolutions in the Security Council and the General Assembly condemning the Grenada invasion.[37]

THE ENMESHING OF ACTOR INTERDEPENDENCE AND ISSUE INTERLINKAGE

Mansbach and Vasquez distinguish 'two types of perceived linkages that fuse stakes into issues — stake and actor.' 'A stake linkage entails a perception that proposals involving two or more stakes represent the same preferred values' or are instrumental to them. 'An actor linkage . . . involves a heightened realization that competition for different stakes involves the same friends or foes.'[38] They suggest that this provides a dichotomous variable to classify the type of issue dimension. In this they are mistaken. As they say, 'discerning dimensions (linking stakes) may be possible by using Guttman scaling, cluster-bloc analysis, or factor analyses.'[39] The starting-point for all these methodologies is that one must have a data matrix in which the rows are the various actors and the columns are the various stakes. Each cell entry represents an actor's attitude to a stake. There will only be an issue dimension if there are patterns to the data by which *both* the rows *and* the columns can be arranged. One is impossible without the other. Therefore it is meaningless to describe an issue dimension as being either a 'stake dimension' or an 'actor dimension'.[40] The cold war appears to consist primarily of rivalry between the USA and the Soviet Union, but it is impossible to take a position on the issue without indicating an attitude to communism and to capitalism. Similarly, apartheid appears primarily as a human rights issue, but it is impossible to take a position without forming an attitude towards relations with the South African government. While issue dimensions may be classified by types of stakes, types of actors, numbers of stakes, numbers of actors, etc., 'actor linkage' and 'stake linkage' are not a basis for classification of issues.

Mansbach and Vasquez have made a distinction not between types of issues, but between the two causal processes which have generated issues. The ideological nature, the legal independence and the legitimacy of the governments which were established in the enemy states of the Second World War provided a series of stakes which were perceived as being related and generated the cold war. This was what we have designated as a set of cognitive linkages producing issue interlinkage. By 1973, every one of the various stakes in the

European cold war issues (except for the future of West Berlin, which became a dormant issue) had been authoritatively allocated mainly by the Helsinki Final Act.

But the issue interlinkage had created a dimension of such salience that it had determined the mutual evaluations by the industrialized countries of each other and had created two institutional coalitions, NATO and the Warsaw Pact. This was what we have designated as a set of cognitive dependencies producing actor interdependence. These patterns became so constraining upon the main actors that the cold war dimension remained, even as some of the issues were resolved. New issues such as the future of Palestine, decolonization of Portuguese Africa, civil wars in Central America and (amazingly) the government of Kampuchea have been perceived by at least some actors as cold war issues. These issues have had insufficient cognitive linkage and have produced sufficiently different alignments to make only a minor contribution to reinforcing the cold war cognitive interdependence. However, the Soviet invasion of Afghanistan, military rule in Poland, the arms race in Europe and the shooting-down of the Korean airliner are for the time being enough to sustain a minor version of the cold war. Cognitive issue interlinkage and cognitive actor interdependence feed back upon each other.

Bargaining linkages will also generate cognitive interlinkage. In the late 1960s, Israel's expansion of its control over territory had great salience for the Arabs, while Rhodesian UDI and the other Southern African issues had great salience for the Africans. Eventually a grand bargain of mutual support was struck, thus linking the issues. From 1970, the Non-Aligned Movement took institutional shape and cognitive actor interdependence also grew. This turned the issue linkages into more than bargains, when a 'Declaration on the Struggle for National Liberation' defined Palestine as a colonial question 'exactly the same as the situation in Southern Africa.'[41] This was now a situation of cognitive issue interlinkage. To the extent that the positions have been internalized by the individual actors, the move from bargaining linkages to cognitive linkages is more constraining and hence will have more of an impact upon policy outputs, because the linkage has changed from being of instrumental value to being of intrinsic value.

FROM NATIONAL POLITICS TO GLOBAL POLITICS

The significance of these processes is that they bridge the gap which is traditionally assumed to exist between domestic and international politics. The relations between different actors, which may be covered by the concept of actor independence, are part of the subject matter of international relations. The relations between the positions adopted on a variety of different policy questions, which may be covered by the concept of issue interlinkage, are part of the subject matter of the domestic politics of an actor. If there are persistent and extensive causal processes operating whereby the dynamics of interdependent systems of actors change issue linkages for an individual actor, and if changes in issue linkages can also feed back to change relations in an interdependent system, then the domestic/international distinction may become invalid.

The traditional basis in state-centric power theory for distinguishing international relations as a separate sub-discipline within political science is the axiom that states are autonomous entities with governments which are able to control activity within the state and free to pursue whatever external policy they wish, subject only to assessments of costs and benefits due to the actions of other states.[42] Traditional theorists can accommodate to some uses of the term inter-dependence. As Reynolds and McKinlay comment: '. . . if all relations or transactions . . . imply some mutual dependence, the concept of interdependence adds nothing unless it refers to mutual dependence of a wholly new range or nature or complexity.'[43]

The first point to arise is that cognitive, common fate, actor interdependence, such as voting in the UN, *is* 'mutual dependence of a wholly new nature.' Intergovernmental organizations are a phenomenon, with few exceptions, new to this century, having expanded the range of their activities dramatically since 1945. Many environmental, technical and resource questions are also totally new to the last few decades and create non-cognitive, common fate interdependence. Of course, none of these forms of common fate, actor inter-dependence threatens the continued existence of the state.[44] It is always possible to opt out of the constraints by abandoning the original policy objective, but doing so too frequently or on too important a question may threaten the existence of the government.

Secondly, it would seem that there is at least a good prima facie case, worthy of empirical investigation, that the 'range and complexity' of resource interdependence has been substantially increasing this century. The same is true for cognitive interdependence, though here we should note that it is not just the undoubted increase in the number of governmental, intergovernmental and transnational actors in the global system which is important. The critical research question is how much all the actors appeal to other actors from other countries in order to mobilize support.

Perhaps, if one considers a single form of interdependence on a limited range of policy questions, the traditional Realist paradigm does not seem to be seriously weakened. This chapter has emphasized the cognitive processes, but they are only a part of the phenomenon of interdependence. It is widely accepted that economic exchanges produce an extensive economic interdependence. However, it is not so widely agreed that this is of fundamental significance and that, as the Global Politics paradigm asserts, it affects state-centric assumptions. What totally blurs the international/domestic boundary is the complex interaction between international actor interdependence and domestic issue interlinkage.

The British economy is thus subject to resources interdependence on inflation via import prices, on unemployment via demand for exports, on the exchange rate and on interest rates via the money markets. At the same time, these questions are related domestically to each other, both cognitively and via resources. As a result of this interlinkage, such questions as the levels of taxation and the levels of personal incomes become subject to international actor interdependence and there is little meaning to the idea that there is a distinct entity, the British economy, which can be controlled by the British government.

Cognitive processes can at times become significant by their interaction with other forms of dependence. Thus we have already mentioned the cognitive issue linkage for the Americans of the Grenada invasion to international law on the use of force and the cognitive dependence upon support from other Caribbean countries. Equally, those Caribbean countries wanted the invasion to take place but were resource-dependent upon the US government for both armed personnel and logistics. This interdependent set of eight governments was formed by three rather different processes.

THE REALITY OF COGNITIVE INTERDEPENDENCE

Even if the theoretical implications of actor interdependence and issue interlinkage on economic questions are not fully accepted, most people have little difficulty in conceptualizing a world economy. A similar argument, that there is little meaning to the idea of a distinct British political system in which only domestic actors set the political agenda, is much more controversial and it is doubtful that many academics or politicians, let alone 'people on the Clapham omnibus', ever think of a global political system based on cognitive processes alone being a substantial contribution. The major exception might be in our perceptions of world communism. Few would deny that communist parties in Western Europe were at their strongest in 1945 because of Soviet prestige as an ally in the war and communist involvement in the resistance movements fighting fascist governments. The cold war and particularly the Soviet intervention in Hungary in 1956 reduced both public support and active membership for Western communist parties, while the Sino-Soviet split and the invasion of Czechoslovakia in 1968 both split the parties and helped to produce Eurocommunism. These events are an archetype of the impact of cognitive interdependence in which changing patterns in the evaluations actors make of each other can occur, with country boundaries being relatively insignificant and non-governmental, sub-national actors being affected.[45]

Yet why should we not also take it for granted that the changing status of the external allies and enemies, which relate to governments via all the processes of diplomacy, has its impact upon the status of each government, both in the world at large and among its home public? The media have long been reporting 'foreign affairs'. In some countries the press and broadcasting can be controlled by the government and in others an informal social orthodoxy prevails, but even so the main evaluations of those in other countries can often be deduced from what the government says or does not say. The new feature of the post-1945 global system is the availability of foreign travel, foreign visitors, foreign radio broadcasts and international contact by telephones for ordinary people. Of course, tourism and other exchanges of people can be tightly controlled, some radio stations can be jammed (but not all simultaneously), and telephones can be completely cut, but surprisingly few such restrictions are imposed and a cost is involved, including the implicit admission that the government is of low status. The expansion of global communications is a substantial new factor in global politics.

What is extremely rare indeed is for a government to refuse to have any dealings at all with any external actors. China during the cultural revolution and Iran for some periods after the Islamic revolution are the only examples which come readily to mind and in these cases external actors still remained important reference points for domestic debate. Equally striking is the fact that in most governments the Foreign Minister is a very high status appointment, usually the highest-ranking minister after the President and/or Prime Minister.[46] Activity on foreign affairs can also be a significant form of participation in domestic politics: aspiring American presidential candidates often undertake a lengthy foreign tour at an early stage in their campaigning: Mrs Thatcher first established a clear image for herself as the 'Iron Lady': in many countries the easiest way to attack a politician is to suggest that he or she has an 'unhealthy' relationship with a foreign embassy. All these factors suggest that cognitive actor interdependence might be the norm rather than the exception. Just as we can talk of world communism, should we not also think in terms of world liberalism, conservatism and socialism? And for that matter are there not common reference points for world debates on human rights, development, racism or disarmament — such as Amnesty, the International Commission of Jurists, Pinochet and Amin, to illustrate for just the first issue?

Cognitive issue interlinkage can occur between foreign policy issues and domestic issues not only because there are obvious practical direct connections (these situations would tend to be covered by economic issue interlinkage), but also because there are powerful symbolic connections. To take a hypothetical example, nothing could make a person who had supported apartheid in South Africa into a credible member of the Commission for Racial Equality in Britain. The real-world examples which have an impact can often be far more complex to understand than this. Attitudes to unilateral nuclear disarmament and membership of the European Community are the best indicators one could have as to which faction of the Labour Party a person supported. Although there are no compelling reasons of logic for these two issues to relate so strongly to the left/right dimension, they do so with such powerful effect that they provide a major part of the explanation for the recent division of the party and the formation of the Social Democratic Party. Similarly, for the Conservative Party of the 1950s and 1960s the deepest divide was not caused by any domestic question, but by the Suez crisis. Britain is no exception in this. Foreign policy questions contributed in a major way to the fall of Lyndon Johnson, Jimmy Carter, Nikita Khrushchev and to the collapse of the Fourth Republic in France. Even a ruthless and efficient military dictatorship, that of the Greek colonels, collapsed, like a pack of cards in 1974 upon a foreign policy failure.

If such major effects are to glaringly obvious, ought we not to be looking for means of assessing whether other effects are occurring continuously? How much did the Falklands War contribute to the Conservative victory in the British election in June 1983? How much did the government's response to the Brandt Report and the Cancun summit lead Conservative voters who are active in the churches to rethink their attitudes to other aspects of the government's economic policy? How much impact did the Pope's visit to Britain have upon policy in Northern Ireland? Because we have neither a regular standardized set of attitude questions included in the opinion polls nor a clear understanding of the dynamics of attitude change, it would be a major and difficult research project to try to relate attitudes to foreign and to domestic questions. That the research would be difficult is, however, no grounds for assuming that cognitive issue interlinkage is not a significant phenomenon.

One feature of the development of a new paradigm is that it generates new research questions. Cognitive actor independence, unilaterally-imposed and bargain linkages, and cognitive issue interlinkage are all concepts that contribute to an issue-based, Global Politics paradigm. This analysis has also clearly

106　*Peter Willetts*

generated a new set of research questions of considerable complexity.

NOTES AND REFERENCES

1. R.O. Keohane and J.S. Nye, *Power and Interdependence: World Politics in Transition* (Boston, Little, Brown, 1977), pp. 8 and 10. The speeches of K.K.S. Dadzie, former UN Director-General for Development and International Economic Co-operation, have been circulated as various editions in the UN Department of Public Information series DPI/DESI NOTE/. The speeches of Sir S. Ramphal have been published in S. Ramphal, *One World to Share. Selected Speeches of the Commonwealth Secretary-General, 1975-79* (London, Hutchinson Benham, 1979).
2. The nearest that Keohane and Nye come to giving a definition of interdependence is on p.8 of *Power and Interdependence*. Rosenau does not give a definition, but says 'four characteristics seem salient as central features of all the diverse issues of interdependence.' These are complexity, the involvement of non-governmental actors, fragmented governmental decision-making and the necessity for multilateral co-operation for management of the issues. Rosenau also objects to interdependence being 'conceived as confined to essentially economic processes.' See J.N. Rosenau, *The Study of Global Interdependence: Essays on the Transnationalization of World Affairs* (London, Frances Pinter; New York, Nichols, 1980), pp. 43-5 and 23-9, quote from p.23.
3. For a conservative approach to UN decisions, treating them as of doubtful legal significance, see J. Stone, *Confict through Consensus. United Nations Approaches to Aggression* (Baltimore and London, Johns Hopkins University Press, 1977); and J. Stone, 'Palestinian resolution: zenith or nadir of the General Assembly?', *International Law and Politics, 1* (1975), 1-18. For increasingly strong acceptance of the UN as a source of law, see respectively, I. Brownlie, *Principles of Public International Law* (Oxford, Clarendon Press, 2nd edn., 1979), pp. 14 and 696; R. Higgins, *The Development of International Law through the Political Organs of the United Nations* (London, Oxford University Press, 1963); and J. Castaneda, *Legal Effects of United Nations Resolutions* (New York and London, Columbia University Press, 1969).
4. When textbooks discuss the UN they tend to emphasize the use of the veto in the Security Council, without considering the political costs involved in using a veto or for how long a veto can be sustained against repeated tabling of the same or similar texts. At the same time the existence of Article 25 of the Charter, making decisions of the Security Council binding, is usually given little attention, despite the many situations in which it has been invoked. Article 2(7) on domestic jurisdiction and Article 51 on collective self-defence are frequently quoted, but usually in an abbreviated form which omits restrictions upon their invocation.
5. *The Times*, London, 28 October 1983: 'Outrage and dismay at UN despite Dominica revelation'; 'Scoon arrives home amid controversy'; 'Mystery over text of invasion request'; and 'Barbados says US first to suggest raid.'

6. It had been widely believed that the US government wished to intervene in Grenada from 1979 onwards, as was evidenced by the dispute between Jeane Kirkpatrick and the Non-Aligned Movement leading to the Moynihan amendment to the Foreign Assistance Act of 1981. Thus it appears strongly as if the legal changes made possible what was already desired.

7. G. Allison, *Essence of Decision: Explaining the Cuban Missle Crisis* (Boston, Little, Brown, 1971); A. Beichman, *The 'Other' State Department* (New York, Basic Books, 1967); M.H. Halperin and A. Kanter (eds), *Readings in American Foreign Policy: A Bureaucratic Perspective* (Boston, Little, Brown, 1973); M.H. Halperin, *Bureaucratic Politics and Foreign Policy* (Washington DC, The Brookings Institution, 1974).

8. N. Leites, *The Operational Code of the Politburo* (New York, McGraw Hill, 1951), and A. George, 'The "operational code": a neglected approach to the study of political leaders and decision-making', *International Studies Quarterly, 13* (1969), 190-222.

9. George, ibid.

10. G. Sjoblom, 'Some problems of the operational code approach', pp.48-9, in C. Jonsson, *Cognitive Dynamics and International Politics* (London, Frances Pinter, 1982), pp. 37-74.

11. R. Axelrod (ed.), *Structure of Decision. The Cognitive Maps of Political Elites* (Princeton, NJ, Princeton University Press, 1976). The methodology is outlined in Chapter 2 and the Appendices.

12. Ibid., p. 72.

13. Ibid., p. 65.

14. R. Jervis, *Perception and Misperception in International Politics* (Princeton, NJ, Princeton University Press, 1976).

15. L. Festinger, *A Theory of Cognitive Dissonance* (Evanston, Ill., Row, Peterson, 1957).

16. J.D. Singer, 'The level of analysis problem in international relations', in J.N. Rosenau (ed.), *International Politics and Foreign Policy: A Reader in research and theory* (New York, The Free Press; London, Collier-Macmillan, revised edn., 1969), pp. 20–9.

17. C.E. Osgood, G.J. Suci and P.H. Tannenbaum, *The Measurement of Meaning* (Urbana, Ill., University of Illinois Press, 1957).

18. In the first example given in Figure 4.1, C is Cuba choosing between Britain and Argentina. If Britain had had a left-wing government when it launched the Task Force in April 1982, it is not beyond the bounds of possibility that Cuba would have sided with Britain rather than Argentina on the basis of a left/right evaluation instead of taking Argentina's side on a nationalist/imperialist evaluation. This would lead to the deduction that the USA would have sided with Argentina — not an impossibility given the American anti-colonial tradition.

19. It would be interesting to see whether taking voting positions in the UN General Assembly on the most salient roll-call(s) for each delegation, to derive their evaluation of other delegations, would identify particular delegations as being more likely to change their voting in subsequent years, on particular less salient issues.

20. We may note that it is impossible for there to be cognitive dissonance for anybody in the results of any *one* United Nations roll-call considered in

isolation. All those casting the same vote (e.g. Yes) are mutually supportive and identically differentiated from those casting other votes (e.g. Abstain). Cognitive dissonance can only arise when there are unexpected differences in the patterns on different roll-calls or between one roll-call and other sources of data, such as exchanges of diplomatic messages outside the UN.

21. The currently emerging paradigm, to which it is hoped this chapter makes a contribution, does not yet even have a widely recognized name. The Open University 'World Politics' course team tended in their preparatory work to talk of the 'pluralist perspective', though the relevant section in their reader for the course is headed 'The politics of interdependence and transnational relations' in M. Smith, R. Little and M. Shackleton (eds), *Perspectives in World Politics* (London, Croom Helm, 1981). M. Banks in 'Ways of analysing the world society', pp. 195-215 of A.J.R. Groom and C.R. Mitchell (eds), *International Relations Theory, A Bibliography* (London, Frances Pinter, 1978), refers to 'the international relations paradigm'. R.O. Keohane and J.S. Nye advocate a 'world politics paradigm' in *Transnational Relations and World Politics* (Cambridge, Mass., Harvard University Press, 1972). R.W. Mansbach and J. Vasquez advocate an 'issue paradigm' in their book, *In Search of Theory: A New Paradigm for Global Politics* (New York, Columbia University Press, 1981). P. Willetts has chosen the label *'Global Politics Series'* for books with Frances Pinter Ltd, contributing to the new paradigm.

22. The government of Sweden provides a striking exception in that they have established an Ambassador to NGOs. See Chapter 8 of P. Willetts, *Pressure Groups in the Global System: The Transnational Relations of Issue-Orientated Non-Governmental Organizations* (London, Frances Pinter, 1982) for a description by O. Dahlen of his own work.

23. There are a few other institutions which bring together governments and NGOs but they are not political coalitions formed on a voluntary basis. In the International Labour Organization and the International Red Cross, membership of the NGO (except for the ICRC) stands or falls with that of their government. The International Air Transport Association is more like the IUCN, but only commercial airlines, government or private, may join and not other government agencies or NGOs concerned with air transport. Membership by liberation movements in intergovernmental organizations is true coalition formation, but apart from the PLO's membership in five IGOs it is a rare phenomenon.

24. W.H. Riker, *The Theory of Political Coalitions* (New Haven, Conn., Yale University Press, 1962).

25. For a simple graphical representation of the growth of the decolonization coalition from 1961 to 1964 to 1970 in the United Nations General Assembly, see P. Willetts, *The Non-Aligned Movement: The Origins of a Third World Alliance* (London, Frances Pinter, 1978), pp. 162-4.

26. Morgenthau specifically asserts that UN decisions will reflect external power capabilities: 'In large measure, ... the distribution of material power between the nations seeking support for a policy and the nations whose support is sought will decide the extent to which the former must give way in order to gain that support.' H.J. Morgenthau, *Politics Among*

Nations (New York, Knopf, third edn., 1960), p. 495. Riker, op. cit., also explicitly applies his theory to the United.Nations.

27. J.N. Rosenau (ed.), *Linkage Politics* (New York, The Free Press, 1969), p. 44.

28. The same question of Cuban troops in Angola was also unilaterally imposed as a linkage to the future of Nambia by South Africa upon the Western Contact Group and the Front-Line States. The fact that the Security Council's rejection of 'South Africa's insistence on linking the independence of Nambia to irrelevant and extraneous issues' only came after much discussion in Southern Africa and in the diplomatic system generally does mean there was a linkage in the political process. (The quote is from UN Security Council Resolution 539 (1983) of 28 October 1983.) In other words, even the rejection of a claim to linkage involves a linkage process incurring expenditure of time and resources to reach a decision and legitimize a decision of rejection.

29. The result was the Conference on International Economic Co-operation held in Paris in various sessions from December 1975 to June 1977 with twelve non-oil-producing developing countries, as well as seven members of OPEC and eight Western delegations, and with a negotiating process divided into four commissions on raw materials, development and international finance, as well as on energy.

30. As Malta is not of high status and is peripheral to Europe, cognitive interdependence did not operate to make Malta's agreement to the final text essential and the issue of the Mediterranean seemed too peripheral to force a cognitive linkage.

31. Mansbach and Vasquez, *In Search of Theory*, op. cit. (note 21), p. 59. Emphasis in the original.

32. Ibid., p. 110.

33. J.A. Vasquez and R.W. Mansbach, 'The issue cycle: conceptualizing long-term global political change', *International Organization, 37*, 2 (Spring 1983) 257-79. Quotes from p. 261.

34. Mansbach and Vasquez do accept that 'relative power is issue-specific', (*In Search of Theory*, p. 197; see also pp. 201, 211 and particularly 215-16), but the fact is often not apparent in their book and not at all apparent in their *International Organization* article. They regard status as a 'systematic quality determined in the context of all issues and all actors' and hence is a form of 'overall power' (*In Search of Theory*, p. 216). Status is clearly a theoretically important attribute of actors, but it would be more effective in promoting an issue paradigm not to relate it to the imprecise and redundant concept of power.

35. Mansbach and Vasquez, op. cit. (note 21), p. 123.

36. For more details of the UN and the Falklands issue, see P. Willetts, 'Latin America, the United Nations and the Non-Aligned Movement', in J.W. Hopkins (ed.), *Latin America and Caribbean Contemporary Record Vol. II* (New York, Holmes and Meier, forthcoming). One should also compare the two drafts of the resolution tabled by the Latin Americans, A/37/L.3 of 1 October 1982 and A/37/L.3/Rev.1 of 1 November 1982.

37. The draft resolution tabled by Guyana, Nicaragua and Zimbabwe in the Security Council received 11 votes in favour, 1 against and 3 abstentions

on 28 October 1983 and fell because of the USA's veto. Resolution 38/7 of the General Assembly was passed with 108 votes in favour, 9 against (USA, six Caribbean countries, El Salvador and Israel) and 27 abstentions.

38. Mansbach and Vasquez, op. cit. (note 21), p. 60.
39. Ibid.
40. Ibid., pp. 197-203.
41. O. Jankowitsch and K.P. Sauvant, *The Third World without Superpowers: The Collected Documents of the Non-Aligned Countries, Volume 1* (Dobbs Ferry, N.Y., Oceana Publications, 1978), pp.207-13. Quote from p. 209.
42. For example, see F.S. Northedge, *The International Political System* (London, Faber and Faber, 1976), especially Ch. 6.
43. P.A. Reynolds and R.D. McKinlay, 'The concept of interdependence: its uses and misuses', in K. Goldman and G. Sjostedt, *Power, Capabilities, Interdependence: Problems in the Study of International Influence* (Beverly Hills, Sage, 1979), pp. 141–66, quotation from p. 159.
44. For an argument that the United Nations has changed the nature of statehood, see P. Willetts, 'The United Nations and the transformation of the inter-state system', in B. Buzan and R.J.B. Jones (eds), *Change and the Study of International Relations: The Evaded Dimension* (London, Frances Pinter, and New York, St. Martin's Press, 1981).
45. The preliminary investigation of the global activities of one type of non-governmental group suggests that cognitive interdependence might operate for them. See P. Willetts, *Pressure Groups*, op. cit. (note 22).
46. Some governments do not have separate Foreign Ministers and the portfolio is held by the head of government. It may be surmised that in these cases the head of government wishes to avoid giving too much prestige to a subordinate. In communist governments the Foreign Minister is not of quite so high a status, perhaps because responsibility for foreign affairs is shared with party officials who deal with relations with foreign communist parties.

5 Power and Interdependence:
A Realist Critique

RICHARD LITTLE

INTRODUCTION

Three main lines of argument will be developed in this chapter. First, it will be suggested that international relations specialists have been much too eager to accept that the recent spate of literature on interdependence marks a completely new departure in the discipline. Both advocates and critics of the concept have agreed, apparently without question, that the idea of interdependence is incompatible with the established Realist or power political approach to international relations. It will be argued here, to the contrary, that Realists have always, implicitly or explicitly, accepted that interdependence is a central dimension of political interaction.

The failure to appreciate the importance of interdependence in the context of power politics has arisen in part because of the propagation and acceptance of a stereotyped view of Realism. But this is not the only reason why interdependence has been dissociated from Realism. In a second line of argument, it will be suggested that the general theoretical literature on power which exists in the social sciences has tended to concentrate almost exclusively on the idea of power as an asymmetric or causal phenomenon, thereby failing to consider the relevance of interdependence for the analysis of power.

The third line of argument suggests that the new school of writers on interdependence, in their anxiety to dissociate themselves from Realism, have, ironically, relied upon the asymmetric conception of power and ignored the Realist conception which has been developed in the context of interdependence. As a consequence, it is the Realists who have most to say about the relationship between power and interdependence.

Despite the link between power and interdependence which can be identified in the Realist literature of international relations, it remains the case that this is an area of thinking which continues to be under-explored. The chapter concludes that although Realism, or power politics, represents such a long-standing approach to the study of international relations it is mistaken to believe that all dimensions of this approach have thereby been fully examined. The easy acceptance of a distinction between power politics and interdependence indicates that the significance of interdependence in the analysis of power is a dimension which has not been self-consciously appreciated by Realists and it will be suggested that there is room for future developments.

THE CRITIQUE OF REALISM

During the 1970s, it was widely proclaimed by both academics and practitioners that 'the very nature of world politics is changing'.[1] The changes were attributed to interdependence and for a decade interdependence became one of the most prominent ideas in the analysis of international relations. Many empirical indicators of interdependence were identified. They ranged from the expanding number of non-governmental organizations to the growing political importance of economics in world affairs.[2] But in more general terms, interdependence was considered to denote both greater complexity and an element of common fate in international relations.[3] Neither of these features of interdependence was considered to be compatible with the Realist image of an international arena occupied by autonomous states pursuing their conflicting interests. The elevation of interdependence to a pivotal position in the analysis of international relations, therefore, ostensibly inaugurated a new approach to the discipline and necessitated a reassessment of Realism. The Realist ideas and models apparently so relevant at the onset of the cold war were now considered outdated and unable to account for the changes taking place in the international arena. Indeed, Realism, so the argument ran, was responsible for generating inaccurate images of world politics and giving rise to counter-productive policies.[4]

A dichotomy therefore was established between Realism and interdependence and it was generally assumed that the Realist approach to international relations was unable either to describe or explain interdependence. A closer examination, however, reveals a major cleavage, dividing the new schools of thinkers on interdependence. Although there was general agreement that Realist assumptions must be abandoned in any attempt to account for interdependence, two different and, indeed, incompatible reasons underlay this apparent consensus.

According to one school of thought, Realism was no longer adequate to account for contemporary developments because, when interdependene prevails, power is not an important feature of social relations. Doran, for example, has insisted that interdependence implies the comparative absence of power politics.[5] From his perspective, interdependent relationships are characterised by co-operation and consensus. Interdependence, he argues, precipitates a high degree of reciprocity and as a consequence the exercise of power is excluded from social relationships.

There is, however, a serious flaw contained in this line of argument. In endeavouring to dissociate interdependence from Realism, this school of thought commits the fallacy of the misplaced dichotomy.[6] Conflict and co-operation are not, as seems to be supposed here, extremes at the two ends of a continuum. Almost all social situations involve both co-operation and conflict. Moreover, it is also erroneous to suppose that power is exercised exclusively in conflicts and is eschewed in co-operative relationships. The leader of a mountain rescue team may have the full co-operation of his team and yet may frequently be required to exercise power. The resort to power is likely to be even more frequent in the acephalous conditions found in the international arena. This dimension of the complex warp and woof of social reality has never been lost sight of by Realists. Morgenthau, for example, believes that through the instrument of diplomacy it is possible to achieve 'peace through accommodation'. Nevertheless, diplomacy is still identificd as an 'element of national power'.[7] Morgenthau, therefore, would be unlikely to condone the proposition that conflict and co-operation are largely independent phenomena and that power is associated with one but not the other. The reason given here to justify the disjunction between Realism and interdependence, therefore, relies on a formulation of power which is inadequate. It also misrepresents the role of power in Realist thinking.

The centrality of power in social relationships has, however, been acknowledged by Keohane and Nye. They have, as a consequence, established a very different approach to

interdependence, where it is accepted that the growth of
interdependence does not undermine the significance of
power. Nevertheless, the crux of the argument still purports to
invalidate the Realist approach to international relations.
Complex interdependence, according to Keohane and Nye,
has made certain basic Realist assumptions about power
untenable. They argue, first, that the task of calibrating power
resources has become much more difficult; second, that power
resources can no longer be 'automatically translated into
effective outcomes'; finally, that with the growth of complex
interdependence, non-state actors have come to have an
increasingly important and unpredictable effect on the
outcome of any international bargaining process.[8]

In practice, it is doubtful if Realism does have any major
difficulty coming to terms with these putative products of
complex interdependence. Realists have never claimed that
power could be easily calibrated. On the contrary, the sources
of power have always been depicted as multi-faceted and
difficult to gauge. By the same token, Realists have also always
acknowledged the problems associated with utilizing power
resources to good effect.[9] And while Realists no doubt believe
that the role of non-state actors has been exaggerated, even
here, they would generally accept it is an empirical question
which may need to be investigated. The apparent divergence
between the Realists and the advocates of complex interdependence, therefore, rests upon an over-simplified or
stereotyped view of Realism.

THE REALIST CRITIQUE OF NEW INTERDEPENDENCE

For a brief period it appeared as if Realism was going to be
relegated to the history of ideas, with nothing relevant to say
about the contemporary world. However, although temporarily
winded by the criticisms, the Realists quickly recovered and
replied to their detractors. A good deal of the Realist responses
focused on interdependence. But two very different lines of
reply were developed reflecting a major epistemological and
methodological division within the Realist camp. It is
necessary, briefly, to describe the division before examining
the ways that Realists have responded to their critics.

The epistemological divide runs all the way through the social sciences and separates reductionists from holists. On the reductionist side of the divide, human society is regarded as an 'aggregate of human actions' and explanations are couched in terms of the language and concepts of the individuals who make up society. On the holistic side of the divide, society is regarded as a 'totality' or a 'whole' and explanations are couched in terms of properties which describe the whole.[10] As a consequence, therefore, the individuals who make up a society may be quite unable to understand the language or the nature of the explanations for human relationships developed by social scientists.

The Realist study of international relations has always seemed to occupy a twilight zone between these two epistemological positions. The actors are states, not individuals, and so the basic units of analysis are in the first instance cast in holistic terms. However, almost invariably the state is anthropomorphized and is treated as a rational actor. It is the interactions among these rational actors that create an international society.[11] The new wave of literature on interdependence has not attempted to make any fundamental change to this ontology. Initially, Keohane and Nye were tempted to disaggregate the state, depicting it no longer as a totality, but rather as an aggregate of subnational and transnational actors.[12] The enthusiasm for this development, however, rapidly waned as they began to contemplate the complexity of the resulting anlysis. When Keohane and Nye fixed upon the idea of interdependence, it was, once again, a phenomenon to be identified among states.

Returning to Realism, we find that the divide between holists and reductionists is easy to identify. The explanations of reductionists are cast in terms of the characteristics and motivations of the state.[13] Holists, on the other hand, treat the interactions amongst states as a system and they account for these interactions in terms of properties of the system.[14] Both schools of thought have criticized the new wave of interdependence literature. The reductionists have developed two lines of criticism. In the first place, it is argued that Realism has been presented in a distorted light. Fromkin insists, for example, that Realists have no difficulty in acknowledging the growing level of co-operation which can be observed in the

international area. At the same time, he denies that this
development excludes a potential for conflict. As a Realist he
observes 'more cooperation between countries than there has
ever been before and more competition.'[15] He is, therefore, well
aware of the false dichotomy established by writers such as
Doran who presuppose that while interdependence generates
co-operation, power must precipitate conflict.

The second area of criticism levelled by the Realists of a
reductionist predisposition is that the recent analysis of
interdependence distorts reality. Fromkin insists that when
Keohane and Nye assert that 'recourse to force' has declined
since 1945, as the result of interdependence, they are simply
failing to confront reality.[16] He asserts that in international
relations 'whenever the tangled web of cooperative and
competitive international dealings break down in an irrecon-
ciblable conflict, the issue tends ultimately to be decided by
warfare, whereas in domestic politics it would be decided by
litigation or legislation.'[17] As far as the reductionists are
concerned, therefore, the new interdependence school has
developed a perspective on international relations which is
either idealized or one-sided. In either event, it fails to provide
an adequate account of the underlying factors which motivate
states.

Holists of a Realist disposition are also critical of the new
interdependence school, but for rather different reasons. Waltz
has provided the most important holistic attack on the
interdependent school of thought and, indeed, has concluded
that 'If one is thinking of the international political world, it is
odd in the extreme that "interdependence" has become the
word commonly used to describe it.'[18] From this perspective,
therefore, it is inappropriate to describe the contemporary
international arena in terms of interdependence. The importance attached to interdependence, according to Waltz, has
arisen for two 'reasons': first, because it has been defined as an
economic rather than a political phenomenon and, second,
because it has been defined in reductionist rather than holistic
terms. His disagreement with the new brand of interdependence
literature, therefore, is 'conceptual not empirical'.[19]

Waltz argues in the first place that interdependence has
generally been associated with sensitivity. Events in one part of
the world can have an immediate effect on another part of the

world. A riot in Iran can lead immediately to a decline in stock-market prices in London. But this and all other examples of sensitivity reflects an essentially economic view of the world, according to Waltz. He admits that the global sensitivity to economic factors 'may never have been finer', but considers that a different focus is required to understand political events.[20] A political conception of interdependence emerges only when it is defined in terms of mutual dependence which thereby precipitates reciprocity among the interdependent parties. However, Waltz believes that the level of reciprocity among states will always be low in comparison to the level of reciprocity experienced within states. Within a state, there are many different kinds of units which make demands upon each other. However, states are remarkably similar and the absence of functional differentiation, as a consequence, reduces the overall degree of reciprocity.

Nevertheless, Waltz does acknowledge in the second place that there can be interdependence in the international system and that the level of interdependence can affect the behaviour of states. He denies, however, that interdependence can be understood, or even described, in terms of international activity. The growth or decline of trade, therefore, can tell us nothing by itself about interdependence. Attempting to develop explanations in terms of state behaviour is an error of reductionism. Only a holistic approach can provide an adequate understanding of interdependence. For Waltz a holistic approach must be couched in terms of the structure of the system. In international politics, the central structural feature is the 'distribution of capabilities' among states.[21] Waltz argues that over the last fifty years, the distribution of capabilities in the international arena has changed dramatically. The arena has become bipolar in structure, with the emergence of two superpowers which are highly self-sufficient in both economic and military terms. There is, therefore, little room for mutual dependence or reciprocity in their relationship and it is for this reason that Waltz argues that the system is not now characterized by interdependence.

Let me now summarize what I have argued so far. First, I have suggested that two distinct but incompatible reasons have been advanced to explain why Realism cannot contend with the idea of interdependence. One reason given is that interdependence promotes co-operative relations and power, the central concept employed by Realists, can only account for relationships which are characterized by conflict. At the other extreme, it is accepted that there is a link between power and interdependence but it is asserted that the character of power is transformed by interdependence in ways which cannot be accommodated by the Realists.

For their part, Realists are also divided by their response to the challenge laid down by the new advocates of interdependence. The reductionists argue that there is a complex relationship between conflict and co-operation and that both processes are influenced by power. As a consequence, Realists believe that while they can account for both violent and peaceful behaviour, the new advocates of interdependence are unable to account for the persistence of conflict in the international arena. The holists have come to the even more dramatic conclusion that inter-dependence, far from becoming the dominant characteristic of the international arena, is diminishing in importance. Only the failure to adopt the correct level of analysis has obscured this otherwise obvious fact.

It is clear from this brief review, therefore, that far from being mystified by the idea of interdependence — as has been suggested by critics of Realism — the Realists have been able to advance a powerful defence of their position. The defence does not involve a refusal to accept the idea of interdependence or to acknowledge the phenomena associated with interdependence. Although the conclusions about interdependence reached by the holists and the reductionists diverge, this is not unusual in the social sciences. Moreover, the distance between the two positions has been exaggerated by Waltz. Reductionists can readily accept that relations between the Soviet Union and the United States are not characterized by interdependence, but still insist that interdependence is a characteristic, for example, of the North Atlantic community. In any event, there are no grounds for thinking that Realists are unable to accommodate pheno-mena associated with interdependence. The dissociation between interdependence and Realism is a myth.

REALISM AND INTERDEPENDENCE

Although the Realists have managed to undermine the

suggestion that a power approach is unable to accommodate interdependence, they have done so on the ground staked out by their critics. As a consequence, they have obscured an important, earlier discussion where the relevance of inter-dependence for Realism had already been firmly established. The earlier discussion had, moreover, taken account of the criticisms levelled by the new wave, that Realists failed to appreciate the importance of co-operation and the complexity of international power relationships. This well-established exploration of interdependence took place in the literature of strategy, developed in the 1950s, and was explicated in Schelling's classic text *The Strategy of Conflict*.[22]

Schelling developed crucial insights about both strategy and conflict in the context of interdependence. He demonstrated persuasively that conflict generally involves both co-operative and competitive forms of behaviour. Even wars, he argues, almost invariably require a degree of co-operation. It was, for example, in the interest of all parties not to use gas during the Second World War. In most social situations, therefore, while 'conflict provides the dramatic interest, mutual dependence is part of the logical structure and requires some kind of collaboration or mutual accommodation.'[23] The mix between conflict and co-operation provides the opening for strategy, which seeks to identify how 'mutual dependence can be exploited for unilateral gain.'[24]

The essential characteristics of strategy are clearly revealed in the matrix used to describe the game of chicken, played by American youths in the 1950s. Two youths in cars would drive towards each other along a straight highway. The 'chicken', who lost the game, would swerve at the last minute to avoid a crash but, at the same time lose face. In this game, the strategy involves persuading the other party to swerve in such situations. However, the best course of action for each participant depends upon what he expects the other participants to do. No individual actor, therefore, is in a position to dictate the outcome of a conflict. The parties involved have no alternative but to anticipate the responses of others, and their own behaviour is thereby conditioned by these expected responses.[25]

Strategy, as a consequence, is concerned with the disposition to act, rather than with action itself; it is concerned with threats

Driver A

	Drive on	Swerve
Driver B Drive on	Crash	A loses face
Swerve	B loses face	Both lose face

Figure 5.1   The game of chicken

and promises rather than with punishments and rewards. The outcome is determined by the intersection of two independent decisions. Schelling argues, therefore, that strategy requires a theory of interdependent decisions and he insists that such a theory is nondiscriminatory as between conflict and the common interest, and between its applicability to potential enemies and its applicability to potential friends. For Schelling, interdependence is not defined by co-operation, but by the idea of common fate. This does not mean that the parties will necessarily experience the same outcome, but rather that the parties are mutually dependent upon decisions reached by each other. For Schelling interdependence also involved power, because strategy, the main product of his theory of interdependent decisions, involves mutual attempts to influence behaviour. The relationship between interdependence and power can, however, be most easily demonstrated by examining a situation where the role of power is excluded, as happens when an individual pits his wits against nature.[26]

Consider, for example, the perennial British dilemma of whether to go out without an umbrella. The dilemma can be cast in the form of a matrix, although very different from the one used to describe the game of chicken. If a lady takes out an umbrella she will be either dry if it rains or inconvenienced if the day is sunny. On the other hand, if she leaves her umbrella, she will be unencumbered if it is sunny and wet if it rains. The dilemma however, does not involve either power or interdependence because there is no way that the weather is affected by the individual's decision. By the same token,

Weather

	Sun	Rain
Umbrella	Inconvenienced	Dry
No umbrella	Unencumbered	Wet

Individual

Figure 5.2   The British dilemma

although the individual's behaviour is obviously influenced by her anticipation of the weather, no rational individual believes she can affect the weather. Power, therefore, does not enter into the equation.

We shall return to Schelling's analysis of power and interdependent decisions later. What I have tried to do in this section is to demonstrate that there was a working conception of interdependence within the Realist tradition which had been fully articulated twenty years before the new wave of writers tried to identify interdependence as a new concept and a new phenomenon. As the result of castigating Realism, the new wave have failed to make use of this earlier conception of interdependence and have deprived themselves of some important insights about the relationship between power and interdependence.

TWO COMPETING CONCEPTIONS OF POWER

In this section I want to show how the new school of interdependence, in their effort to dissociate themselves from Realism have been attracted to an asymmetric or causal conception of power which has been extensively used in other areas of the social sciences. According to this conception, however, the new school has, albeit unintentionally, undermined its ability to analyse interdependence which, by definition, presupposes structural symmetry. Ironically, Realists, on the other hand, have always accepted that many relationships within the international arena presuppose symmetry, as is reflected in concepts such as balance and stability. Realists, moreover, have gone on to show, as was seen in the previous section, that when parties are interdependent, a successful exercise of power may not necessarily result in a successful outcome. For example, if both parties survive in the game of chicken, there has been a mutual exercise of power, without either party experiencing a successful outcome. There are, therefore, two very different conceptions of power which have been linked to interdependence. One is associated with symmetrical relationships; the other with asymmetrical relationships.   Those writers among the new wave who believe that power and interdependence are mutually exclusive are, of course, unaffected by the argument developed in this section. However, as shown earlier, there is an important group who accept that it is necessary to establish a link between power and interdependence. In establishing this link, moreover, Keohane and Nye in particular are very anxious to ensure that their own position should not in any way be confused with Realism. The distinction which they establish is made, in the first instance, in epistemological terms. Realists, they argue, rely upon a holistic conception of power. 'In the traditionalist view', they say, 'to know the distribution of the resources that provide power capabilities is to know the structure of world politics; and if we know the structure, we can predict patterns of outcomes.'[27] Such an approach is seen, with the development of interdependence, to be no longer adequate.

Most Realists, however, would agree that a holistic approach is insufficient to understand international relations. As discussed earlier, many Realists rely upon reductionist explanations. However, as will become clear, they do not, as a consequence, regard the formulation of power employed by Keohane and Nye as entirely satisfactory. Keohane and Nye define power as 'the ability to get others to do something they otherwise would not do.'[28] In the context of interdependence, however, they acknowledge that there is a need to distinguish further between two dimensions of power. The first is sensitivity, which they associate with a contagion or demonstration effect, where behaviour in one country is copied in another. This dimension certainly does not conform to a common-sense view of power, since there may have been no desire on the part of the initiating state to see the behaviour copied. It seems odd, for example, to describe nuclear proliferation in terms of the exercise of American power. Yet the formulation of power as sensitivity leads to this conclusion.

The second dimension of power identified by Keohane and

Nye relates to vulnerability and arises when interdependence is asymmetric. In this context, then, power is exercised when one state is able to influence the behaviour of another more vulnerable or dependent state. Keohane and Nye insist, however, that asymmetry in dependence does not guarantee control; it simply generates the potential to affect the behaviour at the unfavourable end of the asymmetry. This conception of power certainly accords better with a common-sense view of power but, at the same time, it seems to distance us from the concept of interdependence. The idea of asymmetry encourages the idea that power is a one-way phenomenon. Interdependence, on the other hand, presupposes that power can be exercised by either party in a relationship. In an endeavour to accommodate symmetrical relations, it is argued that power is not a fungible commodity and, as a consequence, a state may be vulnerable on one issue, but not on another. However, this is not quite the same as demonstrating the role of power in a situation of mutual dependence.

The failure of the new wave of writers to develop a conception of power which can be extended to interdependence has arisen primarily as the consequence of their desire to establish a break with Realism. The Realists have always been interested in what sociologists call intercursive power or, to use a term more familiar to international relations specialists, balance of power.[29] They have never been content, in other words, with an asymmetric or one-way conception of power. Morgenthau has made this position clear. He argues that power relates to 'men's control over the minds and actions of other men'. But when he comes to define political power he insists that it relates to 'mutual relations of control'.[30] So Morgenthau is advocating a conception of power which is cast in terms of interdependence.

Instead of relying upon this conception of power, Keohane and Nye have been drawn to an analysis of power which has been established and developed beyond the boundaries of international relations. By defining power as the 'ability to get others to do something they otherwise would not do', they are tapping an important body of literature which equates power with a cause-and-effect relationship. Indeed, Nagel, one of the proponents of this conception of power, insists that 'Most modern theorists treat social power as a relation between human beings in which the effect must be the *behaviour* of the person controlled.'[31] Power, as a consequence, is identified in causal terms. From this perspective, power is considered to characterize a one-way or asymmetric relationship. A power relationship exists when a stronger party causes a change in the behaviour of a weaker party.

Although extensively employed, some fundamental problems have been associated with the attempt to define power relationships in terms of cause and effect. In the first place, it is unable to contend with situations where the exercise of power presupposes an anticipated reaction. For example, in the game of chicken, the drivers are trying to anticipate each other's actions. If one does swerve, it is because he has anticipated that the other driver intends to steer a straight course. Common sense suggests power has been exercised. Yet the causal view of power excludes the role of anticipated reactions, because it is not possible for an effect to precede the cause.[32]

A second problem relates to unintended consequences. This difficulty has already been referred to in the context of the contagion effect. A second example can make the same point. If a state increases its military budget in an attempt to increase its security only to find shortly afterwards that its nearest rival has undertaken a similar action, then it can be inferred that the response of the rival was an unintended consequence of the initial action. Such cases do not satisfy our common-sense understanding of power and yet within the causal approach the first state has exercised power over the second state.

A third problem with the causal conception of power has been raised by Waltz who argues that the attempt to define power in terms of getting people to do something they would otherwise not do is 'odd'. He goes on, 'we are misled by the pragmatically formed and technologically influenced definition of power — a definition which equates power with control.'[33] Power, he says, may not always be successful because a power relationship can be affected by the 'structure of action', as the game of chicken illustrates. For Waltz, therefore, the causal conception of power confuses process with outcome.

A re-examination of the Realist theory of interdependent decisions reveals that these problems can be resolved relatively easily and, at the same time, demonstrates how power can be related to interdependence. Realists start from the premise that the relationships amongst states are characterized by inter-dependence. As a consequence, any outcome is dictated by the intersection of independent actions precipitated by the actors involved. An outcome cannot be achieved unilaterally. For example, to end a war requires, except in extreme cases, the co-operation of the parties involved in the conflict.[34] Moreover, in most circumstances, it is the vanquished who will determine when the fighting comes to an end. Because Realists have always been very sensitive to this conception of interdepen-dence, they have also recognized the need to define power in terms of mutual or reciprocal relations of control.

A very clear example of mutual control can be observed in the context of a limited war where a state in the war deliberately limits its actions in order to ensure that a third party is not tempted to intervene. The threat of intervention limits the level of fighting, which in turn discourages intervention. By the same token, deterrence theory rests on the idea of mutual control. In these two examples, each side modifies its behaviour on the basis of expectations about the behaviour of the other party.

Anticipated reactions, therefore, do play a role in the Realist conception of power. But it is also the case that this conception can accommodate the idea of unintended consequences. This is possible because of the relationship identified between unintended consequences and anticipated reactions. There is an important distinction to be drawn between an outcome which is anticipated but unintended and between one which is unintended and unanticipated. In the latter case, the question of power does not enter into the equation, whereas in the former case it does. Two examples can clarify the difference. First, take the game of chicken, when two drivers, both believing that the other is going to swerve, end up with a head-on crash. Here the outcome is anticipated, albeit unintended. But it is, from the Realist perspective, a power situation because both parties have endeavoured (and they believe successfully) to influence the behaviour of the other party. Second, take a crash on a dual carriageway, where one driver has unintentionally driven across the divide. Here, from the Realist perspective, the question of power does not arise because the outcome was neither intended nor anticipated.

As Waltz indicates, therefore, there is a need to

distinguish process from outcome. The interdependent conception of power employed in strategy makes very clear that the process involves mutual power calculations. As a result of the power process, however, a variety of very different outcomes may emerge, as the game of chicken reveals. First, there may be a mutual exercise of power, and both drivers swerve. Second, there may be an unsuccessful exercise of power and the drivers crash. Finally, there may be a successful unilateral exercise of power, and only one driver swerves.

The failure to take account of mutual power calculations can lead to important misrepresentations of reality. For example, suppose two men are walking along a pier and one is blown into a turbulent sea. He cries that he cannot swim and the other man jumps into the water in a rescue attempt. According to the causal conception, power has been exercised by the apparently helpless individual in the sea. Defining the situation in this way, however, excludes the possibility of describing the action of the man on the pier as heroic or, alternatively, foolhardy.

The analysis in this section indicates therefore, that there are some very major weaknesses with the causal conception of power. However, the overall problem, from the standpoint of the international relations specialist, is that it presupposes a one-way or asymmetric conception of power. Although such relationships do exist, they are unusual. Keohane and Nye appear to recognize this point. They argue, 'There is rarely a one-to-one relationship between power measured by any type of resources and power measured by effects on outcome.'[35] However, by restricting themselves to an asymmetric framework they fail to develop any proper appreciation of the relationship between process and outcome. The interdependent conception of power comes much closer to achieving this end.

CONCLUSION

In this chapter I have examined the relationship between power and interdependence. The recent literature on interdependence has made two conflicting claims: first, that the role of power is incompatible with interdependence and, second, that the role of power changes dramatically in situations of interdependence. Both of these viewpoints, however, make the additional claim that the Realist approach to international relations is unable to accommodate the idea of interdependence. I have tried to argue that this claim is false because Realist writers, and in particular Schelling, have done a great deal to develop a theory of interdependence.

The attempt to dissociate Realism and interdependence has had an important consequence which becomes apparent when attention is focused on the concept of power. The new school of interdependence, which accepts that power continues to play an important role in interdependent relationships, has argued that the analysis of power becomes more complex as relationships become more interdependent. However, in endeavouring to steer clear of the way Realists have examined power, they have been drawn towards the asymmetric conception of power, defined in cause-and-effect terms, which prevails in other areas of social science. It has been argued that the analysis associated with an asymmetric conception of power is inconsistent with the essential characteristics of interdependence.

Realists, on the other hand, have always accepted that relations amongst states are characterized by interdependence and have developed a concept of power which is compatible with interdependence. For the Realist, power is not simply associated with capabilities, but also reflects the logic of the situation in which parties find themselves. When parties are interdependent, the intersection of their independent decisions dictates the outcome and determines whether or not an exercise of power has been successful.

Although it can be shown that Realists have examined power in the context of interdependence the examination is generally implicit rather than explicit. There is a need for the relationship between power and interdependence to be explored more systematically. As we have seen, most areas of social science have tended to shy away from an analysis of symmetrical relationships. However, the attempt by Kelly and Thibaut to develop a theory of interdependence represents an important exception.[36] They develop a wide variety of ideas, which could usefully be extended to the analysis of international relations.

The purpose of this chapter has not been to suggest that power relationships can only be understood in the context of interdependence. Obviously, it is possible to extend the idea of power to dependent or asymmetric social situations. However, it is being suggested that power also plays a crucial role in that important area of social relationships characterized by interdependence and that Realists have gone at least some way towards providing an analysis of this role. The attempts by the new wave of writers on interdependence to distance themselves from Realism has had the effect of obscuring the contribution that Realism can make to the debate and has thereby deprived the discussion on interdependence of some important ideas.[37]

NOTES AND REFERENCES

1. R.O. Keohane and J.S. Nye, *Power and Interdependence: World Politics in Transition* (Boston, Little, Brown, 1977), p. 3.
2. Ibid.
3. J.N. Rosenau, *The Study of Global Interdependence* (London, Frances Pinter, 1980), sees greater complexity as a crucial dimension of interdependence. E.N. Haas, *Tangle of Hopes: American Commitments and World Order* (Englewood Cliffs, Prentice-Hall, 1969), associates interdependence with common fate. He argues that nations are 'interdependent to the point of being unable to deal with epidemics, mail, diet, culture, cherished beliefs, and peace except through common institutions', p. 3.
4. R. Rothstein, 'On the costs of Realism', *Political Science Quarterly, 87* (1972), 347-62.
5. C.F. Doran, 'Oil politics and the rise of co-dependence', in D.W. Orr and M.S. Soroos (eds), *The Global Predicament* (Chapel Hill, University of North Carolina Press, 1979), p. 198.
6. See M.J. Levy, ' "Does it matter if he's naked" bawled the child', in K. Knorr and J.N. Rosenau (eds), *Contending Approaches to International Politics* (Princeton, Princeton University Press, 1969), pp. 95-6.
7. H.J. Morgenthau, *Politics Among Nations* (4th edn.) (New York, Knopf, 1974), p. 519.
8. Keohane and Nye, op. cit., p. 223.
9. See Morgenthau, op. cit., Ch. 10.
10. This analysis is based upon A. Levinson, *Knowledge and Society* (New York, Pegasus, 1974), p. 2. He, however, uses the terms Individualism and Collectivism. A review of the historical development of the debate can be found in J. O'Neill (ed.), *Modes of Individualism and Collectivism* (London, Heinemann, 1973). An extension of this debate to international relations occurs in K.N. Waltz, *Theory of International Politics* (London, Addison-Wesley, 1979).
11. For a discussion of the paradoxes and ambiguities associated with the role of the state in international relations, see A. Vincent, 'The Hegelian State and international politics', in *Review of International Studies, 9* (1983), 191-205.

12. R.O. Keohane and J.S. Nye (eds), *Transnational Relations and World Politics* (Cambridge, Harvard University Press, 1971).
13. For a clear exposition of a reductionist's position, see Morgenthau, op. cit., 'To give meaning to the factual raw material of foreign policy . . . we put ourselves in the position of a statesman . . .', p. 5.
14. See Waltz, op. cit.
15. D. Fromkin, *The Independence of Nations* (New York, Praeger, 1981), p. 135.
16. Ibid., p. 134.
17. Ibid., p. 135.
18. Waltz, op. cit., p. 144.
19. Ibid., p. 145.
20. Ibid., p. 141.
21. Ibid., p. 97.
22. T.C. Schelling, *The Strategy of Conflict* (Oxford, Oxford University Press, 1963).
23. Ibid., p. 83.
24. Ibid., p. 84.
25. Ibid., p. 10.
26. Ibid., p. 83.
27. Keohane and Nye, op. cit., p. 224.
28. Ibid., p. 11.
29. See, for example, the discussion by D. Wrong in *Power: Its Form Bases and Uses* (Oxford, Blackwell, 1979), pp. 10-13, and D.A. Baldwin, 'Power and social exchange', *American Political Science Review, 72* (1978), 1229-42.
30. Morgenthau, op. cit., p. 28.
31. J.H. Nagel, *The Descriptive Analysis of Power* (New Haven, Yale University Press, 1975), p. 12.
32. See Nagel, ibid., however, who attempts to place anticipated reactions into a causal framework.
33. Waltz, op. cit., p. 192.
34. This argument can even be extended to the termination of the Second World War. See P. Kecskemeti, *Strategic Surrender* (Stanford, Stanford University Press, 1958).
35. Keohane and Nye, op. cit., p. 11.
36. H.H. Kelley and J.W. Thibaut, *Interpersonal Relations: A Theory of Interdependence* (New York, John Wiley and Sons, 1978).
37. See, for example, R. Rosecrance, 'International theory revisited', *International Organization, 35* (1981), 691-713, who concludes that while Waltz, op. cit., has developed a theory of power we still need to develop a unified understanding of power and interdependence.

6 Interdependence — an Ideological Intervention in International Relations?

JOHN MACLEAN

INTRODUCTION

This chapter is an attempt to work out some of the relations between, on the one hand, concept formation and academic authority in the study of international relations, and, on the other, international practice. The general theroetical starting-point for the enquiry is the assertion that relations between social theory and social practice are always, and trans-historically, problematic, but cannot be established wholly in the realm of theory. That is to say, in understanding the 'real' world of international relations we may not assume that what is 'real' is constituted exclusively in what is empirical. Neither can we take declared central concepts as given and unalterable, even in so far as they may represent valid abstractions.[1] If the proposition is accepted that social reality and theories about it are both socially constructed and, further, that this process of social construction involves complicated reciprocal relations between cognition and materiality, then explicit attention to the theoretical assumptions and implications of our views about the world may be seen in principle as capable of bearing with it practical consequences for how the world is in fact organized, or how it may in the future be organized.[2]

The discussion of the concept of 'interdependence' which is currently, if somewhat controversially, prominent in the discipline, is interesting, for I cannot yet conclude that this concept, for all its prominence, has much advanced our capacity to analyse and explain seriously pressing and threatening world problems. More precisely, and perhaps more controversially, I cannot see that, as presently constructed, this concept may ever do so, and it is this assertion, with its theoretical and substantive implications, that I will be discussing in this chapter. In order to do so, I will begin by examining the nature of the orthodox attempt to obtain consistent non-contradictory usage of the concept of interdependence by means of apparent agreed and abstracted ahistorical definition. I will argue that this attempt has (at least) three important, negative consequences for explanation but that these are, at the same time, important positive factors in the maintenance and reinforcement of substantive inequality in international relations. I will not be arguing that this is an intentional maintenance, although I would wish to deny that relations of inequality are wholly unintentional or 'natural'. The point here is that some part of their causation and reproduction is not reducible to explicit aims and attempts by observable actors, themselves differentially involved in these relations of inequality. What I aim to show, therefore, is that the discipline of international relations, by accepting the re-emergence of interdependence,[3] has tacitly but powerfully continued the tradition of prominent empirico-analytic theory, and has made the recovery and reformulation of a critical and normative mode of explanation of international issues more difficult.

The central paradox I will be exploring here is this: the concept of interdependence is prima facie a compelling one, in that it seems to capture immediately and powerfully the appearance of concrete, intense and widespread interaction between identifiable entities in the world. Yet it is also usually posited as the defining, or essential condition of the contemporary world conceived of as a whole system.[4] To put this another way, the increasing prominence of the concept represents some recognition of the increasingly and apparent unseparated quality of international relations practice. However, in seeking to define the concept as a step towards theory, in relation directly to actors (units), the discipline has reinforced that theory which sustains a view of world developments, and their explanation, as atomized or separated. I will refer to this aspect of the argument more concretely below when I locate it within the context of recent conflicts within the United Nations Educational, Scientific and Cultural Organization (UNESCO).

It is these two features, namely the acceptance of the concept of interdependence as given, or descriptively appropriate, and the attempt to define it directly in relation to international actors, that together provide an initial basis for evaluating the prominence of the concept, and discussion about it, as an ideological intervention in international relations, both at the level of theory and of practice. In the second part of the chapter, I will aim to show how this is so. Further, I will argue that to establish the work on interdependence as ideological, even if convincing, is not at the same time necessarily to invalidate it. Rather, I will contend that this may open up the concept to the possibility of explaining some parts of international relations, in terms of their appearance (presentation) and of underlying relations of causality. It is this latter conjunction that seems to me the core requirement for reconstituting international theory as critical, normative knowledge.

It may be useful to say something at this stage about the context within which the contemporary idea of critical, normative knowledge has developed. Perhaps the major aspect of this is a denial of the claim that knowledge is identical with science, although accepting the latter as one possible form of knowledge. This is itself based on two further connected claims. First, that it is mistaken to suppose that the world appears wholly external and objective to us, as a universe of raw data, events or movements, one whose relations and connections can be grasped fully from those events and movements. Second, and closely connected to this, that knowing subjects play an active part in constituting the world they know, but they may do so without full realization of this and/or without an objective of performing what constitutes their real interests. On this view, knowledge and activity may be interest-constituted, but this is likely to be more the interests of groups which are socially dominant than interests appropriate to equality and the enhancement of freedom of thought and of practice.[5]

This general line of argument in social theory was developed as a critical response within Marxist thought, to the assumed causal (objective) prominence of the mode of production, in particular the capitalist mode of production, and is identified very clearly and unambiguously with the work of the Frankfurt School.[6] Briefly, the view was developed, in particular by Adorno, Marcuse and Habermas, that modes of production not only provide structures for appropriate values, institutions and ideologies, but, more importantly perhaps, that dominant ideologies become universalized and penetrate everyday interpretations of how the world works in such a powerful way that they not only arise out of a particular mode of production, but they are also causally necessary to it. Such a view demands, much more than some strands of Marxist thought, an exposition of particular historical stages of the relations between thought, discourse and the prevailing mode of production, in order that the puzzling phenomenon of large-scale relations of dominance and subordination might be understood as founded in cognitive as well as material aspects of inequality. This position has been developed most within critical theory by J. Habermas, and although much criticized for seeming to reduce political and social power to speech acts and forms of individual psychological states,[7] there is a powerful basis available here for reassessing the relationship between the thought and practice of international relations: between ideology and material conflicts. Thus the long-laboured assumed distinction between the discipline of international relations (the realm of the theoretical) and the activity of international relations (the realm of the diplomat, the military leader, the company president — in general, the practitioner) may be specified in different form. This different form refuses to take the appearance of inequality and disintegration in international relations as either given or as a pathological condition. It questions whether or not the discourse and theory of international relations is itself part of the relations of inequality it often assumes itself methodo-logically and objectively separated from.[8]

Finally, in the third section of the chapter, I will aim to sub-stantiate concretely the relations between concept formation as ideology (the 'theoretical') and the maintenance of substantive inequality in international relations (the 'practice'). I will do this in relation to the demand for a New International Information Order within UNESCO. The aim, put in more authoritative words, will be to 'grasp the reality of interdependence',[9] which reality, I will argue, is one of hegemonic international relations, as much serviced and reproduced by discourse and texts as by overt expressions of coercion and control.

THE PROBLEM WITH 'THE PROBLEM'
OF DEFINITION

The problem of definition is really two distinct but related problems. The first is the wide diversity of meanings attached to the concept of interdependence in international relations literature.[10] This is, or can be, a serious problem to the extent that it constrains analysis. For if a concept can have as many meanings as there are offerings explicitly about it, it is then a concept with little or no specificity of application. This of course does not mean that it cannot have such a specificity, merely that it has wide but ambiguous and unclear currency. An analogous problem can be seen to surround the use of the concept 'alienation' in social theory. This, too, has gained widespread currency, such that it has entered common language usage. At the same time there still remain the differing, but nonetheless specific and technical constructions, to be found, for example, in Durkheim and Marx, where the concept does identify particular conditions and does advance understanding of those conditions.[11] The important point, as far as interdependence is concerned, is that this concept does have immediate appeal as seeming to capture descriptively the extended complexity, both quantitively and qualitatively, of contemporary international relations activity. It thus has potential specificity that carries with it the possibility of powerful explanation.

The problem, though, is that there has not been much progress, over a decade, in realizing this potential specificity of application in the case of the concept 'interdependence', even though there have been some wonderful, failed attempts.[12] The question arises, therefore, as to why concern continues, in spite of little clear explanatory reward. Can it be, simply, that the concept 'interdependence' has such attractive initial force as to produce continuing adherence and/or a powerful fashion? I doubt the issue can be left there — it may be the case indeed that the concept 'interdependence', like 'balance of power', is maintained as central precisely because it does lack specificity, can cover an infinite set of empirical concerns, and thus prevents achievement of the explanatory power it seems to promise. Again, to repeat an earlier disclaimer, this is not an argument implying intentionality within the discipline, a conspiracy to prevent explanation. But it may be seen as an unintended consequence of the way in which we do, generally, go about the business of definition in the discipline.

The second problem of definition is not nearly as widespread in its recognition. Indeed, it is probably at best contentious, and at worst misconceived, but I think worth explicit consideration. The argument here is of much wider origin and application. This second problem of definition is a derived one and not simply a particular function of the concept 'interdependence'. More precisely, it is a general difficulty about modes of abstraction.[13] What is required is a more specific account of the way in which the general problem of abstraction from particular empirical events is related to attempts to define what is meant by interdependence in international relations. What is common among attempts to obtain a working definition of interdependence, both in the concept's re-emergence in international relations literature[14] and attempts to clarify and operationalize it,[15] is a coherent convention about what constitutes definition, and that this convention is rooted in the requirements of the dominant empirico-analytical tradition within the study of international relations. The specific demands of this orthodoxy lead to a definitional concern with obtaining a basis for consistent, non-contradictory usage that is abstract in so far as it does not refer directly either to a particular location or to a particular time. The assumption further is that if these conditions are met, the concept has then been constructed also as objective, inasmuch as it does not in advance depend upon some possible normative content,[16] and as capable of validation in so far as it refers indirectly to some specified empirical activity.

Part of the difficulty of advancing our knowledge of complex real relations in the world is not just a consequence of their increased complexity, but of those steps we take initially to make this complex reality manageable intellectually. If the content we are pressed to give to definitional abstraction is a content that derives more, and in some cases only, from established and authoritative traditions of scholarship than it does from out of the particular historical stage of international relations activity itself, then it might no longer seem so surprising that a concept like 'interdependence' can gain such widespread attention and application.

The problem for the student, then, becomes one of re-translating questions of logical contradictions and consistency away from their construction as only epistemological issues of hypothesis formulation and counter-factuals, back to their connected status as problematic conditions of the social world; away from internal criteria of the logical status of utterances about the real world, and back to concrete, historically specific analyses of structured relations. A clear implication of all this, of course, is that the establishment of such an orthodoxy has allowed in a set of a priori assumptions that are better understood as reified analytic categories, within a scholarly convention. This sounds, as it stands, extremely critical and negative. It is negative in respect of possible explanation, but is not wholly negative. To put this differently: if it is the case that the concept 'interdependence' captures something quite real about international relations, that is their intensely relational and holistic quality, but at the same time, and through its manner of construction as an analytic concept for explanation, it tends to remove or obscure other real aspects of international relations (for example, the latter's stratified structure), then such a concept might be shown to have real, positive consequences for the perpetuation of that stratified structure as an unintended consequence.

The capacity to obscure is the first of the positive/negative consequences referred to in the introduction. Part of what I mean here is what Waltz tellingly referred to in the following way:

The American rhetoric of interdependence has taken on some of the qualities of an ideology. The word 'interdependence' subtly obscures the inequalities of national capability; pleasingly points to a reciprocal dependence and strongly suggests that all states are playing the same game.[17]

What I have in mind further is also shown in the Waltz claim, namely the tendency to define the concept in relation to actors. This slide towards methodological individualism is the second consequence of the way in which the concept has generally been defined. This is again negative with regard to explanation, but positive with regard to the continuation of stratified international relations. What is stunning to me is the ease with which the concept 'interdependence' initially can be taken to refer to the whole system, as a condition of international relations in their totality (indeed it is often posited as such, as has been indicated above); and yet attempts to define and refine the concept for analysis so often adopt a reductionist approach whereby interdependence (and dependence, etc.) become actor variables.[18] To this extent, explanations of the development of interdependence as a concrete process, that include causal reference to structures and processes of the whole system, are not allowed in. In other words they are removed methodologically in the process of constructing international relations as relations between abstracted, that is atomized, parts, and this is a method of disaggregation. This exclusion is general within the development of Western international theory but the inappropriateness of it, in respect of explanation, appears particularly stark in the case of 'interdependence'.[19]

A third consequence of the way in which interdependence has mostly been defined is to remove from related explanations the historical aspects of change in international relations activity. For, by requiring that definitions of concepts can lead to identification of regularity and uniformity in social reality, the history of social and political relations are stripped of explanatory force. These consequences are in themselves difficult enough barriers to the recovery of international theory as a critical and normative enterprise, within which problems of war, starvation, unequal distribution and oppression generally might be explained, and within which the possibility of change might be considered. But the issues of obscurantism raised within the problem of definition are even more complicated than this.

Part of the difficulty of advancing the study of inter-dependence is compounded by the apparent tension raised by the concept's re-emergence between the Realist/traditionalist view of the world and that view implicit or explicit within the interdependence literature.[20] This tension represents a competition between competing paradigms of how the world works. Keohane and Nye put this issue succinctly:

We believe that the assumptions of political realists, whose theories dominated the post-war period, are often an inadequate basis for analysing the politics of interdependence . . . . Three assumptions are integral to the realist vision. First, states as coherent units are the dominant actors in world politics . . . . Second, realists assume that force is a usable and effective instrument of policy . . . . Third, realists assume a hierarchy of issues in world politics, headed by questions of military security: the 'high politics' of military security dominates the 'low politics' of economic and social affairs . . . . Transnational actors either do not exist or are politically unimportant.[21]

Keohane and Nye prefer to place their view of interdependence against the Realist view of the world at the opposite end of a continuum bounded by two extreme ideal types, rather than as a competing and mutually exclusive paradigm. This is quite consistent with their own reductionism which, although empirically richer than that of the Realist, state-centred 'high politics' view, is really no more than an augmented actor-orientated view. Epistemologically, therefore, it is not really distinctive from the Realist position.

It is this conclusion that offers a clue as to a further possible reason for the prominence of interdependence studies within the discipline. However, if it is accepted that there are apparent real differences between the Realist view and the interdependence view of international relations, as far as their respective research questions and empirical scopes are concerned, but little or no difference in their epistemological assumptions, then the following argument is possible.

The re-emergence of the concept 'interdependence' in the discipline of international relations represents, on the one hand, an attempt to respond to clear and pressing empirical developments in international relations activity which cannot be accounted for within the excessively narrow and reductionist Realist view without, on the other hand, removing or calling seriously into question the authority of the empricist view of knowledge, upon which it is based. That is, part of what is represented by the prominence of interdependence, but with little explanatory gain, is a recasting of empiricist epistemology through the emergence of a new orthodoxy, wherein the classical Realist model of inter-state political relations is substantially modified by the addition of liberal modes of economic analysis.[22]

To the extent, then, that examination of the content of problems of definition with the concept 'interdependence' can show the possibility of an underlying maintenance of a particular, non-neutral orthodoxy about what constitutes knowledge, and the exclusion or relegation of competing modes of explanation, the initial basis for understanding the prominence of the concept 'interdependence' as an ideology is made. Importantly, it is also made so far in terms of what constitutes ideological content for the empiricist tradition itself.[23] However, this in itself is not enough to complete the claim for an ideological intervention as a concrete development. The latter must include some further discussion of the relations between interdependence and power in the domain of international relations practice, as well as that of method.

It should be clear by now that this conception of ideology is an expansive one, and this will be explored next. Although the notion of an ideological intervention is not identical with empirical, observable attempts to establish one set of values over another, as a basis for discourse and action — for example the intellectual and theoretical basis of the United Nations Charter — it does not exclude the latter. Indeed, it may often be the case that explicit, documented and articulated ideologies are themselves a necessary part of the appearance of separated entities, coming together from time to time in situations of so-called strategic interdependence, or of joint gain. The appearance, of course, is that ideas are equally presented, as though of equal formal status in relation to the structures of power. What is left out of the account on this view is the possibility that some ideas are, not because of their content particularly, already oppositional, while others are representational of the prevailing orthodoxy, or at least complementary with it. This is not only a matter of cognition or reason, it is material, too. It is this extension to the argument so far that I turn to in the next section.

INTERDEPENDENCE AS AN IDEOLOGICAL INTERVENTION

The discussion so far has been concentrated explicitly on those aspects of concept formation that allow the exposure of interdependence as ideological in relation to method. However, if I am to establish the concept's significance as an ideological intervention in international relations, the connections between theory construction and substantive international relations activity must be identified. Some initial qualifying comments need to be offered here first.

The empirical world is relevant in the sense that part of the difficulty of defining the concept 'interdependence' refers to the tension between structures (the holist aspect) and actors (the unit aspect). There is a tendency within the literature to introduce this dichotomy in mutually exclusive terms. If linked to the first of this pair, analysis is biased towards the system as a whole, and difficulties then arise in specifying not only what are the appropriate empirical interactions covered, but what are the causal links between these and the structures of interdependence. If linked to the second, analysis is then biased towards the actors and difficulties arise in specifying what, out of a range of actor interactions, constitutes interdependent behaviour in terms which do not reduce to capabilities, properties, motives and characteristics of the actors themselves, and which can be distinguished from, say, 'interconnectedness'. If interdependence is a systemic, that is, structural component, it must relate causally to actor interactions, but must also be marked off from them.[24]

The failure to cope clearly with this requirement is, I think, a large part of the long-standing definitional problems with the concept. It does also highlight the difficulty of explaining what international actors do, by looking only at what they seem to be doing. More than this, it is my view that the attempt to construct theories about interdependence, when based in the empirico-analytical view of knowledge, is bound to fail, for it cannot allow causal status to interdependence conceived of as an international structure, because part of any structure, if it is systemic, is not reducible to the empirical. Now this is not at all an argument for metaphysics or an attempt to remove the empirical. Clearly, to do the latter would be absurd. Any social theory must refer to, and deal with, contingencies which cannot be known in advance on the basis of abstract necessity,[25] and must not privilege itself with a withdrawal from empirical research.

The point here, though, is that, first, it is possible to construct validation tests of claims about the world without necessarily holding to the claim that these tests must be only derived from an external empirical world that is claimed to be co-extensive with the 'real' and which can thus be said to be equivalent to the real.[26] Second, it is reasonable to suppose that the causal effect of structures (in this case interdependence) is to impose constraints upon action, even where such constraints may not be (even indirectly) observable. This idea of determination is not necessarily deterministic, in the sense of an a priori assumption, incompatible with intentionality. The latter is more properly called predetermination. Necessity in social relations can operate by way of the intentional activity of actors but in relation, at the same time, to social structures that set conditions for that activity. These structures cannot be known in advance or constructed ideationally through definition. They can only be exposed through a conjunction of theoretical construction out of, and tested by, concrete historical research.

It is clear by now, I think, that my argument about the difficulties of constructing and explaining the already empirically appealing concept of interdependence within the empiricist tradition of knowledge has led me to a positive evaluation of Marxist method as an alternative. And, on this view, what is real is concrete, but not identical with the empirical. The concrete object is so not simply because it has material existence, but because it already exists at the same time in complicated sets of relations with other concrete objects.[27] The move here is now clearly towards the real world, more specifically, the real world of interdependence.

In order to show how it is that the concept 'interdependence' is an ideological intervention, I will firstly say what conditions need to be met for this, and then relate these to some concrete aspects of international relations activity in the area of knowledge and information. In passing, though, I want to indicate briefly what I meant earlier by my preference for the re-emergence of the concept interdependence, rather than its emergence. First, within the discipline of international relations some early writings, for example Mitrany or Angell,[28] identify and reflect upon aspects of international relations that revealed features of interdependence separate from state actors, namely, economic transactions and the irreducibility of people as social agents, nowhere fully autonomous. Second, interdependence understood as mutual dependence or mutual self-interest has a very long history in economic thought. Classical economists, for example Smith, proposed in models of perfect competition that action based on selfish preferences would somehow serve the common good and provide overall net benefits by means of market mediation. Keohane and Nye are quick to refer to this relevant history.[29] However, the point here I think is not so much that an exclusive focus on joint gain may obscure the distribution of those gains (although it may), but that the principle of mutual dependence (or comparative advantage), in taking the relevant units as separate, but needing to meet in the market in order to obtain their supposedly separate needs, allows for the assumption that both parties stand in an equal relationship to the market and obscures the possibility that the market itself may be already structurally biased towards one party rather than the other. In Keohane and Nye's terms, i.e. distribution, the question they are concerned with (and they admit it as 'the old question of politics, who gets what?')[30] is necessarily an empirical question. In this respect it is an extremely limited conception of power.

First, it is confined to overt conflicts of interest — it is bound to focus on behaviour in the making of decisions over which there is an observable conflict of interests. Second, what it cannot admit of is the structure of the interaction (in this case the market place) constructed as a determination of, or constraint upon, the way in which one of the parties conceives of its subjective 'self'-interest in the first place. That is, the structures within which supposedly separate actors meet with separate but interdependent needs may reinforce the interests of one party as against the other, so that an objectively subordinated actor constructs its needs and interests subjectively in relation to those of a dominant actor.[31] (It is interesting that the idea of interdependence as mutual benefit between separated actors has emerged recently, and publicly, in the form of the two Brandt Reports. Although there has been quite intensive criticism of the underlying assumptions of those reports,[32] there has also been much positive reaction to them, as grasping clearly the relevance of contemporary interdependence, and offering the possibility of a way out of difficulties through emphasis upon mutual interests.) As far as seeing these historical examples as ideological interventions is concerned, this quality inheres in concepts to the extent that they do refer to some empirical aspect of social behaviour, and thus to actors and their interactions, but at the same time they operate to hide the real relations within which those interactions are determined. A paradigm example of this notion of ideology is that of the wage-form, articulated and analysed by

Marx in *Capital*. This is not a theory of ideology, separate from its object of enquiry. Rather, Marx's method entails the exposition of how it is that the perceived forms of social reality provide an apparent and thereby plausible justification for their social reproduction. Ideology in this sense is a reference not to causal relations, between an explicit value system programmed for action and then applied to an external socio-economic reality, but to the ways in which social reproduction reproduces systematic distortions of real relations. Thus, in *Capital*, the wage-form seems empirically to identify a fair exchange of equivalents. The worker sells his/her labour power to the capitalist for a certain period of time, and the apparent costs of that labour power enter, along with the costs of the means of production, into the capitalist's calculation of profitability. If, though, the accumulation of capital cannot be explained on this apparent (and partly empirical — the wage labourer does receive 'real' money in his/her hand) view, because the wages given cannot account for the additional value added and then realized through sale, then the wage-form may be constructed as hiding the real relation between the capitalist and the worker, namely that, although paid, the latter is not paid fully for his/her labour. The relation is thus an exploitative one, but this cannot be derived on purely empirical grounds. In this sense, the construction of the wage-form is ideological in the sense of distorting reality, and it is at the same time an intervention materially, in that it reinforces the reproduction of empirical social relations of a particular form, where power operates structurally.[33]

The question now is, can interdependence be shown as a substitution instance of the Marxist paradigm? I think it can, but this must be done in relation to concrete international activity. First, to posit that international relations are relations of interdependence is to construct as real the separateness of the units involved, while allowing in principle that no one actor is fully independent in relation to all others. What this means empirically is that any named actor, in order to achieve its perceived interests and/or objectives, must construct these in relation to those of other named actors. At the same time, though, it implies that where there are conflicts of interests or mutuality of interests, and competition for the material goods that represent these interests, differential distribution of gains can be explained by reference to differentiated capabilities, and characteristics of the actors, where these attributes are taken initially as given.

Thus, for example, arms sales between states capable of sustaining arms production and those that are not, can appear as evidence for interdependence in international relations, in so far as the initial positions of the parties to the transaction, as supplier on the one hand and receiver on the other, are taken as given. Explanations of these transactions will then develop that remove the possibility of constructing the roles of supplier and receiver as historically developed and, in terms of the power structures that establish the receivers as acting, although formally autonomous, more in the interests of the supplier because the interests of the former are constructed subjectively in relation to the latter. It is the case, of course, that some states, such as India and Israel, are both suppliers and receivers of arms. This complicates the issue somewhat, but does not damage the general argument — no state is both supplier and receiver in the same individual transaction.

Actors, abstracted as relatively autonomous units, appear to come together in interdependent interactions in order to satisfy mutual, if not necessarily identical, needs or interests. If a second-order reductionism is made that these needs, although interrelated, can be separated out for individual units, for example, into economic needs, social needs, cultural needs and so on, then the possibility of hiding general and fully international structures of interdependence may be increased by the very richness of increased empirical detail. Interdependence of arms suppliers and arms receivers can then be confirmed as a relationship rooted more in the national security, use-value aspects of arms transfers than it is in relation to arms as commodities produced privately for profit, and having an exchange value such that the capital invested in their production can only be realized through their sale.

If it can be argued that objectively the interests of less developed economies would be better served by non-purchase of arms, either through the extreme case of complete rejection of externally orientated defensive capability (Costa Rica) or in terms of a movement towards a domestic capability for arms production, then the extent of arms purchases by these states, both quantitatively (amount purchased) and qualitatively (appropriateness of arms purchased to likely defence needs) is called into serious question. The depiction of these transactions as evidence for interdependence as mutual benefit, without systematically structured relations of dominance and subordination, is then also in doubt.

On the face of it, then, the possibility of interdependence as an ideological intervention in Marx's sense can be established, but only when brought into relationship with substantive international relations activity. The arms sales case, though, remains an over-general example. What the rest of this chapter will aim to show is that interdependence as a universal material development is linked inextricably to the development of international organization and that the latter represents part of the establishment of dominant ideas, discourse and practical international government, without the establishment of a formal world state. In other words, I am proposing that, whereas interdependence has been developed in such a way as to obscure and reinforce inequality, it can be more usefully, more realistically and more critically developed as expressing a determining (although not pre-determined) international structure. In order that this view should not be assailed as no more than a grand theoretical assertion, I need to demonstrate what its concrete implications are within a substantive context: to show what the relations are between a hegemonic structural feature, and the directly or indirectly observable features of unit behaviour and interaction.

To move beyond a limited, simplistic view of power and authority which is constructed largely in terms of state capability, and where evaluations of the power of non-state actors are generally based upon criteria that only attach to states, seems to me important. But this does not mean that we remove states and their activities from our enquiry. We should also be careful not to develop an analysis that opposes the concentration upon the state by seeking to replace one assumed dominant actor with another.[34] The re-emergence of the concept 'interdependence' has not supported a more realistic development and extension of the analysis of power and authority. What it has led to is a reinforcement of methodological individualism through an extension of the list of actors that can now reasonably be said to be important units within the international system.[35]

Interdependence seems to capture this quality of increasing complexity well, and so scholars have sought a behavioural content for it, without consideration of whether or not the concept 'interdependence' itself requires initial explanation as a material and historical development. The distinction here might be best demonstrated by the following questions. First, and within international relations orthodoxy, we might ask, how can interdependence be best defined in general terms so that it can become analytical as well as descriptive and, thus, operationalized?[36] The second kind of question we might ask, and it is outside international relations orthodoxy, is this: What must have been the case for interdependence to be established, cognitively and materially? The latter question clearly implies that we cannot establish a content to concepts as though they are separated from the social relations to which they are assumed to refer, and are connected only through a methodological assumption of objective externalities. It also implies that any given set of empirical circumstances represents one possibility (albeit the established one) and allows for the introduction of tolerance of alternatives into our explanations of the world. In contrast, if we take the 'real' world as given (in so far as it is assumed to be objective and external to us), we are likely then to see its formation as natural or unchangeable. Again, if we assume that some set of conditions could not have been other than the conditions that in fact became established, we are then locked into an underlying assumption of predetermined social life. An example of this, very common within contemporary advanced economies, is that method of policy-making which argues relations of necessity or entail-ment between some given (say, the amount of state resources in revenue form) and a particular form of distribution (say, a cutback in social welfare expenditure).

The power of such flawed reasoning cannot be reduced to the coercive power of the state. What needs to be invoked is some description of how readily and easily such arguments identify and presuppose a generalized compliance, or recepti-vity, within the broad social structure. Power, in this sense, must allow reference to who wins in overt conflicts of interest, but is only partial if it does not include extended reference to the process by which possible alternatives are not only not allowed on to agendas but are not even formulated.[37] The theoretical point here is that for explanation to break new ground it must be conceptually innovative, so that the reality referred to may be contemplated differently. This is necessary because the language we use to describe the world is already theory-laden and socially predicated.[38] Consequently, descriptions from the start involve assumptions of the truth of various theories and beliefs. The way we perceive reality is linked to the way we think about reality through the concepts we use.[39]

If theory that involves conceptual innovation does not share a common set of observation concepts with the dominant theory it seeks to replace or qualify, then logic and observation are not sufficient criteria for choosing between competing theories. So it is with the concept 'interdependence'. As long as we continue to assume, as I have outlined above, that the problem of definition is one of identifying the correct slice of reality, then the only new ground that can be broken is restricted to new empirical extensions. In other words, the reality is taken as non-problematic, and this, I have argued, is a distortion of reality.

What I will aim to do in the rest of this chapter is to examine concretely the relations of theory and practice that make up the concept 'interdependence' so that the extent of its intervention ideologically in international relations may be substantiated empirically. Although interdependence is always identified as a general concept, its content must be related to relevant particular items through what R. Cox has referred to in a recent paper on Gramsci's method as 'contact with a particular situation which it helps to explain — a contact which also develops the meaning of the concept.'[40] The empirical context in which I will attempt to develop the concept of interdependence is the emergence between 1974-8 within UNESCO of the demand for a New International Information Order (NIIO) linked as a declared prerequisite to the achievement of the earlier demand for a New International Economic Order (NIEO). On the face of it, these connected claims appear as strongly revisionist, even combative, demands. Yet if we examine the institutional outcome of the NIIO demand, the McBride Report, *Many Voices:One World*[41] (and simply note the title's implication of a coherent whole), we can see that its opening chapter, 'The historical dimension', is already limiting as far as fundamental revision is concerned, in that the history referred to is an isolated history of communications, embedded in a number of general contextual comments, for example, that there *was* an era of imperialism (my emphasis); that there was a struggle on a world scale for democratic rights and national liberation; and that in the late twentieth century there have been broader political and economic changes within many countries and on a world scale.[42] These contextual elements, though, are taken as given, and consequently the Report is unable to offer an analysis of the relations between the world history of communications, and how international relations have developed historically. In this respect the Report is actually more about many voices than it is about one world. And yet throughout the Report, interdependence is an attribute often attached to the programme for a new world order.

What sense, then, can we make of the concept in this context? The evidence is overwhelmingly that the application of interdependence reinforces theory that sustains a view of world developments and their explanation as atomized or separated. To substantiate this indicatively I will refer to one aspect of the development of UNESCO and the NIIO demand, namely, the view that the NIIO demand is the latest evidence of the increasing 'politicization' of functional international organization. I will then reformulate the concept of inter-dependence by reconciling the illustrative aspect above within a totality of international relations, constructed as relations of power and authority, through the concept of hegemony.

INTERDEPENDENCE AND INCREASING POLITICIZATION OF THE UNESCO

The view is quite widespread that the Specialized Agencies of the United Nations (other non-state and functionally specific actors) have become 'politicized'. The view can be expressed in strong or weak form. Clare Wells, in a recent paper for the European Consortium for Political Research, offers some interesting examples of the view, including Henry Kissinger's reference in July 1975 to 'the trend in the Specialized Agencies to focus on political issues. UNESCO and the ILO have become heavily politicized', and George Meany's assertion of the 'blatant, outrageous and unconstitutional politicization of the ILO and UNESCO.'[43] In respect of academic work, Wells refers also to David Kay's view that 'the functional and technical operations of many of the Specialized Agencies have become more and more politicized by the introduction of issues designed to attain political ends extraneous to the substantive, technical purposes and programmes for which they were established.'[44] There is also Richard Hoggart's view from the inside of UNESCO of the growing tendency to 'the distortion of debate by the irrelevant introduction of political issues', which he represents further and with reference particularly to the 'Israel resolutions' of the 1974 General Conference, as part of an 'accelerated, planned and strong politicisation of the Organisation, at the expense of any serious attempt at objectivity.'[45]

A more colourful approach to the issue is that of Randolph Hearst expressed in a syndicated newspaper editorial during 1976:

Today, the threat to a free press is virtually world-wide, and a vast international conspiracy exists, directed by the UNESCO, which is one of the leading Moscow-directed anti-democratic agencies operating out of Paris under the banner of the UN. We must not allow this Marxist branch of the UN to isolate us and the Western world from the rest of this shrinking planet.[46]

The view, in its various manifestations, and whether weak or strong, is deeply flawed but powerful none the less. If it can be shown to be empirically and logically incomplete, then its power must be related to something outside the view itself, seen as an expression of how the world is organized.

The politicization view is mistaken on at least three major grounds. First, the strong view that functional international organizations were not political from the outset depends itself upon the assumption of an epistemological division between politics and other behavioural aspects of social activity (economics, culture, leisure and so on) which cannot be sustained in the same way that descriptive empirical references can be offered for those same areas of activity. The theoretical point, that learning how to distinguish between, and how to perform as social agents in, functionally separated areas of our lives (voting, shopping, playing, for example) does not damage the requirement that, in explaining any one of these fully, reference needs to be made to the others, cannot be, and has not been, resolved by the division of labour in academic production. Second, the assumption that political activity (if not political analysis) is necessarily evaluative activity, whereas other kinds of activity, say economics or science, are external to how we think about them, subject to natural laws and thus objective, cannot be sustained either.[47] And this assumption is just as necessary as the first above to allow the distinction between political and non-political, or politics and, say, economics, to be made at all. Neither of these objections has particular effects only upon the concept of interdependence. They are relevant in so far as they are examples of the dominant tendency to analyse complex social wholes in an atomistic way. Clearly, our understanding of interdependence can vary with whether we construct it as a system property or as a function of actor interactions.

In this respect, the view about politicization, because it is an atomistic view, supports the actor-orientated definition much more than it leads us to establish interdependence as a structural property. Thus, for example, in that part of the McBride Report (Part 1, Chapter 3) that deals with 'The International dimension', prominence is given to the debate over the NIIO as a political debate, representing a contingent change, namely a clash of ideas/philosophies between formally separated units. On this formulation, the McBride Commission and its Report become a political solution to a political debate. And, of course, this is a part of the issue and its development. However, an extended analysis of the relations between political positions with UNESCO and the largely private ownership of the means of production and dissemination of knowledge and information would qualify severely the extremely limited notion of interdependence implied by the 'politicization' view.

The third objection to the 'politicization' argument is more directly specific to, and important for, the development of the concept of interdependence, for it refers to the weak view that does allow for the attribution of political interest and content to specialized and/or technical organizations from the start.[48]

'Politicization' on this view is a matter of degree rather than a strict dichotomous development from the non-political to the political. The latter can be argued to be wholly mistaken by extended exposition of the first two objections. Politicization understood as a matter of degree, however, cannot be assessed as wholly mistaken on these grounds. It can be argued to be a limited view of politics because, although recognizing correctly that functional/technical organizations have a politics from the start, the notion of politics utilized is usually one which maintains the separation between politics and other behavioural areas. It is also usually one that assigns an a priori significance to those organizations, like UNESCO, the IMF or the WHO, whose membership is states. What this means, as far as interdependence is concerned, is, first, that the relationship between politics and power is restricted. This is again reinforced by, and itself reinforces, an actor-orientated definition of interdependence. Second, and consequently, interdependence, rather than becoming invested with emancipatory content, remains a static concept that reflects the appearance of separation. As with the two Brandt Reports, interdependence is seen as a developed feature of state interaction, often as though synonymous with interconnectedness, but separated from substantive problems that confront the world.

Part III, Chapter 4 of the McBride Report, 'Images of the world', lists crucial general problems facing the world today, including protection of the environment, rational use of natural resources, employment, inflation, defence of human rights, problems of less developed states, and peace and disarmament.[49] From this general pessimistic context, seven problem areas are then singled out for further discussion: war and disarmament; hunger and poverty; the North–South split; the East–West conflict; extensive violation of human rights; equal rights for women; and, finally, *interdependence and co-operation* (my emphasis). So interdependence is presented both as a problem and, in other parts of the Report, as a positive aspect of the possibility of an NIIO. Such confusion is reflective of the problem of definition that I referred to in the first section of this chapter, but can be made clear perhaps by examining in a little more detail how adequate this weak view of politicization is as an explanation for the outcome of the demand for an NIIO, and what construction of power it allows. When UNESCO was formally established on 4 November 1946, it had a membership of twenty-one states. By the 1970s, the membership had increased to more than 121 states, and it is this increase, largely consequential upon the speed-up of decolonization since the 1950s, that is identified as a major cause of overt political confict within UNESCO.[50]

The significance of the weak view of politicization in respect of this development, and of the re-emergence of the concept 'interdependence' is briefly this. A distinction is made between the kind of politics of the organization at the time of its establishment and the kind of politics involved in the demand for an NIIO and its outcome in the form of the International Commission for the Study of Communication Problems. The first kind assumes the development of an organization out of a pre-existent consensus. Politics represents here the repeated, rational and reflexive advancement, by separated units, of their distinctive objectives. This takes place within a recognized context of interdependence conceived of as mutual dependence. Success or failure of state objectives is assumed to be a function of state and delegation qualities and capabilities. The interdependent context of this bargaining is not seen itself as a constitutive part of power in international relations.[51] Importantly, though, there is held to be no dispute over the methods and procedures of advancement of these separated objectives, and no dispute over the overall purposes and aims of the organization itself. The validity of this conception will be considered shortly. Against this, the second kind of politics involves a confrontation about the purposes and aims of UNESCO itself and, because focused explicitly on the ideas of the organization, is seen as extending politics from a behavioural practice of bargaining and compromise to an explicit ideological and confrontational mode. Thus, the assumed initial constitutional agreement within UNESCO about 'the unrestricted pursuit of objective truth, and in the free exchange of ideas and knowledge ... and to employ these means (of communication) for the purposes of mutual understanding'[52] is itself threatened, and this can be seen only as introducing an ideological (and thus less worthy) element into the politics of UNESCO. Hence the view of increased, and qualitatively differing, 'politicization'.

If we ask questions identified earlier as the kind of question associated with a critical approach, then we take the issue of the NIIO as it emerged in the 1970s as a starting-point, but we do not accept the first view of politics as given. The questions generated now are these: (a) what must have been the case for this demand to emerge, in respect of the global conditions of information and communication? and (b) what evidence is there to support the view that the explicit ideological aspects of the demand are distinctive of it, and not appropriate to the previous history of UNESCO? The first question demands the establishment of empirical relations between the international state organization with legitimate competence in the field of communication and information, and the extended conditions — institutional, technical, financial, for example — of international communication and flows of information, and much of these conditions are, of course, in the contemporary world located in the private sphere. This does not mean they are fully outside of government or formal political influence, but it does mean that they are not fully within it. The second question demands an analysis of the conditions of the setting-up of UNESCO itself, and I shall deal with this first.

Space does not allow a fully developed analysis, but the important features of the case and their relevance to the question can be shown. First, the condition of the world at the end of the Second World War was explicitly imperial, in the sense of direct political and administrative control, with coercive means, by a small number of centre states over a large number of other countries. Consequently, the concerns, substantively and theoretically proclaimed, in the UNESCO Constitution, actually represent the consensus of certain states already established in sets of relations of explicit dominance and subordination.[53] The possible construction of interests by the subordinated part of the world was disallowed, even though the Constitution, seen as the establishment of universal propositions, provided in principle for formal equality.[54] More theoretically important than this, the evidence of the events and meetings leading up to the establishment of UNESCO, even if we were hypothetically to remove from the immediate post-war world all evidence of formal imperial relations, does not support the view of a pre-existing consensus, but reveals rather more a connection with a larger struggle, namely the establishment of a new liberal international world order, with the USA as the hegemonic state. The establishment of UNESCO, on the evidence, was more a cause of the establishment of a consensus, than it was a consequence, within the wider establishment of international organization, including the United Nations itself, the Bretton Woods system and extending into the European Recovery Programme and the Marshall Aid provisions.

The immediate context out of which UNESCO was established was that of the Conference of Allied Ministers of Education (CAME), which was held in London under the Chairmanship of R.A. Butler, the then President of the UK Board of Education. This met twenty-one times, between 16 November 1942 and 5 December 1945. Within this chronological and institutional framework was the Founding Conference for UNESCO, which met, also in London, between 1 and 16 November 1945. The relevant documents, both in the Public Records Office of the UK and in the UNESCO archives at Paris headquarters, show that, far from being an organization based on consensus and agreement, the emergence of UNESCO represented a fundamental and large shift of CAME objectives and aims, on the basis of an explicit USA intervention. Briefly, the important features of this are as follows. The initiative for the convening of CAME came in a draft memorandum of 8 March 1942 from the British Council to the President of the UK Board of Education, concerning a proposed meeting between the latter and Ministers of Education of Allied countries then in Britain. It included a statement of purpose, 'to see whether some of the problems of education in Europe in the post-war period can now be explored', and a statement of limitation, 'the present is no time for a precise statement of post-war needs, *nor for the construction of some theoretical superstructure*'[55] (my emphasis added).

The memorandum also included reference to professional contacts between European educationalists; provision of emergency accommodation; provision of books, writing materials, apparatus; and it identified overall a clearly limited project, both regionally (Europe) and in terms of competence (narrow and immediate educational needs). There is no intimation whatsoever of a move towards a universal permanent international organization. These limitations were refined and emphasized as the proposal for CAME worked its passage through the Foreign Office and thence, on the latter's advice,[56] by means of the Advisory Panel on External Affairs, through to the central co-ordinating UK body on post-war reconstruction, namely Sir William Jowitt's Reconstruction Problems Committee.[57] The decision of the Advisory Panel to go ahead in the end reveals some important government qualifications to the British Council view which had been expressed in a draft proposal from Professor Ifor Evans. This expressed the broad aims of perpetuating and increasing the dominance of the English language, and of establishing 'the Empire of influence, of leadership, which Great Britain, with her well equipped system of education, her universities, and her widespread language can master.'[58] The Advisory Panel held that

. . . there were objections to exploring the present situation for the purpose of propagating British culture . . . we must avoid giving material for an ideological pro- or anti-British campaign in Europe after the war. The policy suggested could be adopted *without the co-operation of the United States*, but any suggestion of rivalry between London and New York as to which should be the cultural capital of the English speaking peoples must be avoided. *The danger of American participation is that the Americans, because of their numbers and their money, will swamp the British element.*[59] [My emphases added.]

From these initiating discussions, and from the early meetings of CAME, it is quite clear that the UK government envisaged a regional, short-term, instrumental, restricted-competence and consultative body. For example, at the first meeting on 16 November 1942, Butler's opening address from the Chair included the advice that

. . . discussions on these problems could best take the form of periodic meetings between representatives of the Allied Education departments, the Board of Education, and the British Council. At these meetings it would be essential to concentrate on specific and perhaps modest practical issues rather than to enter on wider discussion of nebulous and ambitious plans which might later prove unpracticable.[60]

By the time of the fifteenth meeting of CAME on 10 January 1945, Butler was reported as commenting on the draft of a pamphlet for publication by the United Nations Information

Office, about the aim of CAME to set up a universal inter-national educational organization, as follows:

The first paragraph of this part as at present drafted might give the impression that the formation of the conference had been brought about entirely by the results of the Axis occupation in Europe, *whereas, in fact, those responsible for initiating the Conference believed in the ideal of a United Nations Educational Organization and had had the long-term aspect of the question clearly in mind as well as the more immediate problem of rehabilitation.*[61] [My emphasis added.]

The documents clearly do not support this claim by the CAME Chairman. What, then, explains such a large and dramatic shift? My view on this is that it was largely a consequence of US interventions at the sixth and ninth meetings of CAME. Briefly, at the sixth meeting on 5 October 1943, Ralph Turner of the Cultural Division of the US State Department attended, and he was reported as informing the Conference that 'the work of CAME was being followed with great interest in the US . . . . The question of setting up a United Nations Bureau was one in which the US government would have a very strong interest.'[62] CAME at that meeting adopted the report recom-mending reorganization of the Conference towards the establishment of such a Bureau, and also recommended that the Bureau establish direct contact with the Relief Conference, hosted by the USA in Washington and scheduled for November 1943. More important than this initial enlargement was the ninth meeting of CAME on 6 April 1944, when the USA sent a high-powered, five-person delegation, under the leadership of the then congressman J.W. Fulbright, and including Archibald MacLeish of the Library of Congress, who later was to lead the United States delegation to the London Founding Conference in November 1945.

Fulbright intervened in this CAME meeting before the agenda business, and the USA's intentions regarding the role they envisaged for CAME in the context of US aid policy for Europe was clearly articulated. 'The US government were becoming increasingly aware of the importance of inter-national co-operation in education and were much interested in the purpose of the Conference . . .',[63] Fulbright told members. Gifts were brought: an aid programme to supply liberated countries with material aids and to help with the training of teachers, and assistance with the problems relating to the reconstruction of libraries and archives and to the return of art treasures stolen by the Axis powers. But so were enlargement proposals, namely, the possible establishment, in discussion with CAME, 'of a United Nations organization to deal with educational and cultural problems in the period of recon-struction.'[64] Agreement was reached to set up an 'open meeting', called by CAME and the USA jointly, to be held on 12 April 1944. It was also unanimously agreed that Congress-man Fulbright should be in the Chair. This outcome corresponded exactly with the instructions given to the American delegation.

At the first open meeting, an emergency rehabilitation fund was set up, but the USA as the principal contributor by far, would control its management. Butler's early fears had been confirmed. As US aid policy changed, so, during the London Founding Conference and especially during the San Francisco Conference of April 1945, the conception of an international organization for education and culture as a channel for US post-war aid was changed. The USA considered it more likely that by executing its European aid programme directly and bilaterally such aid would be more effective. The embryonic UNESCO then became offered as a permanent institution, with universal scope and, in principle, universal membership.

The story is larger and more rich than this brief account can impart but, taken as a whole, it allows a reconstruction of the history of the winning of the peace as a real struggle between the advanced metropolitan centres for the prize of establishing the form and the content, both in respect of textual detail (e.g. the ideas and principles of the Charter, the conditions of aid, the concepts for discussion) and of institutional forms and policy (e.g. the UK post-war Labour government under Atlee and the removal of social planning in return for dollars, the scope and competence of the IMF and the IBRD, the conditions of Marshall Aid) of the post-war world order. The politics of the setting-up of UNESCO show not just the settlement of overt conflicts of interest by actors involved in bargaining, but that the conditions of the bargaining itself were redefined. And this is what the establishment of hegemony means — the explicit establishment of concepts, methods and practices linked to the interests of a dominant unit, and hence mediated through it in the context of real (that is, empirical) struggle, but assuming then the status of a dominant orthodoxy which is hardly questioned because it is accepted as a basis for universal application.[65] At this point it becomes structural, for it determines then the construction of interests by those units in a subordinate position or whose interests objectively are not met by the conditions of the orthodoxy.[66] As Robert Cox has argued recently:

> . . . hegemony at the international level is thus not merely an order among states. It is an order within a world economy, with a dominant mode of production which penetrates into all countries and links into other subordinate modes of production. It is also a complex of international social relationships which connect the social classes of the different countries. World hegemony is describable as a social structure, an economic structure and a political structure, and it cannot be simply one of these things, but must be all three. World hegemony futhermore is expressed in universal norms, institutions, and mechanisms which lay down general rules of behaviour for states, and for those forces of civil society that act across national boundaries — rules which support the dominant mode of production.[67]

One needs to add here that these rules not only support the dominant mode of production, but are reinforced and reformulated within it.

International organization, then, can now be coherently argued and concretely established as not necessarily the outcome of agreed order and consensus by units, but as the inversion of this, namely, the means or instruments by which consensus, order (and interdependence) of a particular form became established. UNESCO was already then ideological in its 'politics', not so much in the explicit recent form of the NIIO clash, but in the sense of observing the reality of consensus, order and interdependence. We have now answered the second critical question asked above. This answer, though, together with Cox's quote, also leads directly back to the first critical question, that is, what are the global conditions of information and communication that surround the demand for an NIIO? Part of the answer is given in the reconstruction of the establishment of UNESCO, and it is this — understanding the reality of the demand for an NIIO and of claimed interdependence — which cannot be based on the appearance of political debate alone.

We have seen already how UNESCO, as one item in the establishment of a new post-war hegemony, was structurally connected to states as economic and social entities as well as public/political organizations. As Cess Hamelink has argued forcefully, the McBride Report, although identifying explicitly the fact that concentration of communications technology in a relatively few developed countries and transnational corporations has led to a virtual monopoly in this field, proposes to confront the problem through mainly legal measures. And this, Hamelink argues, is inadequate in relation to the vast politico-economic power exercised in the field of communications by the transnational corporations, involved both as producers and consumers of information. He points out that the commercial activities of the eighty transnational corporations, that between them account for three-quarters of world production and distribution of communication goods and services, have assumed such proportions as to make the communications and mass-media industry the fourth largest in the world after the energy, automotive and chemical industries. Furthermore, the capital intensity of the communication industry leads to a strong interlocking with the world's largest institutional investors, the group of leading transnational banks.[68]

The critique by Third World states of the existing international information order provided an initial basis for a counter-hegemonic move, in that it brought into question the abstract and material distortion of free-flow of information; pointed to the private ownership of the major news agencies (Associated Press, Reuters, United Press International and Agence France Presse) that makes the flow of information in this area a one-way flow; and the extent to which the advanced economies' access to advanced information technology, including direct broadcast satellites and scanning satellites, increases their already-established production and trading dominance.[69] The demand, then, was not just about the imperialism of free-flow of information, and its content reproduction of historical and contemporary structures of control, as a debate about competing ideologies of an explicit kind. It opened up the possibility of a political economy analysis. The evidence, though, of the McBride Report as an outcome, of the USA's threat (December 1983) to withdraw from UNESCO unless the Secretariat would accept an 'independent' financial review (which it now has)[70] and, finally, of academic analyses of the demand, show that the radical potential of the Draft Declaration of 1978 has not been realized. This failure confirms the power of a world capitalist structure, mediated through the policies and practices of Western states (in particular the USA) and of private transnational corporations.

CONCLUSION

What I have tried to do in this chapter is to show, with reference both to the theoretical and practical aspects of international relations, that the re-emergence of the concept 'interdependence' defined in an abstract and ahistorical way, and empirically linked to units of the system (especially states), contributes materially to the maintenance of international relations of inequality and, as such, constitutes an ideological intervention in those relations.

The ideological nature of the contemporary world order has been both threatened and reaffirmed by the demand for a New International Information Order. In particular, interdependence, reasserted as a necessary condition of complex interactions between formally separated units (sovereign states, private institutions and inter-governmental organizations) and continuing the assumption of states as the fundamental actors in international relations, has been demonstrated concretely as an ideological intervention in the sense outlined earlier in this chapter. That is, by contributing to the construction of international relations theory *and* practice, as a 'reality' of separated units, interdependence as a critical starting-point for the description and explanation of the 'one world' we inhabit as a structured, highly-integrated world economy, with causal elements of structural or hegemonic power, is hindered.

What I hope this chapter has also shown, though, is that the possibility of a critical emancipatory theory of international relations, grounded in concrete empirical analysis, is not yet fully removed. Indeed, it is, I think, only through analysis of the construction of dominant concepts and institutional aims that the reality of concepts like interdependence and of the causal significance of international organization can be made available as a different basis for our general understanding of international relations.[71]

NOTES AND REFERENCES

1. For further discussion of this tension, see B. Fay, *Social Theory and Political Practice* (London, George Allen and Unwin, 1975); P. Bourdieu, *Outline of a Theory of Practice* (Cambridge, Cambridge University Press,1977); J. MacLean, 'Political theory, international theory, and problems of ideology', in *Millennium: Journal of International Studies, 10*, 2 (1981), pp. 102-25.

2. For further discussion on this, see R.J. Walker, 'Political theory and the transformation of world politics' (World Order Studies Program, Occasional Paper No. 8, Princeton University,1980); J. MacLean, 'Marxist epistemology, explanations of change and the study of international relations', in B. Buzan and R.J. Barry Jones (eds), *Change and the Study of International Relations* (London, Frances Pinter, 1981), pp. 46-67.

3. I prefer 're-emergence of interdependence' here because, although the current prominence of the concept 'interdependence', and of related concepts like 'linkage', 'dependency', 'globalization', 'mutual interest' and so on can be roughly dated from around 1970, the idea of the 'interdependence' of social relations (and of international relations in particular) has a longer relevant intellectual history than this, as I will show later.

4. See Barry Jones's Chapter 2 in this volume, 'The definition and identification of interdependence'.

5. A more detailed exposition of these three points can be found in D. Held, *Introduction to Critical Theory: Horkheimer to Habermas* (London, Hutchinson, 1980), especially Chapter 11. The original texts for this line of development within Critical Theory are those of J. Habermas, in particular, *Knowledge and Human Interests* (London, Heinemann, 1971) and *Communication and the Evolution of Society* (London, Heinemann, 1979).

6. The Frankfurt School is the popular name given to the members of the Institute for Social Research, founded in 1923 and formally attached to the University of Frankfurt. The most active period of work of its members followed the transfer of the Institute first to Geneva in 1933, and then to Columbia University, New York in 1933, and was coeval with the prominence of Nazism and fascism in Germany. For historical and theoretical exposition, see M. Jay, *The Dialectical Imagination: A History of the Frankfurt School and the Institute of Social Research 1923-50* (Boston, Little, Brown, 1973); P. Slater, *Origin and Significance of the Frankfurt School: A Marxist Perspective* (London, Routledge and Kegan Paul, 1977); and Held, *Introduction to Critical Theory*, op. cit.

7. See, for example, Slater, *Origin and Significance of the Frankfurt School*, op.

cit.; P. Anderson, *Considerations on Western Marxism* (London, New Left Books, 1976); and G. Therborn, 'The Frankfurt School' in *Western Marxism — A Critical Reader* (London, New Left Books, 1977).

8. For more recent general and theoretical discussion around similar points, see, for example, B. Barnes, *T.S. Kuhn and Social Science* (London, Macmillan, 1982); and J. Larraine, *Marxism and Ideology* (London, Macmillan, 1983).

9. See R.O. Keohane and J.S. Nye, *Power and Interdependence* (Boston, Little, Brown, 1977), p. 4. This quote is particularly apt for my aim, as Keohane and Nye go on to declare: 'yet theory is inescapable; all empirical or practical analysis rests on it' (ibid., p. 4). The problem, of course, is what kind of theory does it rest upon?

10. See, for example, Barry Jones's Chapter 2 in this volume and Keohane and Nye, *Power and Interdependence*, op. cit., pp. 8-19; D. Baldwin, 'Interdependence and power: a conceptual analysis', in *International Organization, 34* (1980), 471-506; P.A. Reynolds and R. McKinley, 'The concept of interdependence: its uses and misuses', in K. Goldman and G. Sjostedt, (eds), *Power Capabilities and Interdependence: Problems in the Study of International Influence* (Beverly Hills, Sage, 1979), pp. 141-66; M.A. Tetreault, 'Measuring interdependence', in *International Organization, 34* (1980), 429-43.

11. See S. Lukes, 'Alienation and anomie', in P. Laslett and W. Runciman (eds), *Philosophy, Politics and Society, 3rd Series* (Oxford, Blackwell, 1969), pp. 134-56.

12. For example, Keohane and Nye, *Power and Interdependence*, op. cit.; and L.R. Brown, *World Without Borders: The Interdependence of Nations* (New York, Foreign Policy Association, 1972).

13. See MacLean, 'Political theory, international theory and problems of ideology', op. cit. (note 2), especially pp. 110–13.

14. See, for example, R.O. Keohane and J.S. Nye (eds), *Transnational Relations and World Politics* (Cambridge, Mass., Harvard University Press, 1971); K.N. Waltz, 'The myth of national interdependence', in C. Kindleberger, *The International Corporation* (Cambridge, Mass., MIT Press, 1970); and B. Russett, 'Interdependence and capabilities for European integration', in *Journal of Common Market Studies, 9*, 2 (1970).

15. See, for example, Keohane and Nye, *Power and Interdependence*, op. cit., Chapter 1; Baldwin, 'Interdependence and power: a conceptual analysis', op. cit. (note 10); and Reynolds and McKinley, 'The concept of interdependence: its uses and misuses', op. cit. (note 10).

16. See, for example, Barry Jones's Chapter 2 in this volume.

17. Waltz, 'The myth of national interdependence', op. cit. (note 14), p. 220.

18. See, for example, the Jones and Willetts chapters (2 and 4) in this volume.

19. See MacLean, 'Political theory, international theory and problems of ideology', op. cit. (note 1), pp. 108–10.

20. See Keohane and Nye, *Power and Interdependence*, op. cit., Chapter 2; MacLean, 'Marxist epistemology, explanations and change, and the study of international relations', in Buzan and Jones, op. cit. (note 2), pp. 50-3; and Richard Little's Chapter 5 in this volume.

21. Keohane and Nye, *Power and Interdependence*, op. cit., pp. 23-4.
22. See R.B.J. Walker, *Political Theory and the Transformation of World Politics*, op. cit. (note 2), pp. 34-45; and R. Jones, 'The English School of international relations: a case for closure', *Review of International Studies*, 7, 1 (1981), 1-13.
23. For expanded treatment of this point, see MacLean 'Political theory, international theory and problems of ideology', op. cit. (note 13).
24. cf. K. Waltz, *Theory of International Politics* (London, Addison-Wesley, 1979), pp. 39-41.
25. For enlargement of this point, see J. MacLean, 'Marxism and international relations: a strange case of mutual neglect', pp. 9-25 (Paper for British International Studies Association Annual Conferences, December 1981).
26. Ibid., p. 11.
27. Ibid., pp. 2-21, and cf. Waltz's clear articulation of the cognitive separation of structure and unit necessary for any theory to be systemic.
28. D. Mitrany, *A Working Peace System* (Chicago, Quadrangle, 1966); and N. Angell, *The Great Illusion* (New York, Putmans, 1913).
29. Keohane and Nye, *Transnational Relations and World Politics*, op. cit. (note 14), pp. 10-11.
30. Ibid., p. 10.
31. For an excellent conceptual analysis of these issues, see S. Lukes, *Power: A Radical View* (London, Macmillan, 1974).
32. See, for example, Diane Elson, 'Strategy: the Brandt Report', in *Capital and Class, 16* (1982), but also 'Mrs. Thatcher and the F.C.O. Memorandum to the Cabinet' (reproduced in 'Britain on Brandt', *I.D.S. Bulletin, 12* (University of Sussex), pp. 10-15).
33. For expanded discussion on these points, see MacLean, 'Political theory, international theory and problems of ideology', op. cit. (note 2); J. Mepham, 'The theory of ideology in capital', in J. Mepham and D.H. Ruben (eds), *Issues in Marxist Philosophy, Vol. 3: Epistemology, Science, Ideology* (Brighton, Harvester, 1979), pp. 141-69; J. McCarney, *The Real World of Ideology* (Brighton, Harvester, 1980); and J. Larraine, *Marxism and Ideology*, op. cit. (note 8).
34. For examples of this limited conception of power within international relations, see H. Bull, *The Anarchical Society: A Study of Order in World Politics* (London, Macmillan, 1977); A.A. Said and L.R. Simmons (eds), *The New Sovereigns: Multinational Corporations as World Powers* (New Jersey, Prentice-Hall, 1975); and R.O. Keohane and J.S. Nye, *Power and Interdependence*, op. cit.
35. An important caveat here, which Richard Little's chapter in this volume treats at length, is the sharp implicit or explicit compatability of interdependence with the Realist (traditionalist) view of international relations, particularly in the strategic studies/conflict analysis area which has developed the concept of strategic interdependence. What is further important about the latter case is that strategic interdependence is seen as a function of the relationships, and this is some embryonic concession towards a holist requirement, even if this cannot be carried much further on the Realist view due to the overwhelming methodological dominance within it of actor-based variables.

36. This way of handling the concept is dominant in this volume, too, but for particularly clear and extended examples, see the chapters by R. Barry Jones — 'The meaning of the term, however, remains far from clear and, for any given definition, empirical indicators often ambiguous or elusive . . .' and Richard Little, whose chapter is built around contrasting two broad meanings of the term in the literature, in relation to the Realist view of strategic interdependence.

37. For extended and gripping conceptual analysis of some of these aspects of power, see Lukes, op. cit. (note 31); and R.W. Cox, 'Gramsci, hegemony and international relations: an essay in method', in *Millennium, Journal of International Studies, 12* (1983), 162-75.

38. For extended discussion of these points, see R. Bhaskar, 'On the possibility of social scientific knowledge and the limits of naturalism', in *Journal of Theory of Social Behaviour, 8* (1978), 1; and G. Lukacs, *History and Class Consciousness* (London, Merlin Press, 1971) especially Chapter 1.

39. An important related notion here, quite separate from Marx's method, is the distinction developed by P.F. Strawson between descriptive metaphysics and revisionary metaphysics. The former is concerned to describe the actual structure of our thought about the world, and it differs from orthodox logical or conceptual analysis only in scope and generality. Strawson argues that in asking 'how do we use this or that expression?', the answers, however revealing at a surface level, are apt to assume and not to expose those general elements of linguistic structure which we need revealed. The context for Strawson is the problem of the identification of ourselves. The relevant point, for my argument, is Strawson's argument that demonstrative identification of a particular reference (that is to establish and explain the connection between the idea of a particular in general and its object of reference) is often not straightforward. Names may be sometimes used, but they make no sense Strawson claims without a backing of descriptions which can be produced on demand to explain the application of the name. It may be the case that the particular in question cannot itself be demonstratively identified, but it may be identified by a description which links it uniquely to another particular which may be demonstratively identified. This allows for the possibility of causal items, not in themselves capable of direct identification, indeed only understandable at all in terms of extended sets of relations, and this is a coherent argument for non-observable items quite compatible with Marx's idea of form and appearance traceable through relations of parts of a system with structures of the whole system. See P.F. Strawson, *Individuals* (London, Methuen, 1954).

40. See Cox, 'Gramsci, hegemony and international relations: an essay in method', op. cit. (note 37), pp. 162-3.

41. This is the commercial edition, published by Unipub, New York and UNESCO, Paris, 1980. It is based upon the two formal reports of the International Commission for the Study of Communication Problems, comprising the *Interim Report* (Paris, UNESCO, 1978) and the *Final Report* (Paris, UNESCO, 1979).

42. For a more detailed exposition and analysis of these aspects of the McBride Report, see C. Hamelink, *Communication in the Eighties: a*

reader on the McBride report (Rome, IDOC International, 1980), especially the paper by K. Nordenstreng, 'The paradigm of a totality', pp. 8-16.

43. C. Wells, 'UNESCO and Palestinian education, 1967-71: a precedent for "Politicisation"?', European Consortium for Political Research, University of Lancaster, 1981.

44. David Kay, 'On the reform of international institutions: a comment', in *International Organization, 30* (1976), 533-4, quoted in Wells, ibid.

45. R. Hoggart, *An Idea and its Servants: UNESCO from Within* (London, Chatto and Windus, 1978), p. 58, quoted in Wells, ibid.

46. Quoted in R. Righter, *Whose News? Politics, the Press and the Third World* (London, Burnett Books, 1978).

47. I have argued this more fully elsewhere, see 'Political theory, international theory, and problems of ideology', op. cit. (note 1), especially pp. 117-19.

48. Examples of this include R. Cox and H. Jacobson (eds), *The Anatomy of Influence* (New Haven, Yale University Press, 1974); and E. Haas, *Beyond the Nation-State* (California, Stanford University Press, 1964).

49. McBride, *Many Voices: One World*, op. cit. (note 41), p. 175.

50. There are significant exceptions to this general factor, USSR entry in April 1954 (followed by the Ukraine in May of that year) being notable. But Sweden (1950), Nicaragua (1952), Spain (1953) and Finland (1956) may also be cited.

51. For a highly developed analytical framework based on these kinds of assumptions and applied to a range of discrete UN Specialized Agencies, see Cox and Jacobson, *The Anatomy of Influence*, op. cit. (note 48), especially Chapters 1 and 2.

52. *Constitution of the UNESCO*, Preamble, para. 7.

53. Ibid., Article 1, para. 2(a).

54. Ibid., Article 1, para 1: 'in order to further universal respect for justice, for the rule of law and for the human rights and fundamental freedoms which are affirmed for the peoples of the world, without distinction of race, sex, language or religion, by the Charter of the United Nations.'

55. File ED 42/1, item 1, para. 1, Public Records office.

56. Ibid., Foreign Office reply to Butler, 12 June 1942.

57. Ibid., Items 2 and 3.

58. Ibid., Item 5, document for 20 July 1942 meeting of the Advisory Panel on External Affairs.

59. Ibid., Item 5.

60. File ED 42/2, draft report of meeting of Conference of Allied Ministers of Education, 16 November 1942, para. 1.

61. Ibid., draft report of CAME meeting of 10 January 1945, para. 6.

62. Ibid., draft report of CAME meeting of 5 October 1943, para. 2.

63. Ibid., draft report of CAME meeting of 6 April 1944, para. 1.

64. Ibid., para 2.

65. See Bordicu, *Outline of a Theory of Practice*, op. cit. (note 1), especially Chapters 2 and 4.

66. For detailed expansion of this as a coherent empirical possibility, see also Lukes, *Power: A Radical Analysis*, op. cit. (note 31), especially Chapter 4.

67. Cox, 'Gramsci, hegemony and international relations: an essay in method', op. cit. (note 37), pp. 171-2.

68. For detailed expansion of these conditions, see C. Hamelink (ed.), *Communication in the Eighties*, op. cit. (note 42), pp. 46-52; C. Hamelink, *Finance and Information: A Study of Converging Interests* (New York, Aplex Publishing, 1983); and H. Schiller, *Communication and Cultural Domination* (New York, International Arts and Science Press, 1976).
69. For a recent comprehensive collection of studies of the relationship between political power, trading power and information, see R. Cruise O'Brien (ed.), *Information, Economics and Power: The North–South Dimension* (London, Hodder and Stoughton, 1983).
70. See *Sunday Times*, 8 January 1984.
71. I mean here that the starting-point for critical theory must be things as they are, or at least appear, to us.

7 Atlanticism and North Atlantic Interdependence: the Widening Gap?

MICHAEL SMITH

THE ATLANTIC PARADOX

As many writers about interdependence (including several in this volume) have suggested, the concept has both an empirical and a normative aspect. It is empirical in its application to the extent that it leads to the identification of interconnectedness among actors in the international system, and to the exploration of the mutual dependence which can flow therefrom. At the same time, the idea of interdependence can represent a cluster of normative preferences and assumptions, expressed either in the rhetoric of political leaders or in the prescriptions of authors. Clearly, in many cases, these two aspects of the concept can coexist, however uneasily, in the policies of the 'practitioner' and the analysis of the scholar: as Keohane and Nye point out, the interaction of 'interdependence as fact' and 'interdependence as value' is bound to be an important formative influence in policy responses, and there is no necessary contradiction or divergence between them.[1] On the other hand, there is also bound to be a certain tension between the two 'faces' of interdependence: thus, whereas both Morse[2] and Hanrieder[3] identify the transition from symbolic or 'transcendental' values to more empirical or technical concerns as a major concomitant of enhanced interdependence, both also point out that the transition is nowhere complete or likely to be trouble-free for policy-makers or for analysts.

Therefore, although the growth of mutual dependence between actors in the international system can clearly be expressed both as a fact (empirical) and a value (normative), it should not be assumed that there is a necessary convergence of the two. It is logical to conceive of circumstances in which the growth of mutual dependence as a fact of international life is unaccompanied by any elevation of 'interdependence' as a cherished value on the part of the actors involved; in the same way, it can be seen that it is possible for the prescriptive aspects of the term to be espoused whilst empirical behaviour and practice obstruct the growth of mutual dependence. From this possible tension between the actual and the potential flow at least some of the problems faced by those who actually have to cope with interdependence and frame policy responses to the international setting. There is no less of a problem for the analyst attempting to disentangle the appearance of shared concerns and responsiveness from what may be the reality of tensions and recriminations.

Nowhere are these problems more apparent than in the evolution of relations between the societies of the North Atlantic area. There is no doubt that these societies in their mutual dealings display a substantial amount of interconnectedness and mutual dependence. In the strategic sphere, the co-ordinated defence efforts of the North Atlantic Treaty Organization (NATO) provide tangible and costly proof of the growth of an international network. Economically, the area accounts for a large proportion of world trade, and particularly for processes of exchange in the most dynamic areas of technological and industrial activity, whilst it is here also that many of the most important international monetary transactions occur. The pattern of intense mutual dependence extends also to the political realm, with the growth of attempts at policy co-ordination and an emphasis on the interaction of institutions and elites.

As a result, it has become almost the conventional wisdom that if interdependence exists anywhere at high levels it is most likely to exist in the North Atlantic area. It is in this part of the international system that we are likely to find the strongest empirical basis for the analysis of mutual dependence. Here also, in large measure, will be found other features of what Keohane and Nye summarize in the term 'complex interdependence': a multiplicity of channels for interaction between national societies, an absence of any fixed hierarchy of issues and concerns, the growth of non-coercive methods of interaction to the point at which military force becomes irrelevant.[4] In the North Atlantic arena, participants cannot escape from the fact that issues are interconnected — that the strategic, the economic and the political are inextricably interwoven and that policy has to take account of the resulting complexity. The multiple channels of contact between societies will themselves lead to the proliferation of institutions and devices for the handling or management of the networks which result. Richard Cooper, writing in the late 1960s, well expressed the kinds of conclusions which might be drawn from this situation:

These countries are closely and increasingly linked by ties of trade, technology, and capital. Knowledge of each other's institutions and practices has increased enormously, and the level of mutual confidence in national economic policies has risen to the point of greatly reducing psychological barriers to the movements of capital and the location of production. In short, the major industrial countries are becoming more closely 'integrated'.[5]

Although Cooper was specifically referring to economic aspects of North Atlantic relations, many commentators would extend his point to cover the strategic and political dimensions, for reasons already outlined. In empirical terms, therefore, it appears that the countries of the North Atlantic area manifest a high and consistent level of mutual dependence, arising from the extensive interconnectedness between them.

The place of interdependence in analysis of North Atlantic relations goes beyond this largely empirical perspective, however. It is frequently argued that the countries of the area share more than simple interrelatedness and mutual dependence in terms of transactions and exchange. In this context, the notion of 'Atlanticism' occupies a central place, expressing as it does a belief in the convergence of perceptions and attitudes which transcends the purely tangible. Just as the growth in transactions and interconnectedness supplies the empirical cement of Atlantic interdependence, it can be argued that the cluster of rhetorical and symbolic components which can broadly be described as Atlanticism provide the normative substance for the development of a new type of international community. Such an argument adds an important extra dimension to the analysis of mutual dependence, and promises to explain how the difficulties and tensions of interdependence in a world without community and solidarity might be overcome. To take only one instance; if it is assumed that in the North Atlantic area the empirical and normative faces of interdependence are mutually reinforcing then this has important implications for the ways in which the costs of mutual dependence are handled. The arguments advanced by Baldwin and others,[6] that acceptance of mutual dependence is essentially the result of an informed calculation by the participants that they will gain more from acceptance than they might from defection, may thus need to be modified. After all, if normative convergence provides a kind of intangible bond which is resistant to shifts in the calculus of costs and benefits, the participants in North Atlantic interdependence might stay together when logically they should fall apart.

But do the empirical and the normative aspects of mutual dependence in the North Atlantic area function to such effect? It is clear to the most casual observer that proclamations of Atlantic solidarity and community are frequently belied by the persistence of disputes and mutual recriminations. Although these may seem to be especially noticeable in the 1980s, they have been a characteristic of the area since the early 1950s. In all phases of the development of Atlantic relations problems have been caused by the asymmetry of relationships and perceptions, and by the conspicuous absence of any cumulative progress towards a new kind of international community. There is, to be sure, a great deal going on in relations between the United States and its West European 'partners', but a great deal of this is (as it always has been) rather fraught and sometimes bitter.

Not surprisingly, the result of such seemingly perverse tendencies has been a fairly constant questioning of the premises on which ideas of Atlanticism have been based. To take only a random selection of the queries and complaints: is an 'Atlantic' conception necessarily at odds with the development of 'European' interdependence and integration? How are the 'internationalist' aspects of attention to Atlantic affairs to be reconciled with 'nationalist' or even parochial demands? In general, how are patterns of behaviour and expectations to be framed in a context where the received wisdom and the brute reality seem to diverge so regularly? As can readily be seen, these kinds of questions reflect some of the confusion which can arise when the easy assumption of convergence between empirical and normative aspects of mutual dependence is called into question. In the late 1960s, Stanley Hoffmann poignantly expressed the problem:

Over the years there has developed a certain mythology, a certain Atlantic orthodoxy which stresses, on the one hand, the community of values, political institutions and cultural heritage among members of the Alliance, and, on the other hand, the need for solidarity as the prerequisite for the accomplishment of any of the common tasks facing Alliance members. Such views deserve criticism. For as a description of interstate relations, this exhortatory approach supposes that what has still to be solved, the political problem of cooperation, is already solved, and that what has still to be demonstrated, the need for solidarity, is beyond demonstration. It requires a kind of leap of faith to believe that common values and a broad range of mutual transactions, ie., characteristics of a trans-national *society*, are the determinants of foreign policies, ie., of *interstate* relations.[7]

Nor has the problem diminished during the 1970s and 1980s. As John Pinder puts it: 'The contradiction for contemporary Europeans and Americans is that the fact of being mutually conditioned by each other does not necessarily lead to mutual reliance, confidence or trust, and seems at present to be leading away from them.'[8]

It appears, therefore, that mismatch and lack of 'fit' between the empirical and normative components of mutual dependence are at least as characteristic of North Atlantic relations as are convergence and mutual reinforcement. Indeed, some participants in the debates of the 1980s have concluded that there is a growing mismatch, a widening gap between aspiration or rhetoric and reality, which might eventually lead to the effective dissolution of what some have called a permanent alliance.

In the light of these general observations and questions, this chapter is designed to try and explore in a more searching way the relationships between norms and reality in the conduct of Atlantic relations. The argument takes three main lines: first, an attempt to identify and disaggregate some of the different meanings which have attached to Atlanticism; second, an assessment of the relationship between different 'images' of Atlanticism and the development of Atlantic relations; and, finally, an attempt to identify possible 'models of the future' in Atlantic relations in terms of the relationship between norms and realities.

IMAGES OF ATLANTICISM

There are several initial difficulties in attempting to pin down the components of Atlanticism. At one level, these are the difficulties common to all explorations of the relationship between declaratory and operational aspects of world affairs: does one base analysis on what political leaders or officials say, or what they reveal of their attitudes or assumptions, or on what they do? In the case of Atlanticism, it is often held also that the cluster of notions it encompasses have meant very different things — in both declaratory and operational realms — on the two sides of the Atlantic itself, and that therefore the identification of certain ideas or individuals as subscribing to the notions is a hazardous or even misleading enterprise. Nonetheless, many writers and practitioners clearly believe that there is such a phenomenon as Atlanticism, that is identifiable and that its status has fluctuated throughout the period since 1945, when it could be said that relations between the USA and Western Europe began to mean something distinct in international affairs.

It will be argued here that it is possible to discern three images of Atlanticism, each with its distinct overtones and assumptions, which have fluctuated in salience and effect and which have formed the focus of debate between actors within the North Atlantic area. These images thus have clear significance in the realm of attitudes, perceptions and declaratory policy for the participants in Atlantic relations, but equally clearly their relationship to operational policy and behaviour within the empirical realm of interdependence is open to question. Each image is taken to be composed of four central elements or sets of assumptions, which in general can be identified as follows:

(i) *Assumptions about the type(s) and extent of mutual depen-dence in the North Atlantic area.* This element focuses upon the intensity, scope and development of mutual depen-dence between the societies concerned, and also upon the relationship of international interdependence in the area both to the wider international system and the domestic affairs of participants. Whilst it can readily be established that mutual dependence exists, this component guides judgements as to what are the significant or central and what the peripheral forms of the phenomenon.

(ii) *Assumptions about the roles to be played by participants.* This element identifies the appropriate roles to be played by state and non-state actors in two domains: first, the international arena and, secondly, the domestic. The distinction is important. Within the international domain, national role conceptions and their relationship to performance are the central focus, whereas within the domestic domain, the emphasis is upon the relationship of state to society, expectations of government and the stability or security of policy elites. In both domains, role security and the generation of authority and legitimacy are central concerns.

(iii) *Assumptions about policy styles.* The third component of each image relates to the modes of policy pursued by participants. Again, there are several distinct aspects to this element. In the first place, there is an assumption about what is *possible* in terms of the interaction of national policies — in other words, the degree of policy divergence or co-ordination which is likely. This is closely linked to a second aspect which refers to what is *acceptable* — the boundaries of legitimate behaviour in the eyes of both domestic and international 'constituencies'. In addition, there is often a reference to what is *desirable* in explicitly normative terms. But what is desirable, or even what is acceptable, may be very difficult to achieve, producing the possibility or likelihood of tensions in this area.

(iv) *Assumptions about regime construction, maintenance and change.* The final component of each image relates to the ways in which it is assumed the Atlantic relationship will be 'run': the institutions, rules and procedures which fit the needs of the participants and express their mutual dependence and obligations. Here, the responsibilities of participants (linked to such role considerations as 'leadership' or 'followership') are important. Another concern is the relative significance of power relationships and bargaining relationships between the participants. The roles of institutions and the techniques seen as appropriate for multilateral management form a third area of interest, along with the informal influence of elite consensus and shared values in the maintenance or decay of the government arrangements.

The first image: Atlantic Community

Perhaps the longest-standing and most firmly-rooted image of Atlanticism is that which focuses on the development of an Atlantic Community. There is a long history to the kinds of ideas put forward by advocates of Atlantic Union in the late nineteenth and early twentieth centuries,[9] but the emergence of the image was given a substantial boost by the relatively permanent and peaceful engagement of Americans in the fate of Western Europe after World War II.

The mutual dependence component of this image is focused very strongly on what might be termed a 'bottom up' view of the growth of Atlantic Community. Such a community, it is often held, is founded on the cultural and societal affinities of the societies involved, which has caused the spread of common ideas and institutions in the North Atlantic area. From each side of the Atlantic, it is said, the other side looks 'most like us', or at least 'more like us than anyone else of significance.'[10] Quite often, this is because patterns of migration and cultural transmission literally mean that 'us' and 'them' are inextricably intermingled.[11] More specifically, the elites of the participating societies are alike, and demonstrate mutual responsiveness born out of a shared history and shared values. This pattern of cultural, societal and elite commonality is bolstered further by a mass of transactions and transnational networks which bind the societies firmly (ever more firmly) together and constitute a basis for effective social communication leading to a true community.[12] Industrial society, industrial culture and the networks to which they give rise are a sure basis for this evolution:

The achievement of high levels of industrialisation, which distinguishes the North Atlantic area from most of the rest of the world, has heightened the economic interdependence and enhanced the sense of community, or interrelatedness, among Atlantic peoples.[13]

Often this idea of 'community resting on multiple interdependence' is given an almost mystical or inevitable quality, highlighting the common fates of the participants:

The Atlantic Community represents the heart of industrial civilisation [and] generally shared political and spiritual values that tend to bind its members together, however imperfectly. For all the stresses in Euro-American relations, historical experience has clearly demonstrated that their fates are inexorably intertwined.[14]

Within the context of multiple interdependence and nascent community, the roles of the participants are fairly easy to discern but not necessarily uncomplicated. In a real sense, it is assumed that the peoples of the area will unite on a transnational basis to form an integrated community. However, the role of governments has to be accommodated. In the international arena, their function appears to be that of a conduit for the needs, expectations and transactions generated by the peoples. Within the domestic context, another important aspect makes itself felt: governments are themselves a symbol of the convergent social and political values espoused by the North Atlantic peoples, and are held to share qualities of liberal pluralism, with representative institutions of a markedly similar nature in different societies. In the end, it might be held that some kind of 'gentle revolution' will erode their national distinctiveness, leading to the amalgamation of the societies and their institutions in a kind of federal or neo-federal context.[15] In this process, the role of national (but also 'Atlantic') elites is immensely important: they are the vanguard of the otherwise largely informal march.

Not surprisingly, the issue of policy styles in this image is treated as an expression of the implicit assumption of overall convergence. Indeed, the nature of multifaceted mutual dependence almost demands a convergence of policy styles, with leaderships and elites necessarily 'speaking the same language' and responding to many of the same symbols. Shared domestic priorities reinforce the international convergence thus set in motion, and elite responsiveness forms a vital cement. On a spectrum of policy styles from 'divergence' to 'integration', the assumption is that strong co-ordination at least is both practical and desirable (indeed, almost unavoidable) and that integration is the ultimate probability.

The underpinnings provided by convergent social needs

and expectations in conditions of intense mutual dependence are translated into distinctive assumptions about regime construction, maintenance and change. In a real sense, the underlying regime is indissoluble, but at the same time there is an obvious need for appropriate institutions to channel the forces of social community. A form of spillover and gradual integration on the grand scale is sometimes postulated, with the institutional architects on hand to provide the expression for the growth of solidarity and the handling of common problems.[16] In flavour, the framework is held to be multilateral and permissive — a kind of international pluralism to match the domestic pluralism which is at the core of this first image.

A 'first image' version of Atlanticism, then, is an image of progressive pluralistic integration based on social responsiveness and social transactions within a permissive framework. It must be noted, however, that there is a central tension in the image, lying essentially in the coexistence of assumed cultural convergence with institutional and political separatism. For this reason, several writers have pointed out the dangers of mistaking politically expedient co-ordination and collaboration for cumulative convergence. One such in the early 1970s found himself wondering whether the North Atlantic peoples could 'transcend the Cold War';[17] another, more recently, pointed out a central tension which is not unrelated to the second image presented here:

In a sense, America's postwar commitment to Western Europe has been based on the assumption that the United States and Western Europe are, in fact, part of a common Atlantic Community. Behind this view has lain not only cultural sympathy but also fear of what an unattached Europe might become.[18]

The second image: Atlantic Hierarchy

It is not uncommon to find writers on the Atlantic area using the words 'Atlantic Community' and 'Western Alliance' interchangeably. Such a mingling of usages aptly expresses the ways in which ideas of a pluralistic Atlantic world have been interwoven with the image of an Atlantic Hierarchy. In this discussion the two images are separated, but it must be remembered that neither is altogether what it seems in isolation.

The idea of an Atlantic area bound together by ties of hierarchy encapsulates a particular view of mutual dependence among its constituent parts. Such dependence is based on and expressed in power relations, particularly in the field of strategic power and security. However, this is not the only domain of mutual dependence which is central to the image. As Calleo and Rowland have pointed out,[19] it is the existence of a distinct power hierarchy in the Atlantic area which both makes possible and interacts with the exercise of economic power in particular. Not only this, but the propagation and implantation of a dominant mode of (American) political and social thinking is also a constituent part of the hierarchy. It can be seen from this that the pluralistic and permissive nature of the context set out in 'first image' thinking is in reality a trick — an illusion made possible by the background of a form of hegemonial power (albeit the hegemonial power in the second image is seen as benevolent and liberal). Part of the reason for this one-sided pattern of mutual dependence lies outside the Atlantic area altogether, since it is the threat from alien forces which provides the rationale for continued acceptance of a profoundly unequal relationship. The point is that everyone involved is aware of the 'facts of life': on the whole, they do not want to escape or deviate because of the unacceptable risks in being caught out in the cold.

Inherent in this background of asymmetrical mutual dependence is the assigning of well-defined roles to the participants. From the very start of the 'Atlantic' era in the late 1940s, it became evident that three central dimensions of discrimination were to be exercised, and accepted more or less willingly by all concerned. The first of these was the distinction between the global role of the hegemonial USA, particularly in the strategic field, and the essentially regional or local roles of all other actors. To be sure, there were rebellions and reluctant submissions among the subordinate powers (especially the British and French), but the iron law of the hierarchy was not to be denied. A second dimension of discrimination was between the nuclear capacity and role of the USA and the non-nuclear roles of others. This has been the cause of more tensions, but it remains essentially intact, since it is acknowledged as the role of the USA to conduct strategic nuclear war, on the basis both of capacity, and of responsibility and

guardianship. The final area of discrimination was between
the roles of 'banker' and 'creditor' in the Atlantic political
economy, based on the institutional and procedural structures
of Bretton Woods as well as on the fact of the dollar's
international financial dominance. An image of Atlantic
hierarchy, therefore, expressed in the declarations of American
policy-makers as well as the writings of scholars,[20] demands a
strict and asymmetrical division of labour, and a downgrading
of attention to a number of purely national or domestic
concerns.

Not only this, but the image has much to say about
acceptable and desirable policy styles. It is the responsibility
and privilege of the top power to exercise its hegemonial
position, through the exercise either of activist 'hegemonial
intervention' or more permissive 'hegemonial abstention' in
relations to the affairs of the subordinates.[21] By the same token,
it is the duty of the subordinates to accept and to be compliant
to the demands of the hegemonial power. After all, the
compliance is for the greater good of solidarity in the face of an
external threat, and can bring more tangible rewards in the
form of aid or privileges. An extension of this quest for
compliance is to be found in the device of 'special' or 'client'
relationships — specially close ties between the hegemonial
power and selected allies or subordinates, which can also have
the (intended or unintended) effects of a 'divide and rule'
policy. Allied to this kind of strategy is the unilateral creation
of linkages between different issues, often as a test of loyalty in
the face of hegemonial demands.[22] All in all, the Atlantic
policy styles encapsulated in this image are a direct function of
intensely asymmetrical mutual dependence, with the USA
framing the right to define the tone and the terms of
participation for the West European participants.

Against this background the process of regime construction,
maintenance and change is likely to reflect the fluctuating
capacity and inclinations of both the USA and the West
European countries — of the USA to exert its dominance, and
of the West Europeans either to comply and collaborate or to
attempt defection. The image assumes that Atlantic regimes
will be an expression of the hierarchy and of the role-
allocations within it, encapsulating the privileges and burdens
which grow out of the fundamental power realities. In contrast

to the permissive and pluralistic framework of a 'first image' Atlantic regime, the second image postulates a structural bias in institutions and procedures; indeed, such a bias is demanded by the requirements of what Keohane has termed 'hegemonic stability'.[23] It is consolidated and rationalized by a process of more or less veiled coercion, on the basis of the perceived external threat or the USA's threat to withdraw the privileges and protection accorded to subordinates. By the same token, of course, the erosion of hegemony, because of changing relative capabilities, a decline in perceived external threat, or fluctuations in the will of all concerned to fulfil their allotted roles, will render fragile the regime itself. In such circumstances even the hegemonic power might feel the temptation to defect.

To a large extent, the second image outlined here can be seen as a direct contradiction of the first ('Atlantic Community') view of Atlantic relations. In place of pluralism, it postulates hierarchy; in place of a 'bottom up' construction, it is firmly 'top down'; in place of evolutionary and progressive amalgamation, it bases its view on conservative and coercive stability. To this extent, the image might broadly be seen as 'realist' in its assumptions and implications, but there have been those who consider its very 'realism' misleading both for analysts and for policy-makers.[24] The alternative, however, is not simply a nebulous pluralism. This is where the third of our images embraces a distinctive set of assumptions and prescriptions.

The third image: Atlantic Partnership

In contrast to images built either on assumptions of pluralistic social community or on ideas of international hierarchy, the third image to be presented here is founded on the notion of more or less equal partnership between the USA and Western Europe within the Atlantic system. The idea of 'Atlantic partnership' is often associated with the attempt by American policy-makers in the 1960s to accommodate their perceptions to the emergence of an integrating Western Europe, but it has both broader and more particular referents.

To a certain extent the Atlantic Partnership image centres around a conception of mutual dependence which matches the requirements of 'complex interdependence' as laid down by Keohane and Nye.[25] Not yet an amalgamated community, nor still a unified hierarchical system, the North Atlantic area is essentially heterogeneous as to actors, channels of communication and procedures for management. Interdependence is not, therefore, primarily to be seen in terms of cultural or popular feelings of community; nor is it to be confined to the realm of security and alliance, although that forms part of the environing conditions for its development. The mutual dependence which is envisaged or identified is broadly to be found in the economic and technical fields, fostered by the massive growth of communications and transactions which has undoubtedly taken place in the North Atlantic area. Communications and transactions, though, are by no means an end in themselves, or the sole building blocks of a broader unity. The role of governments persists, and there is also a search for authoritative institutions which can provide the framework for further expansion of the already burgeoning interconnections. Central to this image of mutual dependence is a vision of relative symmetry — in itself, enough to distinguish this image from that of 'Atlantic hierarchy'. The symmetry, it is assumed, is not to be 'legislated into being' or merely declared to exist; it is grounded in the growing economic force of a uniting Europe, and in the recognition of common tasks demanding common action and regulation.[26]

It is clear from this that such a vision or image demands distinctive roles of the participants (which here are clearly a relatively wide range of actors under the joint 'umbrella' of the USA and the EEC). The emergence of these views at the beginning of the 1960s demanded the forging of new roles both for the USA and for a Europe which at that time was only hypothetically united. On the part of the USA, there was a requirement that a relatively symmetrical partnership should be accepted, as the basis for authoritative regulation of both immediate and long-term concerns.[27] At the same time, there were major implications for the role of the existing national states in Western Europe and for the creation of a European identity.

These implications could not be ignored, since they came flat up against the processes of national reconstruction and revival in both the economic and the political fields which were seen as major gains from the existing model of Atlantic relations. If a European entity were to be created, capable of acting in the political and even the strategic as well as the economic realm, then this would imply a redefinition of the roles of European states in both their domestic and their international arenas. Nor was it self-evident that the emerging calls for Atlantic Partnership were entirely free of misinterpretation and ambivalence. The idea of partnership could be seen in a dynamic and creative light, especially as enhancing the status of the putatively uniting Europe; on the other hand (and the other side), it could be seen as a means of preserving American status in the light of a new and thrusting challenge, or even as providing new weapons with which to preserve the status quo.

One of the foundations on which ideas of Atlantic Partnership rested was (and is) the hoped-for development of consistency and co-ordination in the realm of policy styles. Automatic or instinctive convergence on the lines of 'first image' thinking is not realistic, but then neither is a continuation of the carrot-and-stick methods which John Foster Dulles had attempted in the days of American dominance. New times, it is assumed, need new methods. Central to such thinking is the belief that Atlantic institutions can be constructed to provide a reliable and consistent framework for the management of joint policies. Within these institutions, the emphasis would be on bargaining, compromise and conciliation rather than on confrontation or divergence. Nor is this all: the aspiration is for a form of policy co-ordination which would in principle be applicable outside the strictly Atlantic area. After all, this is in keeping with the preponderant share of that area in world resources and with its connection to the global economic and security complexes.

It almost goes without saying that the activity of regime construction, maintenance and change is a central tenet of the Atlantic Partnership image. In fact, it could be said that the whole line of thought on which it is based grew out of a perceived need for new governing arrangements as between the USA and Western Europe. Whether the perceptions and the needs were the same on each side of the Atlantic is, of course, the question which immediately arises. It is not an assumption of Atlantic Partnership thinking that all conflicts between the USA and the countries of Western Europe will magically disappear. Rather, the image postulates an intense yet friendly competition within an agreed set of governing practices and institutions, which will need amending and adapting on the basis of experience and continuous reappraisal. Given this postulate, it is to be assumed that there will be few basic disagreements about the existence of the practices and institutions themselves. One of the reasons why this is a plausible assumption lies in the further aspiration towards a form of broadly based burden-sharing, in which the costs and benefits of collaboration will be equitably distributed. Such burden-sharing is one of the linchpins of the legitimacy and authority which the regime should generate; another key component clearly lies in the development of a 'potential government' in the EEC, capable of entering into and sustaining a role in the range of Atlantic institutions. Given this set of assumptions, a process of regime change by adjustment and negotiation is not beyond the bounds of reason.

The idea of Atlantic Partnership thus expresses a belief in a broadly based Atlantic system, characterized by heterogeneity yet also by the development of a 'two pillar' edifice of political authority. The sustaining fabric of the partnership is neither instinctive convergence nor coercive dominance; neither an erosion of governmental presence nor an enhancement of some governments' power to intervene and interfere; neither a transnational society nor a structurally biased set of inter-governmental institutions. For these reasons, it could be argued that such an image is more realistic and progressive than the others, but to argue thus would be to overlook a yawning gap between the postulates and the realities of Atlantic partnership.

ATLANTICISM AND ATLANTIC REALITIES

The three images of Atlanticism discussed in the preceding section encapsulate in a simplified and idealized form the notion of a normative component to North Atlantic inter-dependence. As argued at the beginning of the chapter, it is clearly important to establish the extent to which these essentially normative constraints correspond to the realities of mutual dependence in the North Atlantic area. If the area is generally characterized by mutual reinforcement of the normative and the empirical dimensions of mutual dependence, then arguably policy and practice can be built on surer foundations than if the two dimensions either diverge or are in a constantly fluctuating relationship. It is not simply, however, that the size of the 'gap' between the normative and the empirical is significant: the source of the gap, and the means by which one element can be adjusted to the other, is also of major importance. Thus it is necessary to form some kind of judgement on priorities: do ideas of Atlanticism precede the development of mutual dependence in the empirical realm, do they follow it (and thus reflect it), or is there a more complex process of mutual adaptation and interaction?

In this part of this chapter, the relationship between Atlanticism and interdependence will be explored with reference to three phases of North Atlantic relations: first, the period of reconstruction and recovery in Western Europe and the consolidation of the Atlantic Alliance (1945-58); second, the period of increasing fragmentation and rivalry (1958-70); and, finally, the period in which the chances of disintegration seemed to grow (1970-84). The final section will reassess the connection between the normative and empirical aspects of Atlantic relations and briefly attempt to outline some possible future developments.

Reconstruction and recovery (1945-58)

Although this is not the place for a detailed survey of the ways in which the USA and West European countries became entangled during the years after World War II, it is important to point out some of the central features of the situation which had emerged by the early 1950s. In the first place, despite uncertainties in the USA about the appropriate form for Atlantic relations in Western Europe, it was clear that the Americans dominated in every field. Partly, and inevitably, this was a result of the sheer weight of American resources in the strategic and economic fields: only the USA could furnish the military might and the economic muscle to sustain the emerging Western Alliance. This judgement was common to policy-makers on both sides of the Atlantic, and was reinforced by the development of bipolar confrontation with the USSR. As a result, and in consequence also of the perceived fragility of the regimes of Western Europe, a kind of unequal bargain was struck, in which the Americans traded support for West European reconstruction and recovery for the right to 'direct operations' in the emerging cold war. In the strategic field, the consolidation of NATO in the wake of the Korean War confirmed a structural and institutional bias in favour of the USA, although there were mutterings from the French about the extent of American dominance. Economically, as Benjamin Cohen has indicated, the bargain was more complex but nonetheless asymmetrical:

The Europeans acquiesced in a system which accorded the United States special privileges to act abroad unilaterally to promote US interests. The United States, in turn, condoned Europe's use of the system to promote its own regional economic prosperity, even if this happened to come largely at the expense of the United States.[28]

The point was that only the Americans could afford the form of mutual dependence encapsulated in the Marshall Plan and the beginnings of European economic integration; and they were willing to pay at least in part because of the strategic and political privileges they received. The political compliance of a 'supine' Western Europe[29] was underpinned by overt American intervention and manipulation at times, but was also guaranteed by the threat of Soviet expansionism.

This was clearly a very uneven form of mutual dependence, and one which might have been seen as giving the Americans total freedom of manoeuvre or involvement. In fact, although successive US governments were tempted to defect by the gravitational pull of global confrontation or by the perceived misdeeds and failings of their European allies, they did not do so. John Foster Dulles's threat of an 'agonizing reappraisal' of American involvement in 1954, as the Europeans confronted the dilemma of the European Defence Community, may have sounded dramatic but represented no real likelihood of US withdrawal. On the West European side, although the various national leaderships had complicated reasons for subscribing to the arrangements, they generally found themselves able (or compelled) to reconcile themselves to their roles. Indeed, it could be argued that the provision of an American 'umbrella' in the strategic and economic fields allowed some leaderships more autonomy that otherwise they might have achieved.[30] In

this, their task was made more manageable by an understandable desire to concentrate above all on domestic
reconstructions; this meant that the tensions between national
subordination and national autonomy did not surface very
often, but it also meant that there were distinct variations in the
extent to which 'Atlantic' ideas became associated with
internal recovery and the growth of legitimacy.[31]
Despite the early evidence of substantial American intervention (whether purposeful or accidental, malevolent or
benign) in the affairs of Western Europe, this was not the
characteristic policy device of the 1950s. In fact, it could be
concluded that once the framework of the Western Alliance
was set, the Americans practised a form of 'hegemonic
abstention' in some important policy areas (for example, the
establishment of the EEC).[32] On the other hand, the development of 'special relationships' with favoured clients was a
noteworthy feature, often one reflecting the pressures exerted
by the clients themselves as a means more firmly to establish
themselves under the American 'umbrella'. In a sense, the
relationship between every West European society and the
USA was 'special', but the responses (say) of French and West
German leaderships to the fact were markedly different.
Linkage strategies, whether deliberately pursued or not, were a
feature of the period. In fact, the whole framework of the
'alliance' in strategic, economic and political spheres expressed
a consciousness of the need and inevitability of cross-sectoral
linkages.
Given the pervasive nature of American influence in both
the material and doctrinal fields, it might come as a surprise to
discover that there were in fact significant deviations from
'orthodoxy' in many areas by the West European governments.
In the strategic field, despite American pressures, the allies
failed consistently to meet the force levels and contributions
allotted to them. Economically, the persistence of trade
barriers and the unconvertibility of European currencies
constituted major derogations from the Bretton Woods system,
whilst the development of political deviations ranging from
incipient neutralism to misplaced globalism among leaderships or populations formed a source of aggravations to
American policy-makers. This situation really reflected two
forms of limitation on US dominance: first, the fact that in

many respects the Atlantic regime was characterized by *laissez-faire* and a significant lack of systematic institutional development;[33] and, second, the fact that American policy-makers habitually defined 'European' and 'Atlantic' priorities as being naturally convergent.[34]

The fact of the matter was, of course, that there was developing by the late 1950s a 'clash of perspectives' within the Atlantic area, in which European integration and Atlantic collaboration were by no means to be seen as automatically complementary.[35] Indeed, one of the major focuses of an emerging European identity often seemed to be a latent or overt opposition to the USA, and this was to be an important element in the developments of the 1960s.

Fragmentation (1958-70)

During the period from the end of the Eisenhower regime to the installation of the Nixon administration in the USA, the mutual dependence of the countries within the Atlantic area undoubtedly deepened and broadened. One of the most marked manifestations of this trend came in the non-governmental fields of business and commercial activity — these were the years of massive growth in the presence and operations of multinational firms, and a rapid increase in many forms of transatlantic communication. In one sense, this could be seen as adding a new dimension to American dominance in the Atlantic area, but the simultaneous consolidation of the EEC with its capacity for co-ordinated action in the commercial field restored the balance to a considerable degree. The economic realm could thus be identified as showing a tendency towards greater interconnectedness but also greater symmetry as between the USA and Western Europe, although the symmetry was confined to certain relatively narrow areas in the first instance. On the other hand, the strategic field manifested no such tendency, despite the ostentatious deviation of the French and the rivalry between Kennedy and de Gaulle. The fact of the matter appeared to be that it was precisely the continuing asymmetry of strategic relations between the two 'pillars' of the Atlantic alliance that made this kind of defection possible.

None the less, the tensions between Western Europe and the USA in several fields did appear to reflect growing differences of view on a number of important issues. Many of these were connected with the costs of mutual dependence, and seemed to express a growing unwillingness on both sides to sustain the burden of the existing arrangements. Strategically, the problem manifested itself in American attempts to establish a more equitable (from their point of view) apportionment of the costs of alliance. The difficulty was that these attempts coincided with developments in the broader international system which changed European perceptions of the Soviet threat and also brought into question the continued credibility of the US guarantee to Western Europe. The emergence of a more equally-balanced relationship in the strategic nuclear field not only changed European perceptions of their potential conqueror, but also eroded their confidence in the willingness of their protector to come to their aid.[36] Meanwhile, in the economic field the essential ambivalence of many American policies became more apparent: to take only one example, the Trade Expansion Act of 1962 could be presented either as the basis for a new liberalization of world trade or as a weapon for the US President to use against the EEC and its protectionist tariff policies.[37]

The result of these underlying tensions in the development of Atlantic relationships made itself felt in a number of more or less spectacular ways. One of the most dramatic manifes-tations was the confrontation of American and French conceptions and policies, which can in many ways be seen as the product of continuing ambivalence about the relative status of participants in the Atlantic system. The irony of this, and of later European paranoia about the 'American challenge' in the economic and technological spheres, was that the status anxieties of all concerned coincided with the most active preaching of ideas of 'Atlantic partnership'.[38]

It is in this light that the pronouncements of American policy-makers especially have to be viewed. John F. Kennedy's 'Declaration of Interdependence' in 1962 could be seen as a statement of faith in the evolution of an Atlantic partnership, but could also represent the American attempt to discover new ways of stating the boundaries of acceptable behaviour.[39] In Western Europe, the results of many US initiatives during the mid-1960s were increased fragmentation and division, for example as in West Germany between 'Europeans' and 'Atlanticists'. Meanwhile, the EEC was beginning its descent into conservative paralysis, a state characterized by the defence of limited gains in conditions of external turbulence.[40] It is hardly surprising, then, that the structure of the Atlantic system itself became both a stake and a weapon of political combat.[41]

The late 1960s in fact underlined these trends. Although the US/French confrontation continued, it was augmented by the corrosive effects of *détente*, which clouded the boundaries of acceptable behaviour and in the hands of Richard Nixon and Henry Kissinger seemed to place a premium on unilateralism. To this source of uncertainty was added the increasing pressure placed on all governments by challenges to their domestic legitimacy — a situation which militated against the achievement of international policy co-ordination, especially on economic issues. The outcome can be seen as a reaction towards national independence, which was paralleled in the political sphere by the emergence of an American administration dedicated to a very particular vision of the world. This vision, none the less, was couched at least in part in terms of Atlantic partnership and continued convergence:

> The challenge to our maturity and political skills is to establish a new practice in Atlantic unity — finding common ground in a consensus of independent policies instead of in deference to American prescriptions. This essential harmony of our purposes is the enduring link between a uniting Europe and the United States .... European and American interests in defence and East–West diplomacy are fundamentally parallel and give sufficient incentive for coordinating independent policies. Two strong powers in the West would add flexibility to Western diplomacy, and could increasingly share the responsibilities of decision.[42]

When these words were uttered, the basis for much of their relevance had either disappeared or was about to be attacked.

Disintegration (1970-84)

There is a fine irony in that fact that the Richard Nixon who in 1972 was preaching responsible Atlantic partnership had, in 1971, destroyed at least part of its basis. The so-called 'Nixon Shock', in which the convertibility of the dollar was suspended and various discriminatory trade measures were taken, was presented as a means by which the USA could start to act as an 'ordinary country', experiencing interdependence in the same ways and on the same terms as other industrial countries. More colourfully, John Connally, the US Secretary of the Treasury, described it as a means of 'screwing the foreigners before they screw us'.[43] None the less, many of the measures taken in 1971 and after were presented by US leaders as contributing to the continued widening and deepening of Atlantic interdependence, a fact which could be interpreted as a sign of hypocrisy but which might also be revealing of changing economic realities. Having failed to form a 'partnership' by persuasion and negotiation, the Americans during the 1970s seemed bent on re-establishing their position by coercion if necessary. Both in the economic and the strategic spheres, the threat of different forms of 'decoupling' was made, openly or by implication.[44] Clearly, this was not a threat to cut all connections with Western Europe: more accurately, and more significantly, it constituted a threat of unresponsiveness and the potential manipulation of mutual dependence to American advantage. Made most openly by Nixon and Connally, it has been implicit in the policies of all American administrations since 1968.

This American stance reflects a broader reality in the Atlantic arena: the continuation and intensification of mutual dependence in a period when the concerns of governments have become focused more and more on parochial demands, and where the international context has been consistently ambiguous or threatening. Thus, in the economic field there has been continued market independence but this has been subject to profound external shocks and resistant to international co-ordination.[45] In such circumstances, it is a natural temptation for any government to try and shift the costs of adjustment on to others, so as to restrain domestic complaints and buttress fragile authority.[46] Strategic interdependence has continued, but in circumstances where the Soviet threat has become more ambiguous and multifaceted and where the American threat to 'decouple' has been matched in its effects by attempts to 'recouple' (through Pershing and Cruise, for example). Political interdependence has been much in evidence, but not always beneficial, with the scare about 'Eurocommunism' disrupting some relationships whilst the slow-spreading epidemic of governmental inadequacy or abdication has characterized much of the 1980s.[47]

Not surprisingly, one of the effects of these trends has been felt in challenges to the structure of the Atlantic system. The decline of the perceived legitimacy of American attempts to 'lead from the front' has reflected the course of US domestic politics as well as the risks attendant on some of the foreign policies pursued by successive administrations. On the other hand, the failure of the EEC to transcend its image as a 'civilian power', despite the nuisance value of European Political Co-operation, has meant a continued inability to establish a co-ordinated European 'presence' in the Atlantic arena. In the words of David Calleo, the European Community remains 'a supermarket, not a superpower'.[48] On both sides of the Atlantic, it has appeared more often than not that policies are framed with an eye to domestic pay-offs rather than international consequences, and this has not unnaturally reinforced perceptions of duplicity.

The problem of roles and perceived legitimacy has come to have close links with policy styles within the Atlantic area, partly because of the emphasis placed on this aspect by successive US Presidents. Richard Nixon's implied aim that the USA should act as an 'ordinary country' was, to say the least, misleading given the continued dominance and relative invulnerability of his country in many areas of international activity. In fact, the Nixon strategy — and later that of Ronald Reagan — can be seen as relying on the misuse of a privileged position as much as upon the use of 'normal' rules of international intercourse. It is also arguable that American 'ordinariness' is essentially unattainable in the light of their ascribed role in many central issue areas. Such an impression is reinforced by the contrast with the EEC: far from being a nascent European 'government', or constituting the expression of a European 'identity', it has functioned inevitably as a 'partial partner', with a narrow range of co-ordinated policies which in many areas are undermined by the independent actions of its members. American commentators have been wont to attack this feature of European activity, whilst omitting to mention that at least some of it is due to the impact of US policies inside and outside Europe.[49]

In consequence, the Atlantic area has been through what the ancient Chinese curse calls 'interesting times', and seems likely to live in them for the indefinite future. During the early 1980s, the continued impact of uneven mutual dependence has meant that any governing arrangements or rules of behaviour have become fragmented and manipulable. Whilst there have been no direct disputes over the entire structure to parallel those of the 1960s, this is partly due to the fact that the structure is fragmentary at best, dominated by litigation and the 'politics of resentment'.[50] Mechanisms of co-ordination have grown up on an *ad hoc* basis to deal with specific issues or crises, whilst there has been a continuing attempt to proclaim the unity of the Atlantic countries (now including Japan) through such devices as 'economic summits'. This sort of symbolism often exists in a different world from the bitterness and recriminations over the increasingly contested linkages between strategic, economic and political measures and the fears arising out of domestic preoccupations within a turbulent and ambiguous international environment. It is not therefore illogical to argue that the way better to achieve Atlantic collaboration in the 1980s is not to try too obviously,[51] — since the attempt to pronounce doctrinal uniformity or sweeping notions of 'leadership' can itself be seen as self-serving, irresponsible or illegitimate.

ATLANTICISM AND INTERDEPENDENCE: A REASSESSMENT

It seems clear from the brief review of developments in Atlantic relations since 1945 conducted in the preceding section that the relationship between any consistent image of Atlanticism and the realities of North Atlantic interdependence has been tenuous. In this final section there is a twofold aim: first, to reassess the origins and implications of the gap between normative and empirical concerns in Atlantic relations; and, second, to look at some possible 'images of the future' suggested by recent writings, in the light of the conclusions drawn about past trends.

The Atlantic gap

The central components of three images which appeared typically Atlanticist have already been set out: Atlantic Community, Atlantic Hierarchy and Atlantic Partnership. It was seen that these images encapsulated different assumptions about four central issues: first, the nature and extent of mutual dependence between countries in the North Atlantic area; second, the roles to be played by actors in the area; third, the policy styles adopted and expected by the governments and other groups involved; and, finally, the way in which the regime or governing institutions and practices was to be constructed, maintained or transformed. Analytical separation of the three images, it was argued, did not imply that they were unconnected in fact or occurrence, but did highlight their diverse foundations and implications.

What seems clear from the discussion on Atlanticism and Atlantic realities is that there is very little consistent convergence between any of these images and Atlantic realities. In the period 1945-58, it could be argued that there *was* considerable relevance in the image of Atlantic Hierarchy. The Americans dominated, they intervened and manipulated and generally behaved hegemonically. They were assisted in this by a context in which 'Atlantic orthodoxy corresponded to the needs and realities of the bipolar conflict.'[52] But at the same time, substantial derogations and deviations occurred within the Atlantic framework, and the ferment of pluralism seemed to grow even though the hierarchy was not seriously challenged or undermined.

This limited coincidence of image and reality was even so more substantial than that which characterized the period 1958-70. The image of Atlantic Partnership was promulgated and promoted, but reality seemed more like a corrupted version of Atlantic Hierarchy. Some of the corruption clearly arose from internal defections and a reduced level of compliance within the Atlantic system, whilst some arose from a muting of the bipolar conflict which had helped to sustain the relationship of the 1950s. Perhaps even more important was the beginning of a major shift in economic power and impact which posed a challenge both to the initial 'bargain' of the late 1940s and the policy-making creativity of national leadership.[53] The Atlantic image persisted in the language and rationalization of elites, but how far could it be trusted?

In the years after 1970, it becomes even harder to discern any mutual reinforcement of Atlanticism and the realities of Atlantic relations. Whilst interconnectedness and mutual dependence increased, a combination of external shocks and

internal inconsistencies destroyed many of the settled expectations which had sustained relations as late as the 1960s. No
one image could be realistically promulgated or pursued:
indeed, a central feature of the period has been the divergence
between the language espoused by policy-makers or elites and
the reality of behaviour.[54] Quite apart from the misdemeanours
of particular leaderships or other groups, an argument could
be made that an inexorable form of 'generational decay' was
destroying the framework of assumptions on which any image
of Atlanticism has to be based.[55] The result appeared to be an
uneasy blend of 'incomplete pluralism and disintegrating
hegemony',[56] and indications were that the 'Atlantic gap' could
only be expected to widen.

These assessments raise major issues about the relationship
of the normative and the empirical in the analysis of North
Atlantic interdependence. It was suggested at the beginning of
the chapter that the two 'faces' of interdependence can become
disconnected, and that assumptions of normative convergence
could persist even when behaviour diverges. This is clearly the
case in the Atlantic area, and it appears to be the case that
periods of mutual reinforcement between normative and
empirical 'faces' are relatively restricted. Not only this, but the
periods of mutual reinforcement or convergence seem to be
much less frequent in the 1980s than in the 1950s. Hence the
argument that the 'Atlantic gap' is becoming a yawning gulf,
and that attempts to reassert an Atlanticist image of any kind
will only make things worse.

In this light, some important aspects of Atlanticism itself are
sharply illuminated. Most importantly, it becomes clear that
Atlanticism does not represent an abstract or universal set of
normative preferences; rather, it constitutes an interlocking set
of 'actor's models', reflecting political needs, preferences and
responses. This is the case, whichever 'image' of Atlanticism is
at issue. As a result, the relationship of Atlanticism to reality is
predestined to fluctuate according to developments in the
distribution of power and influence among the actors in the
North Atlantic arena, and according to the level of consensus
among policy-makers as to their preferences. Indeed, Atlanticism itself is almost a part of the reality — a stake in
competition or even a weapon of combat in the transatlantic
system. The changing reality of the 1970s and 1980s in

particular has generated a number of centrifugal forces which have undermined consensus between policy elites in the North Atlantic area and reduced expectations about convergent behaviour. Thus it is to be expected that Atlanticism as an image of desired circumstances is markedly less salient in the 1980s than in the 1950s, and that where it is espoused it is open to suspicions or recriminations.

Atlantic futures

Despite the decline of what might be called 'classical Atlanticism', the significance of North Atlantic relations both for the countries concerned and for the broader international system has meant a continued attempt to speculate about the future of the area. There is time here only to touch on three possible 'Atlantic futures', but it is important to stress that in principle these visions of the future can be subjected to the kind of analysis and evaluation conducted in this paper. Each contains assumptions about the nature and conduct of relations between the United States and Western Europe, and each responds in a different way to the developments of the early 1980s.

(i)   *A first future: the end of Atlanticism.* On the basis of the trends described earlier in the chapter, it is quite possible to decide that any concept of Atlanticism is defunct. Some commentators have argued precisely this, emphasizing broad structural trends in the world economy which will create unsupportable contradictions between the USA and Western Europe and eventually lead to a grand restructuring of global relations.[57] Others, from an Atlanticist tradition, have argued that unless something is done to defeat the forces of indifference and introspection there will be a drifting apart of the two 'pillars' in the Atlantic system, responding to domestic preoccupations and a lack of responsible leadership within the system as a whole.[58] These two very different approaches share common ground in that they assume interconnectedness will continue, but they are markedly at odds when they come to consider the roles, policies and institutions appropriate to the future Atlantic system. Whereas one predicts Atlantic 'divorce', the other fears it and argues for a kind of renewed partnership.

(ii) *A second future: Atlanticism reasserted*. It has also been argued that a combination of renewed tension in the international system and active leadership by the USA can restore the Atlantic area to a situation not unlike that of the 1950s. Such a regression would bear out the arguments made by Morse that one way of confronting an intractable environment is to re-emphasize transcendental or symbolic goals, in contrast to the tangible and instrumental goals typical of 'complex interdependence'.[59] The problem here, of course, is precisely that which has been explored by this chapter: will actual behaviour conform to the goals espoused, even in the most tangential way? If Atlanticism was reasserted in its 'classical' form, it would come up against the domestic and parochial pressures, not to mention the ferment of international pluralism, which confronted it before, and might be seen as a self-serving attempt to revalue the stakes of transatlantic interplay. As a strategy of leadership, it would appear to rekindle hegemony and lay itself open to the problems such a situation has created; but it may reflect circumstances in which domestic concerns or the perceptions of policy-makers see no future in non-hegemonic forms of persuasion.[60]

(iii) *A third future: permissive Atlanticism*. More likely than an Atlantic 'divorce' or a reasserted hegemony, according to some analysts, is a form of Atlanticism in which necessity holds the participants together whilst they assert a considerable degree of independence and autonomy. To borrow a phrase from Ruggie, this situation would reflect a kind of 'embedded Atlanticism'[61] in which a series of continuous compromises sustained the system, without forcing upon any of the participants the choice between submission and defection. A generalized 'menu' of Atlantic issues and solutions would exist, within which specific choices or combinations could be available to the actors. Defection would be prevented not by binding commitments or coercion, but by the inevitable constraints of continuing entanglement — the edifice would be self-supporting and would exercise a continuous influence on the participants' perceptions and choices.[62]

Whilst not a full-blown concept of Atlantic Community, it can be seen that this view derives partly from such an image. The difficulty is that it can only really apply at a broad aggregate level: the different power structures and terms of combat in different issue areas will provide a continuing source of tensions and disturbances, although its proponents would argue that the very complexity of the structure would ensure its survival.

CONCLUSION

Whichever 'Atlantic future' emerges, it is almost inevitable that it will not correspond to any simply stated or broadly shared image of the desirable Atlantic world. This chapter has attempted to show why there can be no easy coincidence of image and reality in the North Atlantic area, and thereby to draw attention to some underlying tensions in ideas of interdependence more generally. Although it would be too sweeping to say that the espousal of particular versions of interdependence as a normative image is bound to be contradicted by the facts of interconnectedness and mutual dependence, there are important questions to be asked about the relationship between values and reality. The answers provided by the North Atlantic area are partial and often enigmatic, but are clearly significant.

NOTES AND REFERENCES

1. See R.O. Keohane and J.S. Nye. *Power and Interdependence: World Politics in Transition* (Boston, Little, Brown, 1977), Ch. 1.
2. E.L. Morse, *Modernization and the Transformation of International Relations* (New York, Free Press; London, Collier-Macmillan, 1976), pp. 88ff.
3. W.F. Hanrieder, 'Dissolving international politics: reflections on the nation-state', *American Political Science Review, 72* (1978), 1276-87.
4. Keohane and Nye, op. cit., especially Ch. 2.
5. R.N. Cooper, *The Economics of Interdependence: Economic Policy in the Atlantic Community* (New York, Columbia University Press, 1968), p. 8.
6. D.A. Baldwin, 'Interdependence and power: a conceptual analysis', *International Organization, 34*, 4 (1980), especially 500.
7. S. Hoffman, *Gulliver's Troubles, or the Setting of American Foreign Policy* (New York, McGraw-Hill, 1968), pp. 387-8 (emphasis in the original).

8. J. Pinder, 'Interdependence: problem or solution', in L. Freedman (ed.), *The Troubled Alliance: Atlantic Relations in the 1980s* (London, Heinemann, 1983), p. 67.
9. See E.R. Goodman, *The Fate of the Atlantic Community* (New York, Praeger, 1975), Ch. 1; and D.K. Pfaltzgraff, 'The Atlantic Community — a conceptual history', in W.F. Hahn and R.F. Pfaltzgraff, Jr (eds), *Atlantic Community in Crisis: a Redefinition of the Atlantic Relationship* (New York, Pergamon, 1979), pp. 3-29.
10. See K.N. Kelleher, 'America looks at Europe', in Freedman (ed.), op. cit. (note 8), pp. 44-66.
11. This is brought out in K. Kaiser and H.-P. Schwartz (eds), *America and Western Europe: Problems and Prospects* (Lexington, D.C. Heath, 1979), especially Part I.
12. This is essentially the argument of K.W. Deutsch, *et al.*, *Political Community in the North Atlantic Area* (Princeton, Princeton University Press, 1957).
13. D.K. Pfaltzgraff, op. cit. (note 9), p. 3.
14. Goodman, op. cit. (note 9), p. xix.
15. D.K. Pfaltzgraff, op. cit.
16. Goodman, op. cit.
17. S.A. Scheingold, 'The North Atlantic area as a policy arena', *International Studies Quarterly, 15* (1971), 59ff.
18. D. Calleo, 'Early American views of NATO: then and now', in Freedman (ed.), op. cit. (note 8), p. 23.
19. D. Calleo and B. Rowland, *America and the World Political Economy: Atlantic Dreams and National Realities* (Bloomington, Indiana State University Press, 1973).
20. See Calleo and Rowland, ibid.; Hoffman, *Gulliver's Troubles*, op. cit. (note 7); and S. Hoffman, *Primacy or World Order: American Foreign Policy after the Cold War* (New York, McGraw-Hill, 1977).
21. Calleo and Rowland, op. cit.; and M. Smith, *Western Europe and the United States: the Uncertain Alliance* (London, Allen & Unwin, 1984), Ch. 5.
22. Smith, ibid., Ch. 5.
23. See R.O. Keohane, 'The theory of Hegemonic stability and changes in international economic regimes, 1967-1977', in C.R. Holsti, R.M. Siverson and A.L. George (eds), *Change in the International System* (Boulder, Col., Westview Press, 1980), pp. 131-62.
24. See Calleo and Rowland, op. cit., especially Part II.
25. Keohane and Nye, op. cit., Ch. 2.
26. See Kaiser and Schwartz, op. cit. (note 11), and R.L. Pfaltzgraff, Jr, *The Atlantic Community: a Complex Imbalance* (Princeton, Van Nostrand Reinhold, 1969).
27. This was emphasized, for example, by H. Kissinger, *The Troubled Partnership: a Reappraisal of the Atlantic Alliance* (New York, McGraw-Hill, 1965). See also D. Calleo, *The Atlantic Fantasy: the United States, NATO, and Europe* (Baltimore, Johns Hopkins University Press, 1970); and Goodman, op. cit. (note 9), Ch. 3.
28. B.J. Cohen, 'The revolution in Atlantic economic relations: a bargain

198   *Michael Smith*

comes unstuck', in W.F. Hanrieder (ed.), *The United States and Western Europe: Political, Economic, and Strategic Perspectives* (Cambridge, Mass., Winthrop, 1974), p. 118.
29. Keohane and Nye, op. cit., p. 47.
30. Calleo, 'Early American views of NATO', op. cit. (note 18), p. 20.
31. See, for example, N. Wahl, 'The autonomy of "domestic structures" in European-American relations', in J. Chace and E.C. Ravenal (eds), *Atlantis Lost: U.S.-European Relations after the Cold War* (New York, New York University Press, 1976), pp. 225-48.
32. Smith, op. cit. (note 21), Ch. 5.
33. See Pinder, op. cit. (note 8), pp. 69ff.
34. A. Wolfers, 'Integration in the West: the conflict of perspectives', *International Organization, 17* (1963), 753-70.
35. Wolfers, ibid.
36. This problem is well expressed in Kissinger, *The Troubled Partnership*, op. cit. (note 27).
37. Calleo and Rowland, op. cit. (note 19). See also D. Calleo, *The Imperious Economy* (Cambridge, Mass., Harvard University Press, 1982).
38. See, for example, A. Grosser, *The Western Alliance: European–American Relations since 1945* (London, Macmillan, 1980), Ch. 7.
39. Grosser, ibid. See also Calleo and Rowland, op. cit. (note 19).
40. E. Haas, *The Obsolescence of Regional Integration Theory* (Berkeley, University of California Press, 1975).
41. See K. Kaiser, 'The United States and the EEC in the Atlantic system: the problem of theory', *Journal of Common Market Studies, 5* (1966-7), 388-425.
42. *U.S. Foreign Policy for the 1970s* (Washington DC, GPO, 1972), p. 40.
43. See J.S. Odell, *U.S. International Monetary Policy: Markets, Power, and Ideas as Sources of Change* (Princeton, Princeton University Press, 1982), Ch. 4.
44. See, for example, several contributions in R.N. Rosecrance (ed.), *America as an Ordinary Country* (Ithaca, Cornell University Press, 1976); A.J. Pierre, 'Can Europe's security be "decoupled" from America?', *Foreign Affairs, 51* (1973), 761-77; and Cohen, op. cit. (note 28).
45. Pinder, op. cit. (note 8).
46. A good study of this is R.O. Keohane, 'U.S. foreign economic policy toward other advanced capitalist states; the struggle to make others adjust', in K.A. Oye, R. Rothchild and R.J. Liebar (eds), *Eagle Entangled: U.S. Foreign Policy in a Complex World* (New York and London, Longman, 1980), pp. 91-122.
47. Smith, op. cit. (note 21), Ch. 3.
48. D. Calleo, 'The European coalition in a fragmenting world', *Foreign Affairs, 54*, 1 (1975), 98.
49. E.A. Kolodziej, 'Europe: the partial partner', *International Security, 5*, 3 (1980-1), 104-31.
50. J. Joffe, 'Europe and America: the politics of resentment (cont'd)', *Foreign Affairs, 61*, 3 (1983), 569-90.
51. Kolodziej, op. cit., p. 130.
52. Hoffman, *Gulliver's Troubles*, op. cit. (note 7), p. 391.

53. Cohen, op. cit. (note 28).
54. See, for example, the analysis in M. Kaldor, *The Disintegrating West* (Harmondsworth, Penguin, 1979), Ch. I.
55. See Kelleher, op. cit. (note 10).
56. Calleo, 'Early American views of NATO', op. cit. (note 18), p. 22.
57. Kaldor, op. cit.; and I. Wallerstein, 'Friends as foes', *Foreign Policy, 40* (1980), 119-31.
58. L. Freedman, 'The Atlantic crisis', *International Affairs, 58* (1982), 395-412.
59. Morse, op. cit. (note 2), pp. 88ff.
60. Keohane and Nye, op. cit., pp. 231ff.
61. J.G. Ruggie, 'International regimes, transactions and change: embedded liberalism in the postwar economic order', *International Organization, 36* (1982), 379-415.
62. Ruggie, ibid.; see also Scheingold, op. cit. (note 17).

8 Interdependence, Power and the World Administrative Radio Conference

JOHN VOGLER

This chapter will provide no new conceptualization of interdependence. On the contrary, it proceeds from the conviction that there is a need to evaluate the usefulness of existing approaches in the investigation of contemporary political problems. The new theories of interdependence are to be judged by their performance in the analysis of political relationships from which the question of power can hardly be excluded. They will have demonstrated their utility if and when they assist in providing a more satisfying answer than established Realist approaches to the enduring question of 'who gets what, when and how?' in the international system.

Although it has often been pointed out that interdependencies have always existed, the justification provided for more recent works such as Keohane and Nye's *Power and Interdependence* is that modern conditions require modern theories. World politics is in transition and Realism cannot continue to provide a comprehensive view relevant to 'today's multidimensional economic, social and ecological interdependence.'[1] It is for this reason that an incontrovertibly 'modern' topic has been chosen for analysis. The generation, storage and transmission of information is said to constitute the basis of the emergent global economy in much the same way as coal and steel provided the foundations of the first industrial revolution. The networks of information exchange made possible by the new technologies are truly transnational in their reach. To take but one amongst a myriad of examples, domestic flight booking information for some East European airlines is stored on a computer in Texas.[2] Without labouring the point, there can be few other areas of transnational interconnectedness that accord so well with the rhetoric of global interdependence.

This chapter concentrates on the essential resource upon which the greater part of electronic information exchange depends — the electromagnetic spectrum. The spectrum may be regarded as part of the global 'commons' or 'commons in the sky', as one writer has dubbed it.[3] In the sense that the electromagnetic spectrum is a resource over which no one has exclusive jurisdiction, it is similar to the more well-known 'commons' such as the deep-sea bed, fishery stocks or Antarctica. However, it has a number of notable peculiarities. It does not exist of itself but must be generated by the setting-up of electromagnetic disturbance to form oscillating waves which are then used to carry information. The electromagnetic spectrum comprises the whole range of frequencies potentially available, but for practical purposes of communication we are concerned with the more restricted, but ever expanding, set of usable frequencies known as the radio spectrum. The spectrum may be abused but cannot be depleted; it is infinitely renewable. Its usefulness can, however, be much impaired if it is exploited in a haphazard and unco-ordinated fashion and this constitutes a basic source of interdependence in this area. With the coming of satellite communications the spectrum may be conveniently bracketed with a complementary resource — the finite range of orbital slots for satellites in geosynchronous orbit.

Competition between users of spectrum space and satellite slots is increasingly recognized as posing not only technical but political problems of some magnitude and significance. The relevant governing arrangements, which are now frequently called into question, may be said to constitute a regime which has the International Telecommunications Union (ITU) as its principal organizational component. Fundamental decisions about the allocation and management of the spectrum are taken at the ITU's World Administrative Radio Conferences (WARCs), epic meetings held at twenty-year intervals. Thus there is every reason to select the activities surrounding the 1979 general WARC as a test case for the study of the relationship between interdependence and political power under modern conditions. The 1979 deliberations at Geneva brought about certain changes in the spectrum regime, while avoiding others that had been proposed. The problem is to explain these outcomes and in particular to ascertain whether the concept of interdependence is relevant to such an explanation.

Keohane and Nye have advanced four models of regime change and it is proposed to evaluate these within the context of the WARC. The first model appears, at least superficially, to be apolitical in its assertion that the outcome is simply explicable in terms of economic, and in this case, technological rationality. The second has its basis in Realist thought and the idea that outcomes may be predicted from the overall power structure. In contradiction to this a third, 'issue structural' model posits that outcomes can only be understood in terms of power resources that are specific to the issues under consideration. As far as the WARC is concerned, technical competence and market dominance in the field of telecommunications would prove decisive. Finally, an 'international organizational' model would lay stress on the fact that negotiations were conducted within the framework of the ITU and would advance an explanation couched in terms of the constraints and opportunities provided by its procedures.[4]

Keohane and Nye's major hypothesis is that the relevance of these regime change models will be determined by whether the relationships under study are characterized in terms either of Realism and traditional state power relations or the more modern concept of 'complex interdependence'. If the international spectrum regime may be described in terms of the latter category, then one is to expect that the 'issue structural' and 'international organizational' models will be indispensable to an explanation of the WARC outcome. The preliminary task is to ascertain the nature of interdependence amongst users of the spectrum and their governments and the extent to which the situation approximates to 'complex interdependence'. (See the further discussion of this concept in the relevant section later in this chapter.)

THE RADIO SPECTRUM

Electromagnetic waves travel at 300,000 km per second, the speed of light. They are distinguishable in terms of wave length, frequency and amplitude, there being a direct relationship between wavelength measured in metres (the distance between the peak of one wave and the next) and frequency measured in Hertz (1 Hz corresponds to one cycle or wave passing a fixed point every second). It follows that the shorter the wavelength the higher the frequency. Amplitude constitutes a measure of the size of the wave and the amount of energy carried varies proportionately to the square of its amplitude.

Electromagnetic radiation may be modulated in a number of ways in order to communicate information. In primitive radio this merely involved turning a carrier wave on and off, as with Morse code. Later, amplitude and frequency modulation techniques allowed the transportation of more complex information. In the light of recent developments involving microwave and super high frequencies, it should also be noted that the higher the frequency the greater is the information-carrying capacity. Theoretically, the usable or radio spectrum extends from about 10 kHz to 300 GHz (see Figure 8.1), although by no means all of this vast range of potential frequencies is currently employed. The radio spectrum is conventionally divided into bands differentiated by frequency but also by their signal propagation characteristics and the technology required to utilize them for communication. Propagation is an inordinately complex subject but, very broadly, three types of wave occur in transmissions, the ground wave, sky wave and space wave. Each has different properties at different frequencies and under different geographical, temporal and even climatic conditions. The ground wave, travelling along the earth's surface and thus subject to absorption, will propagate most effectively at low frequencies. The sky wave from an LF transmission will have no use in communication as it will radiate off into space without any reflection. By contrast, high-frequency (short-wave) band transmissions rely on the sky wave to give extremely long-distance coverage. HF radiation is refracted from the ionosphere and can 'skip' around the world, often for very long distances depending on the ambient conditions. Although medium-wave transmission relies heavily on the ground wave, its sky wave can also give rise to serious interference, particularly at night.

In contrast, VHF and UHF transmissions rely solely on the space wave because at these frequencies the sky wave will not be refracted from the ionosphere and the ground wave will attenuate very rapidly. The space wave which forms the basis of UHF/VHF transmission and reception may, in some ways, be regarded as analogous to the beam from the top of a lighthouse as it radiates from the transmitter. However, the analogy is not exact because the range of VHF/UHF transmissions

Wave length	Bands	Frequency	Services
100 km		3 kHz	
10 km	Very low frequency	30 kHz	Time signals, standard frequencies radio navigation
1 km	Low frequency	300 kHz	Fixed, mobile, maritime, navigational LF (long-wave) broadcasting
100 m	Medium frequency	3 MHz	Land mobile, maritime MF (medium-wave) broadcasting
10 m	High frequency	30 MHz	Fixed, mobile land, mobile maritime and aeronautical HF (short-wave) broadcasting, amateur
1 m	Very high frequency	300 MHz	Fixed, mobile land, mobile maritime and aeronautical, TV and VHF broadcasting
10 cm	Ultra high frequency	3 GHz	Fixed, mobile land, mobile maritime and aeronautical, TV broadcasting, radio location and navigation, meteorology and space communication
1 cm	Super high frequency	30 GHz	Fixed, mobile land, radio location and navigation, space and satellite communication
1 mm	Extremely high frequency	300 GHz	
0.1 mm		3 THz	

Figure 8.1 The electromagnetic spectrum

is extended beyond the horizon by tropospheric refraction; hence it is possible to receive from transmitters which are not in direct line of sight. Despite this property, the potential range of VHF and UHF transmissions around the earth's surface is still very limited in comparison to that of lower frequencies, as may be gauged from the location of television transmitters. The 'bending' of the space wave as it strikes the ionosphere diminishes at higher frequencies and thus provides no assistance to the range of transmissions when the Super High Frequency Band (SHF), which lies beyond UHF, is employed. SHF, with frequencies in the gigahertz range provides only 'line of sight' communications on the earth's surface but is now being exploited for satellite up-and-down links. Such high frequencies are particularly suited to this role since the amount of information that may be carried by a transmission varies directly with its frequency.

The general usage of the frequency bands is well known and corresponds to their propagation characteristics and the technical requirements for transmission and reception. LF can provide national coverage broadcasting for a country such as Britain, whereas VHF and UHF provide a multiplicity of shorter-range communications, stereo broadcasting, TV and mobile radio. The HF, or short-wave, band is the most controversial and overcrowded. While it is extensively used for external broadcasting its propagation characteristics also make it an ideal medium for national communications and even telephone networks in the developing countries.

From a political point of view, the technical characteristics of signal propagation at different wavelengths will determine the scope of interdependence and conflict. Thus the HF band, with its world-wide coverage, provides the subject matter for global dispute while MF and LF are matters of regional contention. Similarly, VHF and UHF interference will occur over a more limited area involving only close neighbours.

The most rapid technological development has occurred in the use of the SHF band for satellite communications, the 4, 12 and 18 GHz bands having been allocated to this purpose since 1971. Communications, broadcasting and remote-sensing satellites are most effectively employed in a geosynchronous (stationary) orbit at 23 300 miles from the earth's surface on an equatorial track. This opens up the question not only of allocating spectrum space in the SHF band, but what has become the much more vexed issue of allocating a limited number of orbital parking slots.

THE SPECTRUM REGIME

As in many other areas of global interdependence, the concept of regime — in so far as it implies some form of purposive central management and planning — appears ill matched to the realities of spectrum use and regulation, or rather absence of regulation. Rather, it accords with Susan Strange's view that the 'rules of the game include some national rules, some international rules, some private rules and large areas of no rules at all.'[5]

The institutional framework that has grown up within the ITU is somewhat complex. As far back as the International Radio Telegraph Conference of 1906, participating states recognized that the radio spectrum constituted a common asset and that some form of rational co-ordination of frequency use and technical standards for equipment was the *sine qua non* of international radio broadcasting and communication. The Radio Telegraph Conference was merged into the old International Telegraphic Union in 1932 to form the present ITU. Unlike other UN agencies, this body has no permanent legal status but is based upon a continually renewable Convention which is negotiated at five-yearly intervals by the ITU's governing body, the Plenipotentiary Conference of its state members. This is supplemented by an annual meeting of the Administrative Council's twenty-nine elected members. Three subsidiary bodies have a more permanent existence: the International Radio Consultative Committee (CCIR), the five-member International Frequency Registration Board (IFRB) and the ITU Secretariat based at Geneva (this last is surprisingly small with a staff of 616 and a budget of $US33 million in 1978). Of primary importance to the work of the ITU are the administrative conferences that it sponsors. These are mostly regional in their scope or concerned with specific issues, as in the case of WARCs convened to consider satellite uses during the 1970s. The general WARC, with which this chapter is primarily concerned, has the all-embracing task of allocating the entire spectrum at twenty-year intervals. It would be difficult to overestimate the complexity and magnitude of the task. One indication is provided by the fact that the ITU Secretariat found it prudent to order no less than 96 tons of paper prior to the 1979 meeting!

Under its present Convention, the ITU is directed to

... maintain and extend international cooperation for the improvement and rational use of telecommunications: to promote the development of the most efficient operation of technical facilities in order to increase their usefulness and, as far as possible, to make them available generally to the public: and to harmonize the actions of nations in the attainment of these common ends.[6]

It is important to understand that what this essentially means in practice is that the ITU provides a framework for some limited consensus on the use of airwaves. The restricted scope of the organization and its lack of binding regulatory powers is reflected, as many commentators have pointed out, in the small size, funding and relative obscurity of an organization charged with the oversight of issues recognized to be of fundamental global significance.

The 'rules of the game' are as follows. It is accepted that the general WARC shall agree the allocation of frequency bands to different purposes. Hence the 1979 WARC produced a lengthy revision of the *Radio Regulation Table of Frequency Allocations*, running to some 174 densely-packed pages. Specific frequencies were allocated to over thirty types of service, ranging from amateur radio to satellite identification, without any frequencies being allocated to specific countries. WARC business is conducted through a network of committees and is finally subject to a plenary session of the Conference. In the absence of a consensus, issues are decided by a simple majority, with each state member casting one vote. Majority decisions may, on occasion, be circumvented through the expedient of 'taking a reservation' which, in effect, registers formal dissent and a state's refusal to be bound by a decision. Indications of national disagreement with specific allocations and intent to use frequencies in an alternative manner are recorded as 'footnotes' to the *Table of Frequency Allocations*. It has been observed that the use of this device has greatly expanded in recent years, and particularly during the 1979 WARC.

Assignment of allocated frequencies to particular users is a power that falls within the jurisdiction of national sovereignties. The assignment of a frequency is simply notified to the IFRB which records it in the Master Register after a period of scrutiny in which complaints about interference may be received from other users. The Board does not have its own monitoring facilities nor any powers to enforce compliance with the 'regulations'. As a result, the rules are on occasion flouted by transmitters operating 'out of band' and member states may enter footnotes to the regulations indicating that they reserve their right not to comply. In effect, the system has operated historically on a 'first come, first served' basis. Once registered, the principle of 'squatter's rights' applies to the occupation of certain frequencies, even if, as in many instances, they are not actually used for transmissions. Only in a limited number of cases, for example, the MF band in Europe, have members indulged in co-operative planning to sort out the chaos that may result. Otherwise, what *The Economist* described as 'this creaking relic of the telegraphic age' appeared through most of the 1970s to be resistant to a major overhaul of its procedures.[7]

As to the question of identifying regime change, WARCs have produced changes in spectrum allocation which might on occasion be seen to go beyond mere tinkering at the margin. In present circumstances a major redistribution of spectrum space in favour of the less developed countries, which, it is claimed, have 90 per cent of the world's population but occupy only 10 per cent of the spectrum, would constitute significant change.[8] Fundamental change would occur if the ITU were seen to be shifting towards a general commitment to an active planning and management role in areas such as the HF band and satellite orbits. Many have argued that by analogy with the way in which the Europeans were impelled into a planning conference for MF in the mid-1970s, the extension of such arrangements has a certain inevitability unless major parts of the spectrum are to be allowed to become unusable.

ACTOR INTERDEPENDENCE

The system of radio spectrum usage certainly meets the

criterion of a 'set of actors, where each of the actors is dependent upon one or more of the others in the set.' This became so as soon as the most rudimentary transmitters came on the air at the beginning of the present century. The enjoyment of the benefits of communication was, to a greater or lesser extent, contingent upon the behaviour of others. Just as the original International Telegraphic Union had been founded in 1865 by a number of reluctant governments to cope with the transnational spread of the telegraph through the standardization of equipment, so compatability of transmitters and receivers was on the agenda of the very first meeting of radio users at Berlin in 1903. The immediate stimulus was provided by the rivalry of early wireless companies, Marconi and AEG Telefunken, and in the inconvenience it caused a Prussian prince. In 1902, Prince Heinrich of Prussia was returning from a visit to the USA aboard the liner *Deutschland* when it took his fancy to send a courtesy message to Theodore Roosevelt via the new German ship-to-shore radio with which the vessel was equipped. Much to the chagrin of the Prince, the shore station at Nantucket refused him service on the grounds that it was equipped with the Marconi system (Marconi was at that time attempting to create a monopoly by making its shore stations incompatible with the ship-borne sets of other manufacturers and notably the German Slaby Arco Braun system). An initiative from Berlin soon followed, convening the 1903 conference.[9]

Shortly afterwards, developments in the ability to tune a set, quaintly known as syntony, led to a concern with the use of different frequencies and to the 1906 conference, ancestor of the current WARC. At this early date users were fully aware of the fact of their mutual interdependence in terms of the avoidance of signal interference. This has remained the case ever since, yet the simple statement that the possibility of interference leads to interdependence would require substantial qualification. Clearly, the extent of such interdependence will relate to the number of transmitters that attempt to use a given amount of spectrum space and the technical characteristics of transmissions and their propagation in certain frequencies.

In the most heavily-used bands, MF and HF, there is severe overcrowding and interference resulting from the long-distance propagation of powerful signals. HF frequencies, for example, have for this reason to be allocated on a global basis. In contrast, UHF and VHF can be allocated by region. Similarly, the relatively simple amplitude modulation system used for medium and short-wave broadcasting gives rise to severe problems on account of the amount of bandwidth required. AM works by establishing a carrier wave and then modulating it to produce sidebands displaced at widths of up to 4.5 kHz above and below the carrier. Thus reasonable quality AM broadcasting requires 9 kHz bandwidth, and with great numbers of MF and HF transmitters taking up such large parts of the limited spectrum space available it is easy to grasp the magnitude of the interference problem. There are various ways of managing this interdependence. One solution that has already been mentioned was found in the European Administrative Conference of 1975, which gave rise to a planned attempt to arrange frequency use in the MF band, resulting in the sacrifice of some frequencies by users. (The BBC lost a number of its medium frequencies in this way). An alternative technical solution is to make better use of the spectrum by utilizing improvements in equipment to shift some services higher up the spectrum. A radical technical solution was proposed by the USA to the 1979 WARC, involving the universal introduction of 'single sideband' AM by the end of the century. This type of transmission supresses one sideband, which is then restored by the receiver; its introduction would thus virtually double the available spectrum space at a stroke. Unfortunately, all current equipment including receivers would have to be replaced (single sideband on a conventional receiver renders speech as a passable imitation of Donald Duck). The availability and costs of technical alternatives to the kind of high-level interference and interdependence now experienced in the European MF band, and more significantly in world HF, are very pertinent to the question of relative dependence and vulnerability and will be further discussed in that context.

The 'new frontier' of spectrum use is to be found in the fast developing technologies of satellite communications and the related dispute over the allocation of orbital parking slots. This, perhaps, provides an analogy for the move from relative independence to extensive interdependence that has occurred in the electronic communications system as a whole during the present century. It is estimated that depending on the safety margin allowed, somewhere between 180 and 1800 satellites could function in geosynchronous orbit without collision. At present there are 110 in orbit with a separation of 3–4°. Given the small number of present users they are relatively independent, but by 1985 the estimate is for 300 geosynchronous satellites to be in place. Overcrowding and interference are therefore imminent. As far as the use of the 12 GHz SHF band for up-and-down links is concerned, the USA and Canada are already aware of their interdependence in allocating parts of the band to different uses. Prior to the 1979 WARC, the USA proposed dividing the band into halves, one half allocated to direct broadcasting and the other to fixed-point communications. Canada objected on the grounds that she was developing a hybrid satellite, which unlike US broadcasting and business satellites combined both functions. One of the achievements of the WARC was a complex compromise for the sharing of the 12 GHz band.[10]

COMPLEX INTERDEPENDENCE?

How far is the interdependence that has been described 'complex' in terms of Keohane and Nye's formulation of the concept in contradistinction to Realism? It will be remembered that complexity involves the existence of multiple channels connecting societies, an absence of issue hierarchy and the reduced utility of force. The multiple channels that connect societies are, of course, one and the same thing as the various uses of the spectrum that have been considered. Yet the essential point is that under complex interdependence state-to-state high politics relations do not predominate. International and traditionally domestic issues become intertwined, transnational and non-state actors play a significant role. This certainly appears to be the case in the politics of the spectrum regime. Harold Jacobson summed it up rather neatly in the title of his article on the ITU, 'a pot-pourri of bureaucrats and industrialists.'[11] Private operators have always been well represented since the days of the Marconi and Slaby Arco Braun systems. At the 1927 Washington Radio Conference, eighty state delegations and sixty-four other interested organizations were in attendance. This trend has continued and although non-state actors do not have voting rights in ITU conferences (except in the absence of a state delegation) their role is institutionalized in the organization's consultative procedures. 'Recognized private operating agencies and scientific and industrial organizations' participate actively in the deliberations of the CCIR and attend WARCs.

Modernist views of policy-making under complex interdependence tend to disaggregate the state. Their vision is of a network of competing national and transnational interest groups whose activities blur the classic distinctions between high and low, foreign and domestic politics. It may be unfair to raise the question of the nationality of most of these theorists, but it comes as no surprise to find that the one clear case in which policy-making followed this pattern is provided by the United States. There, an open and pluralistic debate surrounded the formulation of a WARC negotiating position, involving a multiplicity of agencies, corporations and pressure groups. The framework was provided by the State Department but the delegation itself was headed by G.O. Robinson, an academic specialist in telecommunications law. The US delegation of sixty-five members included representatives of many governmental agencies and the armed services, but it also included no less than twenty-two members from private organizations as diverse as Western Union and the National Black Media Coalition.[12] By contrast, the British preparations for the WARC followed the near-universal pattern whereby the state authorities arrogate telecommunications policy-making to themselves. The British delegation was presided over by D.E. Baptiste of the Home Office Radio Regulatory Department assisted by a Foreign Office advisor. The only whiff of public debate was provided by the objections of the mobile radio lobby, although informal consultation with other bodies doubtless occurred and, unlike most countries, Britain's negotiating proposals were published. In this instance, then, there is little evidence for the widespread adoption of procedures which appear uniquely founded on the pluralistic political system of the United States.[13] Yet the day-to-day work of the ITU is so technically complex that many participants must turn to the expertise of specialists often from private and foreign organizations. One example of transnational activity along such lines is provided by the case of a coalition of twelve Latin American states ill endowed with the necessary competence. They were assisted in drawing up their position for the Conference by a number of private groups: the US Public Interest Satellite Association, the Nauman Foundation of West Germany and the British-based World Association for Christian Communications.[14]

Unlike other issue areas which seem highly functional and low politics-orientated, the subject matter of spectrum use must impinge upon the hallowed ground of 'high politics' and state security. The monitoring and direction of communications is increasingly a major prerequisite of governmental control over populations and of the efficiency of armed forces. Similarly, technical developments such as direct satellite broadcasting, which enhance the transnational reach of communications links, are often viewed with trepidation as a profound threat to the maintenance of national sovereignty. Such fears are nowadays widely voiced by Third World countries concerned by the violation of their cultural integrity as well as their political independence. Curiously, however, such matters have not traditionally dominated ITU agendas. This is partly because article 51 of the ITU Convention allows members 'to retain their entire freedom with regard to military radio installations of their army, navy and air forces.' Jacobson was able to conclude in 1974 that in general, 'high politics' and politically symbolic issues dominated only rarely, for example, when the admission of new members was considered, and that this might be explained by the relative obscurity of the ITU.[15] By the late 1970s, any such conclusion would seem dated, if considered in the light of Western press coverage of the WARC, which was full of anxiety that the ITU would be dragged into the arena of North–South ideological debate in much the same way as, in their perception, UNESCO had been debased. The source of this concern was a co-ordinated attempt by the Non-Aligned Movement at its Havana summit meeting of 1979 to 'act jointly so as to ensure that the World Administrative Radio Conference produce results which would be in conformity with the interests of the Non-Aligned Movement, aspiring to establish the new international information order.'[16] This was a significant development but it did not imply the emergence of a clear hierarchy of issues dominated by political and security concerns.

Similarly, the notion of the non-usability of force appears applicable with few reservations. There have been no declarations of war or military demonstrations over the misuse of frequencies and the most coercive activities observed to date involve the jamming of 'subversive' foreign broadcasts. This is not to say, however, that the highly sensitive issue of satellites in geosynchronous orbit, and particularly those which are crucial to the command and control of armed forces, may not one day lead to the exercise of forms of technological *'force majeure'*.

DEPENDENCE AND VULNERABILITY

Although it would be misleading to speak of complete independence or complete vulnerability, very wide divergencies exist between the relative positions of the advanced industrialized states and the Third World. By being first in the field, the developed states have profited from the doctrine of 'squatter's rights' such that they control the lion's share of frequencies. Many assignments are retained even though they have fallen into disuse. By contrast, a large number of Third World states attended a WARC for the first time in 1979 and brought with them a general demand for equity and long lists of specific requirements for spectrum space.

In deliberations on the use of the spectrum, advanced states are relatively invulnerable, to the extent that their expertise and mastery of the new technologies allow them to dominate technical discussion. Their control of advanced communications networks is an additional source of strength. The United States provides the most obvious example. At the WARC more than one hundred US delegates and advisors were employed and:

... nearly a thousand people had been involved in preparing US plans ... with the use of massive computer expertise the US had mapped out a negotiating position covering the entire spectrum from 1 Hz to 387 GHz with a complex set of fallback positions. The delegation had also collected all known facts concerning the positions of other delegations as well as informal information collected in private briefings and everything relevant that could be found out about the members of all the other delegations. The whole of this information could be held on-line and could be retrieved in a matter of moments.[17]

In the face of all this, there is no need to stress the relative weakness of a newly-arrived, less developed member of the ITU with a delegation of one, two or three people. Some amelioration might be achieved through the sort of links enjoyed by the coalition of twelve Latin American states, but this hardly rectifies the imbalance. The dependence of such actors becomes even more acute as suggestions arise for the utilization of higher frequencies or satellite communications in which they will have little or no indigenous expertise and for which all the necessary equipment will be manufactured by the electronic corporations of the developed world.

Perhaps the most important aspect of the relative invulnerability of advanced countries is simply that in circumstances where the scope for independent state or commercial activities is impaired, they possess a range of alternatives. Elsewhere in this volume doubts have been cast upon the soundness of Keohane and Nye's sensitivity/vulnerability distinction. However, their definition of vulnerability dependence has significance here: 'Vulnerability dependence can be measured only by the costliness of making effective adjustments to a changed environment over a period of time.'[18] The technology and resources available to advanced states at worst provides the means for such adjustments to be made, even at some net cost, and at best allows a cost-effective way of reducing vulnerability. In actual terms this means that whereas less developed states remain heavily committed to the use of HF for their national broadcasting and telephone communications, advanced states and corporations have long been able to diversify by moving services higher up the spectrum into microwave, using satellites or even avoiding the electromagnetic spectrum altogether by the use of cable and fibre optics. For advanced users, HF is still of interest for lower-priority services, external propaganda broadcasting, redundant back-up services for the military and increasingly for the new land mobile radio services. All this can be gauged from their negotiating positions at the WARC which, taken together with the demands for the reallocation of the HF band by the Third World, highlight the differential levels of dependence of North and South, where essential communications links are concerned. Many vital services, for economic information or the circuits of the major news agencies, are already owned and

controlled by Northern business corporations anyway, indicating yet another facet of Southern dependence and vulnerability.
As the advocates of the New International Information Order
point out, this technical dependence implies an even more
profound economic and cultural dependence.

The unequal apportionment of the spectrum and the
differences in relative vulnerability of users would appear to
give rise to a global information system which is highly
asymmetrical as between advanced and developing worlds.
Yet there is a sense in which even the United States is
vulnerable in the face of concerted action by the electronically
dispossessed. It is noteworthy that, despite extreme irritation
with the demands of the Third World within the ITU, the
United States delegation at the WARC prefaced its negotiating
position with a firm statement that it would remain in the
organization and had no interest in defecting to set up a rival
organization of 'squatters'. A.W. Branscomb has summed up
the American interest which is also a source of dependence:

Economically, US dependence on telecommunications discourages
ignoring the ITU because of the destructive electronic chaos that
would ensue. More important, US leadership in telecommunications
technology promises substantial economic benefits from a global
expansion of communications.[19]

Thus it is within this context that one can refer to the mutual
vulnerability of users in the face of any degradation in the
spectrum regime. Such mutual vulnerability gives rise to what
Barry Jones, elsewhere in this volume, has defined as 'common
fate interdependence', where users may be dependent upon
one another for desirable outcomes or the collaborative efforts
necessary to secure beneficial developments. It is this countervailing element to the general pattern of asymmetrical
dependence that makes the political process within the ITU
interesting and the outcome of the WARC something more
than a set of foregone conclusions.

POWER AND INTERDEPENDENCE

At the beginning of this chapter it was asserted that theories of
interdependence ought to be evaluated in terms of their
usefulness in the explanation of political outcomes. We may

thus ask whether the concepts of interdependence and vulnerability that have been discussed are in any way necessary to an understanding of what transpired in Geneva at the end of 1979. A framework for this investigation is conveniently provided by Keohane and Nye's four models of regime change. In essence, if either the 'overall power structure' model or the 'economic/technical rationality' model, or some combination of the two, provide a satisfying and sufficient explanation, then the concept of interdependence as advanced by modernist writers has little value. More conventional economic and political analysis will serve. On the other hand, it has been argued that allowing for some serious reservations concerning the unique nature of the US policy process, the politics of spectrum use and management approximate to what has been specified as complex interdependence. It follows that if Keohane and Nye are correct, then 'issue structural' and 'international organizational' explanations of the outcome of the WARC will be required.

The focus of analysis is the outcome of the 1979 conference in relation to the negotiating positions of the participants. There follows a considerably condensed version of both, which concentrates on the general objectives of the United States and the Third World, in so far as it was identifiable as a coalition. It should be noted that this emphasis necessarily obscures many specific divergences of view between the US and other advanced countries and similar disagreements within the Third World camp. Some of these will be mentioned if they appear germane to the argument.

The US position comprised:

1. A general declaration of support for the ITU.

2. Opposition to any general rewrite of the *Table of Frequency Allocations*, coupled with demands for incremental revision and sharing of frequency bands amongst services.

3. A general objection to the planning of frequency use on the grounds that this would be wasteful, inflexible and a restraint to technical innovation.

4. Demands for more broadcasting frequencies in the MF band 1815-60 kHz, to allow the creation of fourteen new private AM stations.

5. More allocation in the HF band to point-to-point and mobile radio and for external broadcasting by the VOA, etc.

6. A universal commitment to the introduction of single sideband equipment by 1995.

7. Reallocation of the VHF and UHF bands towards mobile communications Citizen Band and other commercial uses.

8. A doubling of the SHF space allocated to satellite links from the existing 11.7-12.2 GHz up to 12.7 GHz, dividing this part of the spectrum into two halves, the lower allocated to satellite business systems and the upper to broadcasting satellites. Allocation of frequencies for satellite solar power generation and other scientific purposes.

The Third World position comprised:

1. Voicing general concern over sovereignty violations by the new technologies and the iniquity of spectrum allocation.

2. A reallocation of the HF band in favour of the less developed countries (an Algerian proposal which did not receive complete backing called for a 70-per-cent share).

3. The provision of satellite orbital slots for developing countries regardless of their present capacity to use them. This demand had been made with inconclusive results at the specialized 1977 satellite WARC.

4. A demand for planning conferences to consider the joint management of HF and geostationary satellites.

The outcome of the conference, which met from 27 September to 6 December 1979, was highly complex, mixed and in some ways indecisive. Neither the fears of those who foresaw a collapse into destructive ideological rancour, nor the hopes of those who wished for the creation of some new and more equitable telecommunications order were fully realized. A large number of specific compromises between individual countries were arranged, notably between the USA and Canada, over the allocation of the SHF band. The head of the

US delegation felt able to claim success· in the adoption of proposals to expand AM broadcasting, to increase the portion of the spectrum allocated to satellite use and to protect and allow for scientific uses of the spectrum.

However, *The Economist* was moved to comment that the WARC had allowed the Third World 'to reject many technically sound plans for getting the best use out of the radio spectrum'.[20] This, presumably, was a reference to the defeat of the single sideband proposal, along with the rejection of some US and Western proposals for VHF and UHF. At the same time, the demand for more external broadcasting space in the HF band was only partially met by new allocations above 9 MHz. (The BBC in particular had wanted space around 6 MHz, this being regarded as being more useful in improving World Service reception.) Changes in HF allocation did, in fact, exactly meet the joint proposals put forward by the Non-Aligned Movement.[21] The most damaging outcome from an American point of view was the resolution of the Conference to convene administrative planning conferences on the HF band and geostationary orbit slots. This might be represented as a move towards fundamental revision of the spectrum regime and although it remains an aspiration rather than an actuality, management was placed on the agenda in a way which caused much concern to the advanced users of the spectrum, who had been able to profit by the old permissive rule of 'squatter's rights'.

An analysis of the Conference outcome based upon the exercise of pure technical rationality — akin to Keohane and Nye's economic process model — does not provide a convincing explanation. As Jacobson has pointed out, the long-standing participants in the ITU always used to claim that their deliberations were essentially technical and depoliticized, the pursuit of rational solutions to the problem of spectrum use which were easily assumed to be in everybody's best interest.[22] The idea that interdependence ought to be managed in this way is still very prevalent in the developed world. Glen Robinson, head of the US delegation, frequently criticized the way in which 'sound rational technical argument' was being clouded by 'highly abstract issues of political ideology'. Nevertheless, in the next breath he was prepared to argue that US policy was designed to 'enhance US economic,

social and national security interests.'[23] The apparent contradiction between such eminently political concerns and
exhortation about the pursuit of neutral technical solutions
appears not to have been noticed. Yet E.H. Carr and many
others have long ago noticed and explained the phenomenon.
In his classic attack upon the liberal idealist notion of the
harmony of interests, Carr recognized that *laissez-faire* was the
'ideology of a dominant group concerned to maintain its
predominance by asserting the identity of its interests with
those of the community as a whole.' In the context of trade,
'The tacit presupposition of infinitely expanding markets was
the foundation on which the supposed harmony of interests
rested.' Using the analogy of road traffic, control is unnecessary
so long as the number of cars does not exceed the comfortable
capacity of the road. 'Until that moment arrives, it is easy to
believe in a natural harmony of interests among road-users.'[24]
Such comments would be equally relevant if 'squatter's rights'
and 'technical rationality' were substituted for *laissez-faire* and
frequencies and orbital slots for markets and roads. In the
words of a Costa Rican delegate: 'Freedom of the air is a good
principle among equals but it is inappropriate to the new
realities of communication.'[25]

If technical explanations are not explanations at all, but the
ideology of the powerful, then a Realist perspective might be
pressed into service. Writing in the early 1970s, Jacobson
explained the political processes within the ITU as a combination of purely technical discussion on substantive issues with
occasional aberrations towards power politics when symbolic
or representational issues were under consideration. On such
occasions the outcome might be predicted in terms of a Realist
view of the global power structure. The United States would,
for example, muster its allies to oppose the admission of
Communist China to the ITU. Despite the fact that the ITU is
generally regarded as having become more overtly politicized
during the 1970s, it is difficult to assert that a Realist — or in
Keohane and Nye's terminology, an overall power structure
model — provides an explanation of the 1979 outcome. Had
the overall power balance and pattern of alignments in
international politics been dominant, the negotiation and its
conclusions would surely have been markedly different. Major
powers would have been able to draw linkages from their

military–political strength to the issues at WARC and a combination between the United States and Soviet Union on an issue would have ensured their mastery. In fact, these two powers, as advanced users of the spectrum, were aligned on some issues, for example, in opposition to the convening of a satellite conference, but failed to carry the Conference with them.[26] Perhaps the most striking example of the lack of congruence between general power politics and the deliberations at the WARC is provided by Iran. In late 1979, at the height of the hostages crisis, the USA found itself receiving implicit support from the Ayatollah's regime on the issue of reserving more space in the HF band for external broadcasting.[27]

We are left, therefore, with explanations which are issue-structural or international-organizational in character. In the context of the WARC, an issue-structural explanation would predict an outcome which reflected the relative balance of expertise and strength in communications. If that were to be the case, the developed world with its dominance and mastery in these areas should have been rather more successful than it was, although many of the more intricate decisions of the WARC bear witness to the knowledge and engineering competence of these countries. Up until the late 1970s, the history of the ITU demonstrates this pattern. The stronger states in the telecommunications issue system did dominate and did determine the permissive rules of the game. Issue-structural power was, in effect, exercised under the spurious guise of seeking neutral technical solutions. The rules of the ITU regime gave free play to technically-advanced users to occupy frequencies as soon as it was feasible to use them and to allocate an ever-expanding usable spectrum according to their interests. However, by 1977 it had become clear, especially in the field of orbital slots, that universal satisfaction could no longer result from the unbridled exploitation of the telecommunications commons. The new Third World members of the ITU had begun to grasp the iniquities of spectrum allocation and the implicit injustices stemming from the character of the regime itself. Dependent, vulnerable and lacking in the essential resources for the exercise of issue-structural power, they turned to the only weapon at their disposal, the voting procedures of the organization.

For the Third World bloc this source of international organizational power gave countervailing leverage to offset their own dependence through exploitation of the rules of the ITU. Thus it was that the Havana meeting of 1979 called upon 'broadcasting organizations of non-aligned countries to take necessary joint and coordinated action in international forums concerning issues of common concern, so as to improve the situation in this sphere in favour of the non-aligned and other developing countries.'[28] The first fruit of this approach was a concerted attempt to capture the chairmanship for an Indian delegate at the beginning of the WARC. After a week's wrangling, with the West supporting a New Zealander, a compromise was arranged which installed an Argentinian diplomat, R. Severini, in the chair. More was to follow as large plenary session majorities supported Third World initiatives on the convention of planning conferences for satellites and HF. The United States was also 'swamped' by plenary votes enhancing the powers of the IFRB and disallowing the use of the 200 and 300 MHz bands for satellite communications, reserving them instead for fixed and mobile services used by developing countries.[29]

Thus, the introduction of 'politics and ideology' into the hitherto cosy world of the ITU may account for the way in which 'technically sound' proposals were overcome and planning conferences arranged. But to conclude on this note would be to place too high a value on the achievements of the Third World, many of which remain essentially symbolic. It should be remembered that at least two obstacles stand in the path of their organizational strategy. First, a majority consensus is required and, while this may exist at the level of rhetoric and on broad-gauged issues such as equity in the allocation of orbital parking space, it may not exist when the divergent national interests of individual Third World nations are at odds. Nowhere was this shown more clearly than in the HF debate, where a substantial number of countries wishing to develop their own external broadcast services broke ranks with their Third World colleagues, with the result that the vote against the provision of more broadcasting space in the 6 and 7 MHz bands was only 56 to 54.[30] Second, the strategy must ultimately confront the permissive rules of the ITU which are still in place. Thus, although outvoted, a large number of participants took out footnotes and reservations which are tantamount to a formal declaration that they will refuse to be bound by WARC decisions.

At first sight, Keohane and Nye's 'international organiza-tional' model appears to provide a neat explanation of these developments. An 'issue-structural' approach, although coping well with most of the ITU's work, would not seem able to encompass the ambiguous outcome of the 1979 WARC with regard to the setbacks experienced by the United States and other advanced spectrum users. According to Keohane and Nye, the 'international organizational' model accounts for just such 'failures of the basic structural models.' The model states that: 'Power over outcomes will be conferred by organization-ally dependent capabilities, such as voting power, ability to form coalitions and control of elite networks . . . .'[31] In this sense, Third World majorities in WARC plenary sessions appear analogous to outcomes within the UN General Assembly or in UNESCO debates on the New International Information Order. Yet victories won in such forums are frequently of symbolic importance. They are irritating rather than damaging to the interests of powerful actors in the international system or issue area. As demonstrated by the American notice of withdrawal from UNESCO, the organiza-tion itself may be regarded as dispensable if the activities of a majority of its members become too offensive. Keohane and Nye themselves admit the marginal nature of their 'international organizational' model. Above a certain level of conflict actors will assert their underlying power and the model will become 'largely irrelevant'.[32] What is significant about the WARC is that the votes of the Third World majority do appear to affect substantive issues of importance to other users and carry weight simply because the costs to advanced states of abandoning the ITU are prohibitive. The element of 'common fate interdependence' bound up with the maintenance of the telecommunications regime means that the ITU is not akin to UNESCO. The outcome in 1979 was, thus, only superficially explicable in terms of voting procedures and the 'international organizational' model. Of more fundamental significance was the fact that Third World demands raised the implicit threat of disruption in what might be termed an exercise in 'negative issue-structural power'.

It is certainly too early to make a judgement as to the success or failure of the Third World's campaign for more equity within the ITU regime. Yet, in so far as their strategy at the WARC made an impact, it did so because it rested not upon the traditional sources of strength in international politics, but upon the inherently interdependent characteristics of the global communications system. Developed states and corporations, whatever their resources and expertise, are vulnerable to any threat to disrupt the communications regime itself. The option of escaping this interdependence, of going beyond specific reservations and abandoning the ITU, seems too costly to contemplate.

NOTES AND REFERENCES

1. R.O. Keohane and J.S. Nye, *Power and Interdependence* (Boston, Little, Brown, 1977).
2. See A. Smith, *The Geopolitics of Information* (London, Faber, 1980), p. 129.
3. M.S. Soroos, 'The commons in the sky: the radio spectrum and geosynchronous orbit as issues in global policy', *International Organization, 36*, 3 (1982), 665-77.
4. For a description of the four models, see Keohane and Nye, op. cit., Ch. 3.
5. S. Strange, 'What is economic power and who has it?', *International Journal, 30* (1975), 219.
6. United Nations, *Everyone's United Nations: A Handbook of the UN, its Structure and Activities* (New York, United Nations, 1979), p. 372.
7. *The Economist*, 29 September 1979, p. 91.
8. The estimate is made by R. Carazao in *Intermedia, 7*, 5 (1979), 8.
9. The tale of Prince Heinrich's encounter with the 'new technology' is told in *Wireless World*, October 1979, p. 81.
10. For details, see *The Economist*, 29 September 1979, p. 91.
11. H.K. Jacobson, 'ITU, a pot-pourri of bureaucrats and industrialists', in R.W. Cox and H.K. Jacobson (eds), *The Anatomy of Influence: Decision Making in International Organizations* (New Haven and London, Yale University Press, 1974), pp. 59-101.
12. Details of the US preparations and delegates are given in *Broadcasting*, 17 September 1979, pp. 34-45.
13. See J. Howkins, 'The management of the spectrum', *Intermedia 7*, 5 (1979), 12-16.
14. See *New York Times*, 20 November 1979, p. C22.
15. Jacobson, op. cit., pp. 68-9.
16. Resolution No.6, Havana Conference, 1979, text in P. Willetts, *The Non-Aligned in Havana* (London, Frances Pinter, 1981), p. 194.
17. Smith, op. cit., p. 115.

18. Keohane and Nye, op. cit., p. 13.
19. A.W. Branscomb, 'Waves of the future: making WARC work', *Foreign Policy, 34* (1979), 142-3.
20. *The Economist,* 8 December 1979, p. 83.
21. The Committee on Allocations agreed to reallocate 785 kHz of HF spectrum space to the fixed services of the developing nations; see *Broadcasting,* 3 December 1979, p. 40.
22. See Jacobson, op. cit., p. 74.
23. *Wireless World,* December 1979, p. 45.
24. E.H. Carr, *The Twenty Years' Crisis 1919-1939* (London, Macmillan, 1980), pp. 44-5.
25. *New York Times,* 24 November 1979, p. C22.
26. See *Broadcasting,* 3 December 1979, p. 38.
27. Iran supported British and American proposals, see *The Economist,* 8 December 1979, p. 83.
28. Willetts, op. cit., p. 134.
29. *Broadcasting,* 3 December 1979, p. 38.
30. Ibid., p. 40.
31. Keohane and Nye, op. cit., p. 55.
32. Ibid., p. 58.

A Basic Bibliography on Interdependence

H.R. Alker, 'A methodology for design research on interdependence alternatives', *International Organization, 31*, 1 (1977), 29-63.

Samir Amin, *Accumulation on a World Scale: A Critique of the Theory of Underdevelopment, Vols. 1 and 2* (New York, Monthly Review Press, 1974).

S. Brown, *New Forces in World Politics* (Washington, Brookings Institution, 1974).

D. Baldwin, 'Interdependence and power: a conceptual analysis', *International Organization, 34* (1980), 471-506.

———, 'Power and social exchange', *American Political Science Review, 72* (1978), 1229-42.

C. Fred Bergsten, *Toward a New International Economic Order: Selected Papers of C. Fred Bergsten, 1972-1974* (Lexington, Lexington Books/D.C. Heath, 1975).

W. Brandt, *North-South: A Programme for Survival* (London, Pan Books, 1980).

L.R. Brown, *World Without Borders: The Interdependence of Nations* (New York, Foreign Policy Association, 1972).

H. Bull, 'The Structures that prevent collapse into anarchy', *Times Higher Educational Supplement*, 30 September 1977, p. 13.

R.N. Cooper, *The Economics of Interdependence: Economic Policy in the Atlantic Community* (New York, McGraw-Hill, 1968).

R.W. Cox, H.K. Jacobson (eds), *The Anatomy of Influence: Decision-Making in International Organizations* (New Haven, Yale University Press, 1974).

K. Deutsch *et al., Political Community and the North Atlantic Area* (Princeton, Princeton University Press, 1957).

C.F. Doran, 'Oil politics and the rise of co-dependence', in D.W. Orr and M.S. Soroos, *The Global Predicament* (Chapel Hill, University of North Carolina Press, 1979).

M. East *et al., Why Nations Act* (Beverly Hills, Sage, 1978).

R.B. Farrell, *Approaches to Comparative and International Politics* (Evanston, Northwestern University Press, 1966).

Andre Gunder Frank, *On Capitalist Underdevelopment* (Bombay, Oxford University Press, 1975).

David Fromkin, *The Independence of Nations* (New York, Praeger, 1981).

J. Galtung, 'A structural theory of imperialism', *Journal of Peace Research, 8* (1966), 81-117.

K. Goldmann and G. Sjostedt (eds), *Power, Capabilities, Interdependence: Problems in the Study of International Influence* (Beverly Hills, Sage, 1979).

Ernst Haas, *Beyond the Nation-State* (Stanford, Stanford University Press, 1964).

——, *Tangle of Hopes: American Commitment and World Order* (Englewood Cliffs, Prentice-Hall, 1969).

J. Handelman, M. O'Leary, J. Vasquez and W. Coplin, 'Color it Morgenthau: a data-based assessment of quantitative international relations research', unpublished paper presented to the International Studies Association, USA, 1973.

W. Hanrieder, *Comparative Foreign Policy* (New York, McKay, 1971).

——, 'Dissolving international politics: reflection on the nation-state', *American Political Science Review, 72* (1978), 1276-87.

Alex Inkeles, 'The emerging social structure of the world', *World Politics, 27* (1974), 467-95.

D.A. Kay and E.B. Skolnikoff, *World Eco-Crisis: International Organizations in Response* (Madison, University of Wisconsin Press, 1972).

P.J. Katzenstein, 'International interdependence: some long-term trends and recent changes', *International Organization, 29* (1975), 1021-34.

C.W. Kegley and P. McGowan, *The Political Economy of Foreign Policy Behavior* (Beverly Hills, Sage, 1981).

H.H. Kelly and J.W. Thibaut, *Interpersonal Relations: A Theory of Interdependence* (New York, John Wiley and Sons, 1978).

R.O. Keohane and J.S. Nye, *Transnational Relations and World Politics* (Cambridge, Harvard University Press, 1972).

——, *Power and Interdependence: World Politics in Transition* (Boston, Little, Brown, 1977).

S.D. Krasner, 'State power and the structure of international trade', *World Politics, 28* (1976), 317-47.

R. Maghroori and B. Ramberg, *Globalism vs Realism* (Boulder, Westview, 1982).

R. Mansbach and J. Vasquez, *In Search of Theory: A New Paradigm for World Politics* (New York, Columbia University Press, 1981).

R. Mansbach, Y. Ferguson and D. Lampert, *The Web of World Politics* (Englewood Cliffs, Prentice-Hall, 1976).

M. Mesarovic and E. Pestel, *Mankind at the Turning Point* (London, Hutchinson, 1975).

E. Morse, 'Crisis diplomacy, interdependence and the politics of international economic relations', in R. Tanter and R. Ullman (eds), *Theory and Policy in International Relations* (Princeton, Princeton University Press, 1972).

——, *Modernization and the Transformation of International Relations* (New York, Free Press, 1976).

——, 'Interdependence in world politics', in J.N. Rosenau, K.W. Thompson and G. Boyd (eds), *World Politics: An Introduction* (New York, Free Press, 1976).

——, 'Crisis diplomacy, interdependence, and the politics of international economic relations', *World Politics, 24* (1972), Supplement.

——, 'The transformation of foreign policies', *World Politics, 22* (1970).

J.H. Nagel, *The Descriptive Analysis of Power* (New Haven, Yale University Press, 1975).

F. Northedge, 'Transnationalism: the American illusion', *Millenium, 5* (1970).

R. Cruise O'Brien (ed.), *Information, Economics and Power: The North–South Dimension* (London, Hodder and Stoughton, 1983).

R. Cruise O'Brien and G.K. Helleiner, 'The political economy of information in a changing international economic order', *International Organization, 34*, 4 (1980), 445-70.

J. Pinder, 'Interdependence: problem or solution', in L. Freedman (ed.), *The Troubled Alliance: Atlantic Relations in the 1980s* (London, Heinemann, 1983).

P.A. Reynolds and R.D. McKinley, 'The concept of interdependence: its uses and misuses', in Goldmann and Sjostedt, *Power, Capabilities, Interdependence*, op. cit.

N.R. Richardson, 'Economic dependence and foreign policy compliance: bringing measurement closer to conception', in Kegley and McGowan, *The Political Economy of Foreign Policy Behavior*, op. cit.

R. Rosecrance and A. Stein, 'Interdependence: myth or reality', *World Politics, 26* (1973).

R. Rosecrance, 'International theory revisited', *International Organization, 35* (1981), 691-713.

R. Rosecrance, and W. Gutowitz, 'Measuring interdependence: a rejoinder', *International Organization, 35* (1981), 557-60.

R. Rosecrance *et al.*, 'Whither interdependence?', *International Organization, 31* (1977).

J. Rosenau, *The Scientific Study of Foreign Policy* (London, Frances Pinter, 1980).

———, *Domestic Sources of Foreign Policy* (New York, Free Press, 1967).

———, *Linkage Politics* (New York, Free Press, 1969).

———, 'Muddling, meddling and modelling', *Millennium, 8* (1979).

———, *The Study of Global Interdependence* (London, Frances Pinter, 1980).

———, *The Study of Political Adaption* (London, Frances Pinter, 1981).

B. Russett, 'Interdependence and capabilities for European integration', *Journal of Common Market Studies, 9* (1970).

T.C. Schelling, *The Strategy of Conflict* (Oxford, Oxford University Press, 1963).

A.M. Scott, *The Dynamics of Interdependence* (Chapel Hill, University of North Carolina Press, 1982).

A. Smith, *The Geopolitics of Information* (London, Faber, 1980).

M.H. Smith, *Western Europe and the United States: the Uncertain Alliance* (London, Allen and Unwin, 1984).

Tony Smith, 'The underdevelopment of development literature: the case of Dependency Theory', *World Politics, 31* (1979), 247-88.

Mary Ann Tetreault, 'Measuring interdependence', *International Organization, 34* (1980).

———, 'Measuring interdependence: a response', *International Organization, 35* (1981).

J. Vasquez, 'Colouring it Morgenthau: new evidence for an old thesis on quantitative international politics', *British Journal of International Studies, 5* (1979).

———, *The Power of Power Politics* (London, Frances Pinter, 1983).

A. Vincent, 'The Hegelian state and international politics', *Review of International Studies,* 9 (1983).

K. Waltz, 'The myth of national interdependence', in C. Kindleberger, *The International Corporation* (Cambridge, Mass., MIT Press, 1970).

———, *Theory of International Politics* (Cambridge, Mass., Addison-Wesley, 1979).

J. Wilkenfeld *et al.*, *Foreign Policy Behavior* (Beverly Hills, Sage, 1980).

Dennis Wrong, *Power: Its Forms, Bases and Uses* (Oxford, Blackwell, 1979).

Oran Young, 'Interdependencies in world politics', *International Journal,* 24 (1969).

Name Index

Subject Index